Assessing Children's Needs and Circumstances

The Impact of the Assessment Framework

Hedy Cleaver and Steve Walker

with Pamela Meadows

Foreword by Al Aynsley-Green

Jessica Kingsley Publishers
London and Philadelphia

First published in the United Kingdom in 2004
by Jessica Kingsley Publishers
116 Pentonville Road
London N1 9JB, UK
and
400 Market Street, Suite 400
Philadelphia, PA 19106, USA

www.jkp.com

Second impression 2005

Library of Congress Cataloging in Publication Data
A CIP catalog record for this book is available from the Library of Congress

British Library Cataloguing in Publication Data
A CIP catalogue record for this book is available from the British Library

ISBN-13: 978 1 84310 159 8
ISBN-10: 1 84310 159 9

Printed and Bound in Great Britain by
Athenaeum Press, Gateshead, Tyne and Wear

Contents

List of Figures

List of Tables

Foreword

The Government is firmly committed to improving the lives and health of children and young people and giving all children the chance to succeed. As stated in the Government Green Paper 'Every child matters', 'We need to ensure we properly protect children at risk of neglect and harm within a framework of universal services which aims to prevent negative outcomes and support every child to develop their full potential' (HM Treasury, 2003, p.13). Assessing the needs of children and families is the fundamental starting point in delivering appropriate services to match their needs.

For many children the support offered to them and their families through public and independent services is crucial. Where a child is considered to be a child in need, the Assessment Framework will ensure a holistic assessment of the child's developmental needs, parents' or carers' capacity to meet those needs, and the impact of the wider family and environmental factors. The importance of this approach to assessment has been endorsed by the National Service Framework for Children.

Three Government Departments issued the Assessment Framework for national implementation in April 2000. By providing a common language for all professionals the Assessment Framework supports co-operative work across agencies. It is a transparent approach for working with children and families that enables professionals to identify the strengths and difficulties, and the most relevant services. Good assessments, however, depend on staff having a sound knowledge base, relevant training, and adequate support.

I welcome the publication of this comprehensive research into the implementation of the Assessment Framework and its impact on social work practice and inter-agency collaboration. The challenges to its introduction are clear, but so is the extent to which social workers, their managers, and professionals from other agencies and organisations, welcomed its introduction and saw it as benefiting their work. Perhaps most striking is the satisfaction expressed by the majority of parents who felt that practitioners listened to their views, respected their ideas and involved them in all stages of assessment and planning. This alone should demonstrate the value of using the Assessment Framework when working with children and families.

Professor Al Aynsley-Green
National Clinical Director for Children

Acknowledgements

This research study was done in partnership with 24 councils, and we acknowledge with sincere thanks the many people who gave generously of their time to help with this study. We are especially indebted to the young people and their parents who let us into their homes at distressing times, and willingly answered our many questions fully and honestly. We hope that we have done justice to their views as they hold important messages for all those working with children and families.

We would like to thank managers and practitioners within social services, education, health and the voluntary bodies who met with us, completed questionnaires, and participated in interviews. We are particularly aware that they gave generously of their time during a period of great change compounded by difficulties in recruiting and retaining staff.

This study was commissioned and funded by the Department of Health under the *Costs and Effectiveness of Services to Children in Need* research initiative. We are particularly indebted to Dr Carolyn Davies and Caroline Thomas of the Research and Development Division for steering the research through from the proposal stage to completion.

The study was undertaken with the help of an advisory group chaired by Jenny Gray, then of the Department of Health, and now of the Children, Young People and Families Directorate at the Department of Education and Skills. We would like to express our gratitude for their support and advice. The members of this group were:

Jane Aldgate
The Open University

Anthony Cox
King's College and St Thomas' Hospitals

Gillian Garratt-Frost
Youth Justice Board

Jonathan Corbett
Wales Assembly Government

Ratna Dutt Guys
Race Equality Unit

David Gough
Institute of Education

Clare Lazarus
Regional Co-ordinator

Margaret Lynch
Department of Health

Gaynor Lovell
Barking and Dagenham Social Services

Wendy Rose
The Open University

Phillippa Russell
National Children's Bureau

Ian Sinclair
University of York

Caroline Thomas
Department of Health

Diane Williamson
Sheffield Social Services

We would like to thank the numerous academic and professional colleagues who have discussed issues with us, read drafts and provided helpful comments particularly Wendy Rose from The Open University, Jane Tunstill and Anna Gupta from Royal Holloway, University of London. Most importantly we thank Jenny Gray for her continual encouragement and advice.

Finally, without the tremendous work of every member of the research team this study could not have been done. It is through the efforts of the researchers – Don Nicholson, Sukey Tarr, David Bliss and Jackie Davies – that we were able to gather such a range and quality of information. We would also like to express our gratitude to Jackie Hammond and Caroline Banks who provided the administrative support that held the team together.

Hedy Cleaver and Steve Walker with Pam Meadows,
Royal Holloway College, University of London

Chapter 1

Introducing the Study

> Every child and young person deserves the best possible start in life, to be brought up in a safe, happy and secure environment, listened to and heard, to be supported as they develop into adulthood and maturity, and to be given every opportunity to achieve their full potential. However, too many of our children still miss out.
>
> (HM Treasury, 2001, p.v)

The Children Act 1989 places a duty on Councils with Social Services Responsibility to safeguard and promote the welfare of children. Part III of the Act is the basis in law for the provision of local services to children in need (Children Act, 1989, s17.1).

> Children who are defined as in need under the Children Act 1989 are those whose vulnerability is such that they are unlikely to reach or maintain a satisfactory level of health and development, or their health and development will be significantly impaired without the provision of services. (Department of Health, Department for Education and Employment, Home Office, 2000a, 1.18)

However, assessments of children in need led by social services have tended to focus primarily on issues of abuse and neglect, and the developmental needs and circumstances of children have not always been recognised. Research on children looked after has highlighted the variability of assessments (Sinclair *et al.*, 1995). The framework provided by the Looking After Children materials, and in particular the Assessment and Action Records, has provided consistency in assessing the needs of looked-after children. The *Framework for the Assessment of Children in Need and their Families* (Department of Health *et al.*,

2000a) provides a similar structured assessment system for children in need living with their families. This study examines the impact on professional practice of the new Assessment Framework and places particular emphasis on establishing the effects of this model on experiences of children and families, and the cost of assessments.

The legal context

The majority of children benefit from growing up within their own families, but there may be occasions when outside help is required because parents' problems or their environmental circumstances prevent them from being able to respond to the needs of their children (see, for example, Cleaver *et al.*, 1999). The key principles that underpin the Children Act 1989, found in Part II of the Act, recognise these issues:

- It is the duty of the State through local authorities both to safeguard and to promote the welfare of vulnerable children.
- It is in the children's best interest to be brought up in their own families wherever possible.
- While it is parents' responsibility to bring up their children, they may need assistance from time to time to do so.
- They should be able to call upon services, including accommodation (under s20 of the Children Act 1989), from or with the help of the local authority when they are required.

The notion of partnership between State and families is thus also established in this Part of the Act (Department of Health *et al.*, 2000a, 1.13).

However the Act also recognises that from time to time families experience difficulties and turn to the State for help.

> Parents are individuals with needs of their own. Even though services may be offered primarily on behalf of their children, parents are entitled to help and consideration in their own right… Their parenting capacity may be limited temporarily or permanently by poverty, racism, poor housing or unemployment or by personal or marital problems, sensory or physical disability, mental illness or past life experiences. (Department of Health, 1991a, p.8)

Furthermore, the Government's draft strategy for children and young people recognises that the circumstances and communities in which they live can affect children and young people as much as, if not more than, their parents.

> Stress, illness, poverty, crime or racism are negative experiences that we often relate to adult lives, but for too many young people they are just as likely to be a reality. (Children and Young Peoples' Unit, 2001, p.6, 1.7)

Although many families cope adequately with the difficulties they experience, others, particularly those experiencing multiple and complex stressors, would benefit from the assistance of professional agencies. Section 17 of the Children Act takes a developmental approach to the provision of services for a child in need and places a duty on Councils with Social Services Responsibilities to provide services when:

- he is unlikely to achieve or maintain, or to have the opportunity of achieving or maintaining, a reasonable standard of health or development without the provision for him of services by a local authority under Part III
- his health or development is likely to be significantly impaired, or further impaired, without the provision for him of such services
- he is disabled.

The importance of responding appropriately to the needs of families who experience serious problems is emphasised by recent Government policy.

> All families face pressure in their everyday life and all families want some measure of support. But a small proportion of families encounter more serious problems and need particular help and assistance. We must not ignore their needs. (Home Office, 1998, p.5.1)

The current focus of government policy on children and families is to offer help, assistance and resources at an early stage in order to prevent the development of more serious long-term problems (see, for example, Children and Young People's Unit, 2001; Department of Health, 1998a and 1999a; Department of Health *et al.*, 1999; Department of Health *et al.*, 2000a; HM Treasury, 2001). However, the challenge to service providers, including social services, is to identify accurately and sensitively those families who may require services, and to ensure that children and families receive an appropriate and timely service which results in good outcomes for children. Furthermore, councils have to be confident that the services they provide to children and families are well managed and effective.

> We need to be confident that those children who need local authority care and services really benefit from the experience. (Department of Health, 1998b)

Research evidence

The government's emphasis on holistic assessments of children's developmental needs that take account of parenting capacity and environmental factors is based on evidence from research, inspection and practice. High-profile cases of child injury and death have shown that agencies focused primarily on whether or not abuse and neglect had been perpetrated rather than assessing the child's state of health and development to ascertain if it was, or was likely to be, impaired. As a result, assessments have been incident-driven and resources directed to identifying who had done what, to whom, and when.

The Department of Health's programme of research into child abuse identified a number of issues that were hampering the provision of relevant and timely services to families of children in need and their families. Of particular relevance were the high levels of unmet need that were overlooked by incident-focused assessment procedures. The child abuse research suggests that some 15 per cent of child protection referrals resulted in the child's name being placed on the Child Protection Register. However, the research also revealed that in more than half the referrals families were experiencing levels of adversity that impacted negatively on children's development (Cleaver *et al.*, 1999; Department of Health, 1995a). In addition, the research revealed that:

- social workers failed to identify all the family problems; some problems only came to light during the course of the research
- family problems were recognised but information was not systematically recorded
- family problems were identified and recorded but their impact on children and other family members was not fully understood
- there was no systematic recording of the child's developmental needs
- outcomes and plans were not always specified.

The findings from this programme of research into child protection (Department of Health, 1995a) and a series of Social Services Inspectorate inspection reports (Social Services Inspectorate, 1997a and 1997b) resulted in a policy-led debate on how best to refocus children's social services. The anticipated shift was from a service overly pre-occupied by incidents of child maltreatment to one that focused on the developmental needs of children including cases where their health and development was being impaired through neglect or abuse.

It was anticipated this shift would enable assessments to be informed by research on the impact of parenting and family and environmental factors on children's health and development. For example, the degree to which children are affected by their parents' mental illness is related to the level of their involvement (Rutter and Quinton, 1984). Moreover, research has shown that children are at risk of significant harm when violence, neglect or scapegoating is directed at them. Problems in children's health and development are also found to be associated with being witness to, or participating in, the abuse of a parent. Similarly, the impact on children is aggravated when families are experiencing a number of problems; of particular significance is the presence of family violence (Cleaver *et al.*, 1999; Jaffe *et al.*, 1990; Rutter, 1990; Velleman, 1993; Velleman and Orford, 1999).

It is important to get the balance right and not pathologise all children who live in families where a parent suffers problems such as mental illness, problem drinking or drug misuse, or where there is domestic violence. Indeed, a significant proportion of these children show no long-term emotional and behavioural disorders (Jenkins and Smith, 1990; Orford and Velleman, 1990; Rutter and Quinton, 1984). How children are affected will depend on a combination of individual factors (such as temperament, gender, age and self-efficacy), family factors (such as the degree of parental warmth and the presence of a non-affected parent) and environmental factors (such as the support of wider family and friends, school and neighbourhood resources). Nonetheless, a considerable number of children living in homes where a parent is experiencing problems are children in need and would benefit from services. For some children the effects may be so detrimental to their welfare that they would be better placed in an alternative care context.

Assessments of children have generally focused on parenting deficits. The impact of the environment (see, for example, Jack, 2001) and particularly poverty and inequality (Aldgate and Tunstill, 1995) have not always been sufficiently understood.

> Even the most satisfactory mother could do little to mitigate the insidious effects of grinding poverty. (Parker *et al.*, 1999, p.1151)

There is a growing body of research that suggests poverty has immediate and long-term consequences for children's health and wellbeing, both through its direct impact on the child (see, for example, Gregg *et al.*, 1999) and its effect on parenting (see, for example, Spencer *et al.*, 2001). It could be argued that, if assessments recognised the impact of poverty and deprivation on children and families, practitioners might feel paralysed by their inability to effect structural changes in society. However, professionals who fail to take account of these issues in their assessments of children's developmental needs may hold unrealistic expectations of parents and blame them when they fail to live up to them. This approach may result in a failure to recognise the many strengths families have in combating the effects of poverty and deprivation, and leave parents and young people feeling guilty and unwilling to engage in the assessment process. It may also deprive them of access to necessary services (Children and Young People's Unit, 2001; HM Treasury, 2001).

Many government publications have emphasised the value of identifying and building on family strengths (Department of Health *et al.*, 1999; Department of Health *et al.*, 2000a). However, the publication of government guidance does not automatically bring about changes in the values of practitioners, the way services are provided, or in public opinion. A common public perception is that social-work agencies are there to protect children (or not) from bad or incompetent parents rather than to support families who experience difficulties from time to time. This negative perspective can be influenced by the approach towards children and families that is adopted by professionals and agencies. Research suggests when professionals take a strengths-based approach to assessment, and problems and concerns are not overlooked, families are more involved and see themselves as actors in the process of finding solutions to the issues that face them (Graybeat, 2001).

In order to identify which children are in need and what services they would benefit from, assessment should consider the full range of children's and families' strengths as well as needs and difficulties, including the wider environment and circumstances in which they live. The challenge facing social workers and other professionals is to identify which children and families require support and to what extent, in which areas of their development children are impaired, and what types of service would be most effective. Moreover, it is not necessarily the case that more expensive assessments or services are associated with better outcomes for children (Sinclair *et al.*, 1995). The costs involved in assessing the needs of children and deciding which services should be provided may be reduced by the existence of a structured framework. This was one of the Government's intentions in producing the Guidance *The Framework for the Assessment of Children in Need and their Families* (Department of Health *et al.*, 2000a). This was issued under Section 7 of the Local Authority Social Services Act 1970, which means that it must be followed by local authority social services unless there are exceptional circumstances that justify a variation.

The Assessment Framework

> A framework has been developed which provides a systematic way of analysing, understanding and recording what is happening to children and young people within their families and the wider context of the community in which they live. (Department of Health *et al.*, 2000a, p.vii)

The Assessment Framework was a key aspect of the government's Quality Protects Programme and a further stage in the refocusing of children's services. It provides a consistent way of collecting and analysing information about an individual child to enable a more coherent understanding of the child's world. It guides practitioners when undertaking an assessment of a child to address:

- the child's developmental needs
- the capacity of his or her parents/carers to respond to those needs
- the impact of the wider family and environmental factors on both the child and his or her parents/carers, while ensuring the child's welfare is safeguarded and promoted.

The three domains of the child's developmental needs, parenting capacity, and family and environmental factors constitute a framework within which to understand what is happening to a child. These three inter-related domains incorporate a number of important dimensions (see Figure 1.1).

In exploring each domain and how they interact with each other, professionals undertaking assessments should be better able to establish their individual or combined impact on the current and long-term wellbeing of a child. A full description of the various dimensions within each domain can be found in Department of Health *et al.* (2000a) and Rose (2001).

The Assessment Framework is evidence-based and the following principles underpin the approach taken to working with children in need and their families.

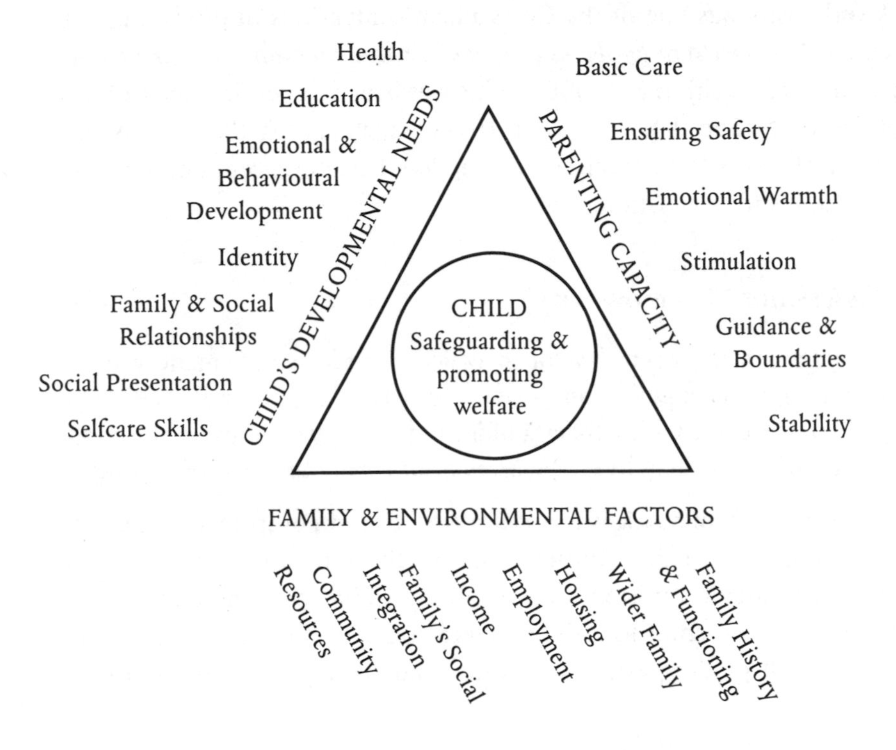

Figure 1.1 The Assessment Framework (Department of Health et al., 2000a)

Assessments:

- are child centred
- are rooted in child development
- are ecological in their approach
- ensure equality of opportunity
- involve working with children and families
- build on strengths as well as identify difficulties
- are inter-agency in their approach to assessment and the provision of services
- are a continuing process, not a single event
- are carried out in parallel with other action and providing services
- are grounded in evidence-based knowledge.

(Department of Health *et al.*, 2000a, p.10, 1.33)

The Assessment Framework was issued under s7 of the Local Authority Social Services Act 1970. This means that it does not have the full force of statute, but Councils with Social Services Responsibilities should comply with it unless local circumstances indicate exceptional reasons that justify a variation.

The publication of the Assessment Framework was supported by practice guidance (Department of Health, 2000b), referral and assessment records (Department of Health and Cleaver, 2000), a set of questionnaires and scales (Department of Health, Cox and Bentovim, 2000b), and by training materials (NSPCC and The University of Sheffield, 2000).

The referral and assessment records

> Good assessments will be essential as a basis for deciding what are the concerns for the child and the family, what needs to change and which services and interventions are needed to achieve this. (Adcock, 1998, p.40)

It is important that assessments focus primarily on the child's developmental needs. Parental issues and environmental factors should be examined in relation to how they impact on the child's wellbeing. A focus on the child also means that assessments should wherever possible involve the child and young person in the process. This will help to ensure assessments identify issues children and young people regard as important.

In order to gather the necessary information and make sense of a family's situation practitioners should also work collaboratively with the child's parents or carers. Because parents often fear the involvement of social services in their lives, sensitive work to gain the co-operation of parents and their commitment to work is crucial for the outcome of plans for the child's wellbeing.

To inform social workers and other relevant professionals about how parental issues and environmental factors impact on children's health and development, and to assist in deciding on the key information to be recorded during an assessment, the Department of Health commissioned a review of current research findings in a number of areas (Cleaver *et al.*, 1999; Dutt and Phillips, 2000; Jones and Ramchandani, 1999; Marchant and Jones, 2000; Pont, 2001; Robbins, 2001; Ryan, 2000; Seden, 2001; Sinclair, 2001). This body of knowledge informed the development of assessment records (Department of Health and Cleaver, 2000; http://www.doh.gov.uk/quality protects). The assessment records were designed to support practitioners when undertaking assessments. They do not replace social workers' professional judgement but offer a systematic way to record and analyse the information gathered during an assessment and to make plans that are then subjected to review.

The development of the referral and assessment records took careful account of the following key policy developments in England and Wales:

- Framework for the Assessment of Children in Need and their Families (Department of Health *et al.*, 2000a)
- Working Together to Safeguard Children (Department of Health *et al.*, 1999)
- The Government's Objectives for Children's Social Services in England (Department of Health, 1999a)
- Children First in Wales (National Assembly for Wales, 2001).

As a result the assessment records for children in need are evidence-based, they operationalise the Assessment Framework and Working Together, they reflect the principles that underpin these documents, and they take full account of the objectives set for children's social services.

The development of the assessment records

The assessment records were drafted, subjected to feasibility studies, and revised in the light of the findings and wider consultation prior to their publication. The first stage was the production of a set of five age-related assessment schedules. These were drawn up at the request of the Social Care Group of the Department of Health as one element of its implementation of Quality Protects (Department of Health, 1998a).

> The Department of Health has commissioned the development of age related assessment records for use by social services front line staff when collecting, collating and analysing information gathered during an assessment of a child and family. (Department of Health, 2000b, p.115, 4.7)

These records are based on the Assessment Framework dimensions, building on the developmental approach to children's needs in the Looking After Children's materials, draw from the findings from research (Cleaver *et al.*, 1999 and others) and from Government statistical requirements.

> The assessment records cannot replace professional skills, but are tools to assist social workers and other colleagues in the process of assessment,

recording and decision making when undertaking an assessment. As such they are designed to help social workers record:

- the child's developmental progress
- each caregiver's parenting capacity
- the impact of family and environmental factors.

(Department of Health, 2000b, p.115, 4.8)

During 1999 these schedules were subjected to a four-month feasibility study, in four English local authorities and three NSPCC child protection teams. The study involved social workers using the schedules when carrying out assessments with families where a child had been identified as a possible 'child in need' as defined by the Children Act 1989. Sixty-six assessments were completed using the schedules. These were audited and a group of practitioners and families interviewed. The feedback from the feasibility study was generally positive, and families and practitioners contributed to the revision of the assessment schedules. Key to the revisions was the feedback from both managers and practitioners that such a detailed schedule was unsuitable for cases that did not involve complex issues.

As a result a separate referral form and an initial assessment schedule were developed. These were subjected to a three-month feasibility study in two Welsh authorities. The study involved the scrutiny of 152 referrals and 57 initial assessments and interviews with service managers and practitioners. The findings from this study informed the revisions to these two records.

The findings from the two feasibility studies and wide consultation with relevant academics, practitioners and policy-makers resulted in the production of the following three records with accompanying guidance on their use:

The Referral and Initial Information record (to be completed in one working day) records:

- initial information about the child and family
- the reason for referral or request for services
- the action to be taken.

The Initial Assessment record (to be completed within a maximum of seven working days of referral) records:

- whether this is a child in need
- what services are required

- whether a core assessment should be carried out next
- the time taken to undertake the initial assessment.

The Core Assessment record (to be completed within a maximum of 35 working days) records:

- details of child's developmental needs
- details of parenting capacity: strengths and difficulties
- family and environmental factors: adverse and protective features
- objectives which are clearly stated and a plan of action
- plans which are subject to regular review (at least every six months)
- the time taken to undertake the core assessment.

The three records operationalise the Assessment Framework and Objective 7 of the Government's Objectives for Children's Social Services (Department of Health, 1999a). The records focus on the inter-relationship between children's behaviour and development, parenting capacity and environmental circumstances. To help social workers identify where services may be needed, the records encourage social workers to explore the strengths and difficulties families may be experiencing, and the health and development of the children.

The assessment records form a coherent system for recording assessments of children in need. This system is aimed at reducing the replication of information. As a result information recorded at the referral stage is not sought again at a later stage in the assessment process. The response from social services departments to a family's request for help or a referral from an agency is critically important. At that point the foundation is laid for future work with the child or family. The recording of information taken at the referral contributes to the first phase of an assessment.

The assessment records, when completed should ensure that:

- information is recorded in a consistent way
- a plan of action with clearly stated objectives is developed
- the most effective services are identified to address the child's needs, including services for parents or bringing about changes in their environment
- the objectives are regularly reviewed.

The assessment records should also act as the basis for reassessment when the child and family's situation changes. Finally, the use of the records will assist councils to collect the required information about their performance under Quality Protects in England or Children First in Wales and other statistical returns to Government and for the own individual management and planning purposes.

The aims and methods of the research

The research explores the ways in which the implementation of the Assessment Framework and the introduction of the assessment records had an impact on social work and other agencies' practice. It is an empirical study carried out over two years that specifically aims to:

- explore the assessment process as set out in the Assessment Framework
- consider whether the assessment records facilitate assessments which consider the child's developmental needs, parenting capacity, and family and environmental factors
- estimate the costs incurred in conducting core assessments using the assessment records.

The study involved 24 councils in England including five Outer London Boroughs, three Inner London Boroughs, seven Metropolitan Districts, three Unitary Authorities and six Shire Counties. This study was replicated in Wales with the exception of the costing element.

Because the research began prior to the required date for implementation of the Assessment Framework (i.e. 1 April 2001), the study needed to incorporate both developmental and research elements. The developmental stage aimed at assisting councils in implementing the Assessment Framework and familiarising social services staff and professionals from relevant agencies with the Assessment Framework and the assessment records. The research element utilised three methods:

1. an audit that examined approximately 100 referrals to social services in each of the participating 24 councils, and all subsequent assessment records
2. postal questionnaires aimed at exploring the perceptions and experience of social work managers and practitioners, and other relevant professionals, including those in health and education services, police and probation, and the voluntary sector

3. an interview study to explore the experiences of children over the age of 10 years, their parents, and practitioners who had been involved in a core assessment.

The research tools used in the study are available as Appendix V on the Jessica Kingsley Publishers website: www.jkp.com.

The study does not set out to evaluate the Assessment Framework but to explore how councils implemented and used it. The Assessment Framework was issued under Section 7 of the Local Authority Social Services Act 1970 and as such it must be followed by local authority social services unless there are exceptional circumstances that justify a variation. A detailed description of the aims and methods of the study can be found in Appendix I.

Chapter summary

When children are in the care of the state, the Looking After Children materials, which are based on research findings, offer a focused and effective framework to assess a child's needs and target resources. Until 2000, however, no such system existed for children in need. *The Framework for the Assessment of Children in Need and their Families* (Department of Health *et al.*, 2000a) offers a structured model of assessment for children in need.

Recent government policy and guidance recognises that, although most children benefit from growing up in their own families, they may need help from time to time. It is acknowledged that the difficulties some families face, both internal (such as parental mental illness or domestic violence) and/or external (such as poverty and inequality), may mean that state support is required to ensure children's wellbeing is not adversely affected.

The difficulties in identifying and mobilising services to these children and families have been highlighted by the findings from a body of research (see, for example, Department of Health, 1995a). This work suggests that focusing on possible child maltreatment has resulted in children's services adopting a narrow, deficit-based rather than a holistic, strengths-based approach to the assessment of children in need and families. Adopting the latter approach not only identifies possible impairment to health and development that may mean the child is suffering or likely to suffer significant harm, but also identifies all the developmental needs of a child. It also enables each child and his or her family to develop a greater understanding of his or her situation and encourages them to participate in the resolution of their own difficulties.

The Assessment Framework was developed as part of the Quality Protects Programme to provide a coherent approach to assessing the needs of children within their family and environment, and to decide how best to respond to these identified needs. The Assessment Framework expects those undertaking or contributing to assessments to focus on the inter-relationship of three domains: the developmental needs of the child, the parents' or carers' capacity to respond to these needs, and the impact of the wider family and environmental factors on children and parents.

To support practitioners in undertaking assessments under the Assessment Framework the Department of Health commissioned Practice Guidance (Department of Health, 2000b), a training pack (NSPCC and The University of Sheffield, 2000), assessment records (Department of Health and Cleaver, 2000), and a set of questionnaires and scales (Department of Health *et al.*, 2000b). The assessment records are evidence-based and support key government policy initiatives such as Quality Protects in England and Children First in Wales. The original draft records were subjected to feasibility studies and amended in the light of the findings and further consultation with policy-makers, practitioners and relevant academics.

The assessment records include:

- the *Referral and Initial Information record* to record initial information about the child and family, the reason for the referral or request for services, and the action to be taken. They should be completed within one working day
- the *Initial Assessment record* which allows practitioners to record whether the child is a child in need (as defined by the Children Act 1989), what services are needed and when, and whether a core assessment should be carried out. The initial assessment is to be completed within a maximum of seven working days
- the *Core Assessment record* which is age-related and records details of the child's development, parenting capacity, and the impact of wider family and environmental issues, and takes a strengths approach to assessments. The objectives of the assessment should be clearly stated and there is section to record the plan and the outcome of the review. The core assessment is to be completed within 35 working days.

The time-scales for completing the assessments are set out in Objective 7 of the Government's Objectives for Children's Social Services (Department of Health, 1999b). The research was carried out over a two-year period, starting in November 1999, and explores the impact of the implementation of the Assessment Framework and the introduction of the assessment records on social work practice, the costs of assessments, and the experiences of children and families. To do this three methods are used: an audit of assessment records; postal questionnaires to social work managers, practitioners and professionals from other relevant agencies; and a case study involving interviews with children, families and professionals. Details of the aims and methods of the study can be found in Appendix I.

Chapter 2

Implementation

> There is nothing more difficult to take in hand, more perilous to conduct, or more uncertain in its success than to take the lead in the introduction of a new order of things, because the innovator has for enemies all those who have done well under the old conditions, and lukewarm defenders in those who may do well under the new.
>
> (Machiavelli, 1469–1527)

Councils with Social Services Responsibilities involved in the study

Implementing the *Framework for the Assessment of Children in Need and their Families* presented a challenge for Councils with Social Services Responsibilities. Previous research has shown that the ability of councils to respond to the challenge of implementing new government policy is dependent on several factors including their structure, systems, staff, skills, style and values (Pascale, 1990; Peters and Waterman, 1982).

Twenty-four councils were involved in the research project and varied on a number of dimensions including their size, location, the population they served and local economic conditions. These are all factors that can affect their ability to implement new working arrangements (Packman and Hall, 1998). The sample included eight London Boroughs, some of which served very diverse populations. For example:

> Council 12 is an inner London Borough serving a population of over 250,000 people. Of this population approximately 22 per cent are under

> the age of 18 years and approximately 7 per cent are under the age of 5 years.
>
> The council has a culturally diverse population. 34 per cent of the resident population are from black and ethnic minority communities, and 39 per cent of service users are from these communities. The council's proximity to national and international rail terminals has resulted in the council having a significant asylum-seeking population (Audit Commission, 2000), who bring with them a range of complex health and social care needs. It is estimated that 110 languages are spoken in the council area.
>
> The local economy is made up of small businesses in the retail, construction, cultural and media sectors. Local people fill a quarter of all jobs in the borough. The council has an unemployment rate higher than the average for Inner London and Greater London as a whole. Almost 50 per cent of those unemployed within the council have been unemployed for over six months (Council statistics).
>
> The council was ranked in the 15 most deprived councils in England in the Department of Environment Transport and the Regions Index of Local Deprivation for 1998 and in the 10 most deprived councils in Greater London Councils by the Audit Commission.

The sample also included seven Metropolitan Districts from the Midlands and North-west. These councils covered areas recovering from the decline in manufacturing and heavy industry that had a profound effect on the local economy and population. For example:

> Council 18 is one of the largest metropolitan councils in the country. It serves a population of over half a million – a figure that is set to grow steadily over the next 20 years according to projections made by the Office for National Statistics. It is estimated that within the total population of 113,000 children, 41,000 are 'vulnerable children' and between 4000 and 7000 are 'children in need'. Of the total population of children and young people aged under 18, 10 per cent are from black and ethnic minority communities most of whom are British-born, but an increasing number are children from asylum-seeker families.
>
> The council has been particularly hard hit by the decline of Britain's traditional heavy industrial base. The restructuring of the steel, coal and engineering industries has meant that the area has had increasingly to diversify its economy. While there have been some successes, unemployment remains above the national average and is concentrated in certain

electoral wards and amongst certain groups – particularly the young and some ethnic minority groups. Other measures of deprivation follow a similar pattern of uneven spread through the city. The social problems associated with unemployment and poverty and the escalation in drug misuse have all impacted on the services provided by the council.

Council 18 stands out as being markedly poorer than the UK average per capita income.

The circumstances of inner city and urban councils contrasted with those of the six Shire Counties involved in the study. For example:

> Council 21 is among the largest counties in England, covering over 125 square miles. Its population is spread widely across 19 communities, centred on ten small market towns and their surrounding rural areas. The population currently numbers around 431,000 and is projected to increase by some 30,000 over the next decade. The child population (under 18 years) is approximately 95,000 (1991 Census data updated). In common with the majority of the shires the black and minority ethnic population accounts for only just over 1 per cent of the total population.
>
> The County has low levels of unemployment as the expanding service sector has more than compensated for the decline in agricultural and manufacturing employment. However, the service sector does have a high level of part-time working, particularly for women. Some high-technology industries are now being attracted to the motorway corridor to the north of the County.
>
> While income levels are close to the national average, these figures conceal a significant dichotomy; some 30 per cent of the population enjoy an annual income of over £40,000, another 30 per cent cope on less than £7000. Their deprivation may also be compounded by rural isolation; 21 per cent of households have no car and many villages have no regular bus service.

The study included smaller councils, both rural and urban, including three Unitary Authorities. For example:

> Council 16 was created in 1998, taking over responsibility for the complete range of Local Government functions including Social Services from the County Council. It consists of five towns and large tracts of countryside. It has a total population of almost a quarter of a million. Information from the 1991 Census indicates that people from black and ethnic minority communities made up 4.2 per cent of the population at

that time. The black and ethnic minority population is significantly younger than the white population. Whereas older people constitute about 14.5 per cent of the total population, only 4.2 per cent of the black and minority ethnic population are over 65. The under-18 population makes up approximately 25 per cent of the total population (Office of National Statistics).

The council as a whole is not an area suffering from high levels of deprivation; however there are a number of wards which suffer from multiple deprivation factors. The level of unemployment was 4.2 per cent in 1998. This is similar to the national average of 4.7 per cent and the average for the region of 4 per cent.

Information gathering

Information on how authorities implemented the Assessment Framework was gathered in a variety of ways. Initial meetings with managers provided valuable information about the situations of councils prior to implementation and the areas where individual councils anticipated difficulties.

In addition, a member of the research team conducted structured telephone interviews with managers involved in the implementation of the Assessment Framework in each council. These interviews provided information on the council's structure, processes and practice prior to implementation, and key aspects of their plans to implement the Assessment Framework, including training and the management of the implementation.

The familiarisation sessions and consultation events proved to be a rich source of information on the issues which arose during the process of implementation and the strategies councils employed to overcome these. Discussions with the link person from each authority and the early and final audits also provided valuable information on how councils implemented the Assessment Framework (see Appendix I for details of the research methods).

The level of change required

The level of the change required to implement a new policy depends upon the nature and scope of the policy (Hall *et al.*, 1975). Hall and colleagues (1975) identified three levels of change that councils may be involved in when implementing a new policy:

1. *Innovation*: this is the highest level of change and involves the development of new services, either as the result of increased

responsibilities or rights, or through an expansion of the council's role into a new area.

2. *Development*: change at this level involves an increase in the level or range of a council's existing service provision.
3. *Reform*: reforms do not involve a council in new or increased activity. This type of change only requires a change in the way that a council provides an existing service, or range of services.

On first consideration the *Framework for the Assessment of Children in Need and their Families* would appear to fall within the category of *Reform*. Prior to implementation, social services were routinely involved in taking referrals and undertaking assessments to determine whether children were in need as defined in the Children Act 1989. Where children had more complex needs that required care or protection, social workers were expected to undertake a comprehensive assessment (Department of Health, 1988; Department of Health, 1991a). In 1988 the Department of Health published *Protecting Children: A guide to social workers undertaking a comprehensive assessment*, commonly referred to as the 'Orange Book', to support practitioners undertaking comprehensive assessments.

In terms of existing policy requirements, therefore, councils with social services responsibilities for children in need were already involved in a three-stage process, broadly analogous with that set out in the Assessment Framework of referral, initial assessment and core assessment.

However, despite the guidance set out in the 'Orange Book' and the requirements of *Working Together*, there was increasing evidence from the findings of Inquiry reports (Department of Health, 1991b; James, 1994; The Bridge, 1995) and inspections (Social Services Inspectorate, 1999) of an absence of assessments in children and young people's social work records. An inspection of recording in six social work departments found that assessments were present in only 57 per cent of children's cases (Social Services Inspectorate, 1999). Furthermore, these inspections also highlighted that there was confusion in the minds of some practitioners about what actually constituted an assessment.

> Social workers kept showing us things they said were assessments, but clearly were not. (Social Services Inspectorate, 1999)

Unlike previous guidance on assessment the *Framework for the Assessment of Children in Need and their Families* was issued under s7 of the Local Authority Social Services Act 1970. This places a duty on Councils with Social Services

Responsibilities to comply with the Guidance unless there are *exceptional* reasons for not doing so. The Assessment Framework also differed from previous guidance on assessment in a number of other ways:

- It introduced clear, mandatory timescales for each stage of the assessment process.
- Each child or young person within a family, referred to social services, should be dealt with on an individual basis. The practice of 'Family' referrals and assessments, which brought together information about all the children and young people in a family within a single assessment, was no longer acceptable.
- Assessment should consider a child or young person's needs, and his or her parent/carer's capacity to respond appropriately to those needs within the context of the child or young person's wider family and environment.
- It required the practitioner undertaking the assessment to see the child or young person as a part of the initial and core assessments.
- Children and families were expected to be participants in, rather than recipients of, an assessment.
- Although social services were the lead agency in the assessment process, assessment and the implementation of the Assessment Framework is viewed as a multi-agency process. To emphasise this point the Assessment Framework was issued jointly by the Departments of Health, Education and Employment, and the Home Office.

When the above requirements are considered alongside evidence from research and inspections on assessment, it indicates that to implement the Assessment Framework councils would have to change both existing practice and processes and the level of assessment services provided. Further, to ensure that services to all children in need were based on a structured, holistic assessment of their needs could involve councils in a re-organisation or re-structuring of existing services. Hall and her colleagues (1975) suggest that an increase in the level of change from *Reform* to *Development* is significant; the greater the level of change required to implement a policy the less likely it is that it will be successfully implemented. Therefore, implementing the Assessment Framework presented councils with a considerable challenge.

In some respects there were more resources available to support the implementation of the Assessment Framework than there had been for much previous new government policy. For example, the Department of Health had commissioned a training pack (NSPCC and the University of Sheffield, 2000), scales and questionnaires (Department of Health, Cox and Bentovim, 2000) and assessment records (Department of Health and Cleaver, 2000) were developed, as well as the funding of a consultation process.

The position of councils pre-implementation

Two key factors were identified by Hall and her colleagues (1975) as having a significant influence on the likely success of any policy: its *legitimacy* and *feasibility*.

Legitimacy

Legitimacy is concerned with whether the agency considers the activity covered by the policy is one they should be involved in. However, in relation to the Assessment Framework the notion of *legitimacy* needs to be taken further. It is not simply a question of whether practitioners believed it was legitimate for the agency to be undertaking assessments on children and young people but whether they felt it was appropriate to undertake assessment in the *way* required by the Assessment Framework.

This aspect of *legitimacy* is particularly significant in social work where there is an increasingly polarised debate about the role of central government in the management and regulation of services. For example, the introduction of performance measures to ensure quality, such as Quality Protects (Department of Health, 1998a) and the Performance Assessment Framework (Department of Health, 1999b), which preceded the Assessment Framework, are seen by some social services staff as mechanisms to improve quality and strengthen the profession, and by others as a way of undermining professional autonomy and centralising control. In meetings with social services staff it was not unusual to find practitioners within a council with views about the role of central government and the legitimacy of the Assessment Framework at either end of this spectrum. Practitioners within dedicated referral and assessment teams were generally most positive about the Assessment Framework whereas those from more specialist teams, such as those for disabled children, frequently questioned the appropriateness of the Assessment Framework for their service users. This suggested that within councils the Assessment Framework would be implemented more successfully in some teams than in others.

Feasibility

The other factor recognised as influencing the success of a new policy is its *feasibility* (Hall *et al.*, 1975).

Feasibility considers whether an agency has:

- the theoretical and technological knowledge
- the resources
- the collaborative arrangements
- the administrative capacity

to implement a policy.

In addition, a council's ability to successfully implement the Assessment Framework may be affected by the level of change it has been subjected to.

The research team used these factors to review the position of councils prior to implementing the Assessment Framework.

THEORETICAL AND TECHNICAL KNOWLEDGE – PRIOR TO IMPLEMENTATION

To gain an understanding of the level of theoretical and technical knowledge within councils in relation to assessment, prior to implementing the Assessment Framework, the following factors were considered:

- the existence of written policies and procedures relating to the process and practice of assessment
- the provision of information on assessments for children in need and their families
- the process of assessment within the children's social services department.

Written policies and procedures

Councils were asked whether they had written policies and procedures relating to the *process* and *practice* of assessments, i.e. written guidance on how assessments should be carried out. The availability of guidance demonstrates a desire by the council to establish consistency and set standards for the conduct of assessments. Practitioners who have experience of working with written guidance on assessment, it is argued, would be in a better position to implement the Assessment Framework than those who did not.

Twenty (83%) councils had written policies and procedures on the *process* of assessment, and 17 (71%) had policies and procedures in relation to the *practice* of assessments.

The provision of information for families

The Assessment Framework places an emphasis on the involvement of children and families in the assessment process.

> It requires direct work with children and with family members, explaining what is happening, why an assessment is being undertaken, what will be the process and what is likely to be the outcome. Gaining the family's co-operation and commitment to the work is crucially important. (Department of Health, 2000a, p.38, 3.32)

The provision of information for families is an important step in developing partnerships with children and their families (Department of Health, 1995b; Thoburn *et al.*, 1995). If families have information about the process and content of assessments, they are in a better position to understand and contribute to the process. Providing families with a copy of their assessment at the end of the process indicates practice that seeks to empower families. The provision of information to families and sharing assessments demonstrates an inclusive approach consistent with the Assessment Framework.

Nine councils (37.5%) provided information for families. An identical number provided families with copies of assessments. However, only four (17%) councils provided families with copies of both. This suggests that prior to implementing the Assessment Framework few councils had a robust approach to inclusive practice and openness with families.

The process of assessment

A council's existing process for assessment had the potential to help or hinder the implementation of the Assessment Framework. Where councils used a two-stage process for assessment it was anticipated that practitioners would be more familiar and comfortable with the concept and practice of initial and core assessments used in the Assessment Framework.

Ten (42%) of the 24 councils in the study had a two-stage assessment process prior to implementation.

Councils were also asked whether they considered their assessment process was consistent with the Assessment Framework and whether they intended to make any modifications on implementation. Twenty-two (92%) of the 24 councils reported that they would be making modifications to their existing assessment processes on implementation of the Assessment Framework.

RESOURCES – PRIOR TO IMPLEMENTATION

To gain an understanding of the resources available to support the implementation of the Assessment Framework two factors were considered: staffing, and the ability to undertake core tasks.

Staffing

Implementation of the Assessment Framework coincided with increasing concern about the recruitment and retention of social workers. This concern culminated in the launch of a national social worker recruitment campaign by the Secretary of State for Health on 19 October 2001. Informal feedback from practitioners and managers to the research team suggested that staffing difficulties were particularly acute among front-line services for children and families.

Fourteen councils across England, including London Boroughs, Shire Counties, Metropolitan Districts and Unitary Authorities, provided information about staffing levels in children and family social services at the point of implementation. Vacancy rates – that is, posts not filled by a permanent staff member – ranged from 1 per cent to 49.5 per cent with an average rate of 22 per cent. Of the 14 councils, 6 were classified by the research team as having comparatively low vacancy rates (below 15%), four were classified as having average vacancy rates (between 15 and 30%), and four as having high rates (more than 30% of posts vacant).

Eight of the 14 councils who provided information about staffing levels employed locum practitioners and managers to relieve staffing pressures. As might be expected, councils with the highest vacancy rates tended to employ locum staff. Locum workers are expensive for councils to employ owing to the cost of agency fees. This may explain why six of the 14 councils did not employ them. Even where a council employed locum practitioners or managers, they were not always able to afford or recruit sufficient numbers to fill all vacant posts. In the eight councils that employed locums an average of 13 per cent of posts remained unfilled. Locum staff accounted for between 2.8 per cent and 42 per cent of all staff in children and family services, with the average rate of 17.5 per cent.

Although the employment of locum workers enables councils to fulfil statutory and other obligations, it does not fully compensate for the lack of regular staff. Their employment will increase the challenge of implementing new government policy and working procedures. This is because locum workers will be less familiar with an organisation's policies, procedures and practice. It is also more difficult for the organisation to include them in planning for implementation or in training programmes, as the employment of locum workers is more susceptible to the financial constraints of any organisation. As a result it is anticipated that councils with a high proportion of locum workers will experience greater difficulties in implementing change at procedural and practice levels than councils with low levels of vacancies.

The ability to undertake core tasks

It is expected that implementing the Assessment Framework will present a greater challenge to councils who are experiencing difficulties in carrying out their duties. The task will be hampered, because these councils have great difficulty in allocating resources to the process of change, for example, in providing staff with the space to internalise the need for change (DiClementi, 1991), or establishing training programmes. Twenty-two (92%) councils reported that they were generally experiencing difficulties in service provision and 16 (67%) reported that services were being restricted to children with high levels of need, such as children in need of protection or accommodation.

For Councils with Social Services Responsibilities core tasks are those which councils have a statutory duty to provide. In children and families social services, statutory work is often interpreted as referring to services for children in need of protection and children looked after, rather than services for all children in need as defined in the Children Act 1989 (Department of Health, 1995a).

Eighteen (75%) councils reported that they were unable to allocate cases. In seven (29%) councils, allocation difficulties did not affect child protection or looked-after cases, but for four (17%) councils unallocated cases included children in one of these groups, and in seven councils unallocated cases included both children in need of protection and looked-after children.

Unallocated cases increased the demands placed on practitioners and managers. Although cases may not be allocated to a specific practitioner, some work must still be carried out. This may be either planned actions, such as reviews for children looked after, or a response to a crisis. In most social service departments this work was managed by teams holding cases. In practice this means that in addition to allocated caseloads team members were also responsible for responding to issues that arose from unallocated cases.

Finally, the impact of unallocated cases involving children in need of protection or accommodation resulted in high levels of stress throughout the organisation because these are some of the most vulnerable children in need of social work services.

COLLABORATIVE ARRANGEMENTS – PRIOR TO IMPLEMENTATION

Collaborative arrangements were assessed by examining councils' strategic planning arrangements and their joint assessment practice.

Strategic planning

The implementation of the Assessment Framework requires collaboration between agencies at a strategic level in relation to referrals to social services and the design and delivery of assessments.

> Improvements in outcomes for children in need can only be achieved by close collaboration between professionals and agencies working with children and families. (Department of Health *et al.*, 2000a, p.vii)

In order to obtain an indication of the nature of collaborative arrangements prior to implementation, councils were asked about the involvement of other agencies in the development of their Quality Protects Management Action Plan. The Quality Protects programme (Department of Health, 1998a) was established by government to transform the management of children's social services and to improve outcomes for children. The initiative established a number of national objectives with performance indicators and targets to assess the performance of councils. Each council was required to draw up an annual Management Action Plan setting out the council's plans and progress in relation to each of the Quality Protects objectives. It was expected that councils would involve other agencies in developing their Management Action Plan. Furthermore, the plan had to be signed by the Director of Social Services, the Director of Education, the Chief Executive of the Council and the Chief Executive of the local Health Council. The Quality Protects Management Action Plan therefore provided good information about a council's inter-agency strategic planning capacity.

The average number of agencies that councils worked with in developing their Management Action Plans was five, with health and education the most frequently involved. Eight councils (33%) were classified by the research team as having comparatively poor levels of collaboration (less than five agencies). Five councils (21%) were classified as having average levels (five agencies), and 11 (46%) were classified as having comparatively high levels of collaboration (more than five agencies involved) in the development of their Management Action Plan.

One positive feature was the level of involvement of service users. Half of the councils had involved parents and/or children in the development of their Management Action Plans.

Joint assessment practice

There was less evidence of collaboration between agencies at a practice level. Nineteen councils reported that they undertook joint assessments. However, only three councils reported that joint assessments were carried out for all groups of children. In the remaining 16 councils it was reported that joint assessments were restricted to three types of situation:

- The needs of the individual child could not be assessed without the involvement of other agencies. For example, disabled children or children in need of protection (11, 58% of councils reported joint assessments in these circumstances).
- Other professionals were working with the parent. For example, children living in families where there were issues, such as parental drug or alcohol misuse (10, 53% of councils reported joint assessments in these circumstances).
- Formal joint teams, such as Youth Offending Teams or Child and Adolescent Mental Health Services, already existed (4, 21% of councils reported joint assessments in these circumstances).

ADMINISTRATIVE CAPACITY – PRIOR TO IMPLEMENTATION

Administrative capacity was assessed in relation to practitioners' access to computers, and existing structures for referral and assessment.

Practitioners' access to computers

The ability to use the assessment records in an electronic format, such as that provided to councils at the point of implementation by the research team, offered a number of advantages for practitioners implementing the Assessment Framework. These included:

- the reduction in repetitive recording because information, such as names and addresses, common to more than one record, only had to be entered once, as they would be automatically transferred to other relevant records

- better presented and easier-to-read records
- greater ease-to-update records
- the ability to print out copies of the record, negating the need for photocopying.

The ability of practitioners to use the records in an electronic format successfully depended on their access to computers. In seven (29%) councils there was at least one computer to every two practitioners (rated by the research group as above average rate of computers to staff). In eleven (46%) councils there was one computer to every two or three practitioners (rated as average rate of computers to staff). In six (25%) councils more than three practitioners had to share access to each computer (rated as having a low rate of computers to staff).

Structures for referral and assessment

The Assessment Framework establishes clear timescales for the processes of referral, initial assessment and core assessment. In order to ensure that these timescales are met, councils must avoid delay between each of these processes, particularly where the decision is made to progress from referral to initial assessment. The structures in place for referral and assessment may hinder or support councils in meeting the timescales. Referral and assessment teams or comparable structures were most likely to minimise delays as referrals and initial assessments are dealt with by the same team.

Seventeen (71%) councils had referral and assessment teams. Two (8%) councils had referral and assessment teams in some but not all areas of the council. Five (21%) councils did not have referral and assessment teams.

The level of change experienced by the council – prior to implementation

The level of change experienced by social services was assessed by considering the number of re-organisations of both Social Services in general and Children and Family Services undertaken in the five years prior to the implementation of the Assessment Framework.

Research suggests that the nature of social services organisations makes change a complex process. In such organisations change will be more difficult to implement successfully and the repercussions of change will take longer to settle down than in other types of organisation (Handy, 1978). The ability to respond to the change required to implement the Assessment Framework will be exacerbated by the extent of change a department has already experienced as:

> in a climate of uncertainty, practitioners are not only likely to resist change, but will also resort to dogma and fashion, responses which can be exacerbated by inexperience or a lack of understanding. (Bullock, 1995, p.94)

This suggests that where practitioners have experienced high levels of change they are likely to be resistant to further change.

Organisational and structural changes however may not result in changes in practice.

> Such action does not necessarily mean that groups or individuals in the organisation will accept the need for change or feel happy about it: in other words such action might achieve compliance without identification or internalisation of the need for change. (Johnson and Scholes, 1989, p.43)

Research carried out by Howe (1986) found that, if practitioners did not understand or accept the need for change in their practice, they returned to previous patterns of practice at the first opportunity.

The 24 councils in the study had experienced a total of 44 re-organisations. All but one council had experienced some form of re-organisation in the five years prior to the implementation of the Assessment Framework. Seven (29%) councils had experienced three re-organisations, six (25%) had experienced two, with the remaining 10 councils experiencing one re-organisation.

Summary points

- Practitioners within dedicated referral and assessment teams generally welcomed the Assessment Framework. However, practitioners from more specialist teams, such as teams for disabled children, frequently questioned the appropriateness of it for their service users.
- Written policies and procedures played an important role in supporting practice and increasing the theoretical and technical knowledge of staff. Twenty-two of the 24 councils had written

guidance on the process and/or practice of assessment prior to implementation.

- Prior to implementation only four (17%) of councils routinely provided information *and* copies of completed assessments to families.
- Twenty-two councils thought their existing assessment process was not consistent with the Assessment Framework and intended to modify it.
- Many councils were experiencing severe difficulties in recruiting and retaining staff.
- Over half of the councils in the study were limiting services to cases where children had high levels of need. Three-quarters of councils had unallocated cases and almost half of the councils had unallocated child protection or looked-after cases.
- Whilst councils indicated a generally healthy level of inter-agency collaboration at a strategic level, the picture was less positive at the level of individual children and families.
- The low ratio of computers to practitioners prior to implementation suggests that many practitioners were not using IT as an integral part of their job.
- Almost three-quarters of the councils in the study had established a referral and assessment team.
- Councils had, with one exception, experienced major organisational change in the five years prior to implementing the Assessment Framework.

How authorities implemented

All the councils (except for one) involved in the research had implemented the Looking After Children System. The Looking After Children System was launched by the Department of Health in 1995, and all or parts of the system is now in use in over 97 per cent of councils in England. The system consists of a research-based theoretical framework to assess the needs of looked-after children and a series of supporting records. Research on the implementation of the Looking After Children System (Jones *et al.*, 1998; Ward 1995, 1998) identified a number of factors which assisted successful implementation. In particular:

- support with implementation
- leadership
- ownership
- cross-boundary working
- training
- technical capacity.

These factors have been used to review the actions taken by councils during the implementation of the Assessment Framework. Also identified is the support provided to councils by the research team during the first phase of the research programme.

Support with implementation

The research design recognised the challenge that implementing the Assessment Framework presented to councils. In response the first phase of the study was developmental, aimed at supporting councils in the process of implementation. At the start of the research programme, members of the team met with senior and line managers in each council to explain the aims and methods of the research, outline the timetable and address any issues or concerns raised. Each council identified a link person who liaised with an identified member of the research team throughout the duration of the research.

To support the introduction of the Assessment Framework the Department of Health commissioned a training pack, *The Child's World* (NSPCC and the University of Sheffield, 2000). *The Child's World* provided an overview of the research, theory and practice that underpinned the development of the Assessment Framework and guidance on its application in practice. *The Child's World* was provided free of charge to all councils. To assist councils and their partner agencies to use the training pack the Department of Health funded a national programme of 'training for trainers' events. Each council was able to send a number of representatives, again at no cost to the council. The training was focused on helping participants to gain an understanding of the conceptual framework underpinning the Assessment Framework and, therefore, did not contain any exercises directly relating to the use of the assessment recording tools.

To support the introduction of the assessment records each council was provided with four half-day familiarisation sessions delivered by a member of the research team. A training pack, *Using the Assessment Records with Children and*

Families (Cleaver and Walker, 2000), was developed. To ensure consistency in the training provided to councils all members of the research team were trained to use the materials in the pack. The *Assessment Records* training pack aimed to familiarise practitioners with the assessment recording tools and to supplement the materials in *The Child's World*. The *Assessment Records* training pack consisted of two modules. Module 1 provided an overview of the research underpinning the development of the assessment records and the content and structure of each record. Module 2 contained a series of case studies to provide practitioners with an opportunity to use the records. To facilitate ongoing training a copy of the *Assessment Records* training pack was provided to each council (see http://www.jkp.com).

In addition to the familiarisation sessions the research team also contributed to a one-day conference or similar event in each participating council. Each council determined when and how they used the support provided by the research team. In some councils the conference and familiarisation sessions supplemented existing programmes already underway. In these councils practitioners were already familiar with the Assessment Framework and staff were able to focus on the recording tools. In others the conference was used to launch the Assessment Framework, often on an inter-agency basis, and the familiarisation sessions planned around it. In a small number of councils, however, the familiarisation sessions were the first training practitioners had received on the Assessment Framework. This was either because no training programme for the Assessment Framework was in place, or because the programme had started but not yet reached all practitioners.

To provide councils with information on the progress of implementation an audit of some 30 core assessments and preceding documentation was carried out in each council within six months of implementation. A report of the audit provided each council with information on how well the Assessment Framework was being used and highlighted areas for further development.

To provide councils with early findings from the research a series of regional seminars were held. A total of 173 social services representatives, 46 health and 26 education professionals attended these events. The seminars also provided councils with an opportunity to discuss common issues and share strategies employed to implement the Assessment Framework. To support the ongoing sharing of information between the research team and councils, and across councils a website was established. This included information for councils relating to the research and contained a notice board that allowed councils to share examples of innovative practice and ideas, policies, procedures and practice guides and other materials to support the implementation of the Assessment Framework.

Leadership

Implementation of the Assessment Framework involved councils in change at organisational, procedural and practice levels. These changes must be carefully co-ordinated and managed to minimise disruption to the organisation and practitioners.

Councils used four strategies to manage the process of change:

1. appointing a specific project officer
2. appointing a specific project officer and developing an implementation group
3. developing an implementation group
4. using existing management structures.

SPECIFIC PROJECT OFFICER

Seven councils appointed specific project officers. These officers were responsible for overseeing the process of implementation and had no other duties. A key advantage of this approach was that the project officer was involved in all aspects of implementation, acted as a link between areas of service or practice and individuals, and had time to focus on details that might otherwise have been overlooked. For example, a project officer had the time and space to support individual practitioners, or focus on areas such as disability where some practitioners needed more guidance to understand the relevance of the Assessment Framework for their service users.

The success of the implementation process depended on the ownership of the change process being located at the right level within the organisation (Horwath and Morrison, 2000). In most authorities the project officers were internal appointments. This ensured that they had a detailed knowledge of the council's existing policies, procedures and structures. A key factor in the success of this strategy was to ensure that the post-holder carried sufficient authority and influence within the organisation. This was achieved when the project officer appointed was already well respected and a member of the senior management team within Children and Family services or was managed by the Head of Service.

SPECIFIC PROJECT OFFICER AND IMPLEMENTATION GROUP

Five of the seven councils where a specific project officer was appointed had also initiated an implementation group to support the project officer. Having both a project officer and an implementation group combined the advantages of co-ordination, communication and the shared expertise of a group approach, with the dedicated time of a project officer who could see through tasks identified by the implementation group.

IMPLEMENTATION GROUP

Twenty councils formed an implementation group to lead the implementation process. Implementation groups were used to:

- identify the key factors that would impact on implementation at a local level
- develop a timetable and plan for implementation
- draw up training programmes to support implementation
- revise policies and procedural guidance
- establish quality assurance arrangements
- develop information for families
- promote ownership.

Implementation groups allowed councils to increase the involvement of professionals from both within and outwith the council in the process of implementation and several included representatives from other agencies.

Several councils also established sub-groups to the main implementation group, which were responsible for leading on specific issues such as training. This enabled councils to make best use of the specific expertise of individuals and widen involvement in implementation.

EXISTING MANAGEMENT STRUCTURES

Only two councils had neither appointed a specific project officer nor established an implementation group. In these councils the implementation process was taken forward by existing management arrangements.

Ownership

> Securing ownership of the system throughout all levels of the organisation is…a necessary pre-requisite of successful implementation. (Ward, 1995)

The implementation of the Assessment Framework required the commitment of staff at all levels of the council. The organisational change necessary needed the support of senior managers, and practice changes could not be achieved without the support of practitioners.

Previous research indicates that staff are more likely to be committed to new policy initiatives and working methods when they have had some involvement in the process of implementation (Howe, 1986; Jones *et al.*, 1998; Ward, 1995). The involvement of staff from all levels of the organisation can further facilitate implementation by:

- assisting in the identification of areas of potential difficulty and in the development of strategies to overcome these
- facilitating effective communication throughout the organisation about the new policy and methods of working
- helping to ensure ownership of the project at all levels of the organisation.

Research on the implementation of Looking After Children (Corrick *et al.*, 1995; Jones *et al.*, 1998; Ward, 1995) identified four key groups within Children and Family Services whose involvement was essential to successful implementation:

1. senior managers
2. first-line managers
3. trainers
4. practitioners.

SENIOR MANAGERS

Senior managers are able to commit the financial and staffing resources necessary to see through change. Moreover, the involvement of senior managers emphasises the importance of the new policy to staff at all levels of the organisation and to colleagues in other agencies. Senior managers, directors or assistant directors were involved in the implementation of the Assessment Framework in 21 of the 24 councils.

FIRST-LINE MANAGERS

First-line managers are crucial in achieving and maintaining changes in practice. They are the link between the objectives of the organisation and outcomes in practice. First-line managers play a key role in *implementing the system and helping practitioners to use it properly* (Corrick *et al.*, 1995, p.23). The importance of first-line managers in implementation appears to have been well understood by councils in introducing the Assessment Framework, and they were involved in the process of implementation in all but one of the councils taking part in the research.

TRAINERS

The involvement of trainers in implementation ensures that training is an integral part of a council's implementation plan. Training can be built into the plan at key points to support or reinforce changes. Training can also be used to keep staff informed and up to date with the implementation process. Training events are a valuable source of information about the impact of changes on practitioners and the degree of progress they have made in relation to changing their practice. The involvement of trainers in the implementation process ensures that this information is fed back to senior and first-line managers, and implementation groups, to inform the ongoing process of implementation. When trainers are not involved in planning the implementation there is a risk that training can be overlooked or lack the clear focus necessary to support change. Eighteen councils involved trainers or training managers in implementation.

PRACTITIONERS

The commitment of practitioners is essential if changes to practice are to be achieved and maintained. Practitioners need to understand why changes are being introduced and how their practice and service users will benefit (Bullock, 1995; Howe, 1986). Involving practitioners in the planning and implementation stages will increase their ownership of the project. Identifying a number of key practitioners in the organisation who were committed to the project proved to be an important resource in informing other practitioners about the project and supporting changes to practice (Corrick *et al.*, 1995; Jones *et al.*, 1998). Eighteen councils included practitioners in the process of implementation.

Cross-boundary working

The Assessment Framework emphasises the importance of inter-agency and inter-professional working to assess the needs of children and to develop effective plans to meet the needs identified.

> An important underlying principle of the approach to assessment outlined in this Guidance, therefore, is that it is based on an inter-agency model in which it is not just social services that are the assessors and providers of services. (Department of Health *et al.*, 2000a, p.14, 1.50)

The level of inter-agency working in councils was influenced by the effectiveness of existing joint working arrangements.

CROSS-BOUNDARY WORKING AT A STRATEGIC LEVEL

At a strategic level there was a significant level of inter-agency working. Eight councils had established inter-agency implementation groups. Inter-agency implementation groups had a number of advantages for councils. As they were established specifically to support the implementation of the Assessment Framework, councils could ensure that membership of the group included key professionals from other agencies with responsibility for, or involvement in, assessment. The participation of colleagues from other agencies helped to increase ownership of the Assessment Framework and promoted a view that the Guidance applied to all agencies rather than only to social services. Nonetheless, councils reported that it was difficult to achieve this sense of ownership across all agencies.

In eight councils the Area Child Protection Committee took the lead in the implementation of the Assessment Framework across agencies. Local Area Child Protection Committees have the lead responsibility for the management of inter-agency working in relation to child protection, and implementation was only one aspect of the committee's work. Feedback from councils suggests that the success of this approach was affected by the way in which the committee perceived the Guidance: that is, whether they viewed the Assessment Framework or their responsibility for its implementation purely in relation to child protection. In some councils this resulted in a view among some agencies that the Assessment Framework was only applicable to cases of child protection.

Three councils had formal links between the internal implementation group established within social services and the Area Child Protection Committee. This ensured that other agencies were kept informed of developments and increased the awareness of the Assessment Framework, but did little to promote ownership among partner agencies.

In four councils implementation remained the responsibility of social services. Often this decision was taken as a result of internal issues relating to implementation, for example a re-structuring of services. In these circumstances some councils felt that it was important that they had their own house in order before involving other agencies.

CROSS-BOUNDARY WORKING AT A PRACTICE LEVEL

At a practice level the Assessment Framework has promoted the development of joint initiatives. Its implementation provided councils and other agencies with the opportunity to review current practice and to take forward new initiatives. One positive aspect of the research programme was that it provided an opportunity and vehicle for councils to share information and developments. Several councils exchanged examples of work they were undertaking to promote inter-agency working, including joint protocols, inter-agency referral records, guidance, and joint assessment policies.

Six councils had developed inter-agency protocols, policies or procedures. These clarified the role and responsibilities of agencies in relation to joint assessments. In some cases documentation was developed to address specific needs or circumstances – for example, where there were parental mental-health issues. In others they sought to clarify how agencies would work together at a local level in accordance with principles of the Assessment Framework.

Six councils had implemented inter-agency referral records that were used to make referrals between agencies. The inter-agency referral records combined elements of the Department of Health's Referral and Initial Information record and the Initial Assessment record. Councils reported a number of advantages from the use of these records. For example, they supported the development of a consistent approach to assessment and information-gathering between agencies. Professionals from agencies other than social services reported that recording information using the Assessment Framework format led, in some cases, to a greater understanding of the child's developmental needs and circumstances and to better targeted referrals. In addition, they ensured that when social services were taking a referral the relevant information about the child and family was available and readily transferable to their own referral record. Finally, the use of inter-agency referral records had no significant impact on the number of referrals received, but had resulted in a significant improvement in the quality of referrals, which enabled more effective decisions to be made, and reduced the need to recontact agencies.

Training

Training played an important role in supporting the early stages of implementation. Feedback from councils indicated that many had used initial training events and seminars to identify issues to be addressed during implementation, keep staff informed of proposed changes, and consult on new procedures and materials. Fourteen councils had training of some form in place from an early stage.

The implementation of the Assessment Framework required attitudinal changes by some practitioners. Such change is difficult to achieve and consequently required much training, and continuing support. It is not sufficient for training to inform staff about the new guidance and introduce them to new procedures and recording formats: it must also win the 'hearts and minds' of practitioners. To change attitudes, practitioners need the opportunity to reflect on the need for change and its implications for their practice (DiClementi, 1991). Moreover, retaining attitudinal changes gained in the sanctity of a training course is difficult when practitioners return to work in stressful situations with little ongoing support (Horwath and Morrison, 2000).

Eight councils offered training at this level. A further eight had used seminars as the primary vehicle for their training. While seminars are effective in providing information, they do not offer an opportunity for practitioners to internalise the need for change. In the remaining eight councils training was still in the planning stages at the time when this information was gathered, albeit after the council had implemented the Assessment Framework.

Feedback from councils cited two reasons why training was mainly delivered through seminars or short one-off training events. The first was that, as with the Looking After Children System, councils underestimated the level of change required by the implementation of the Assessment Framework. The second was that councils, many of which were under pressure as a result of staffing difficulties, found it difficult to release staff for training.

Councils reported that training had proved to be a far larger task than initially envisaged. Training on the Assessment Framework had revealed gaps in existing knowledge, particularly in relation to the analysis of the information gathered during an assessment. However, only five councils had put arrangements in place to address these gaps in knowledge and provide practitioners with ongoing support. These included innovative methods such as:

- practice mentors who worked alongside practitioners
- action learning sets
- regular practice workshops.

Where these arrangements were in place councils reported lower resistance and improvements in the quality of assessment practice.

Technical capacity

As discussed earlier, the research team provided each council with an electronic version of the assessment records. Several of the councils did not have the Information Technology (IT) or technical capacity to use this. In others the version provided was not compatible with the councils' existing IT systems. A number of councils commissioned or developed in-house their own electronic version of the records, generally based on a Word format.

A total of nineteen councils used some form of electronic record. Six made the decision to implement only an electronic version of the records, and a further thirteen implemented some, but not all, of the records in an electronic format. Five councils used only paper versions of the records.

The research suggests that there was not always a good fit between a council's technical capacity and the version of the records used. This mismatch had the potential to lead to dissatisfaction and frustration amongst the staff. For example, to implement all the records in an electronic format requires practitioners to have regular access to computers and a degree of familiarity and skill, because information can only be entered through a computer.

Three of the councils implemented an electronic version of the records with only an average ratio of computers to staff (1 computer to 2 or 3 practitioners). These councils may not have the technical capacity to use electronic records effectively. Four councils with a lower-than-average ratio of computers to staff (1 computer to more than 3 practitioners) used a mix of paper and electronic versions. The low level of IT suggests that practitioners will have difficulty accessing a computer or may lack the experience or training to use electronic versions of the record. Three councils with an average ratio of computers to practitioners (1 computer to 2 or 3 practitioners) made the decision to implement the records only in paper versions. Many practitioners familiar with using some level of IT would be reduced to recording everything by hand, a process that may increase resistance to the system.

Summary points

- The strategies used by councils to implement the Assessment Framework were examined in relation to the following factors: support with implementation; leadership; ownership; cross-boundary working; training and technical capacity (Jones *et al.*, 1998; Ward 1998).
- Councils had considerable support to introduce the Assessment Framework. For example, the Department of Health provided each council with a training pack, *The Child's World* (NSPCC and University of Sheffield, 2000), and held a series of training events to support the implementation of the Assessment Framework. In addition the research team provided different types of support to councils.
- Strong leadership was necessary to carry through the changes that were required to implement the Assessment Framework, because it involved councils in changes at the organisational, procedural and practice level. Councils used one of four strategies to implement the Assessment Framework:

    1. the appointment of a specific project officer
    2. a specific project officer supported by an implementation group
    3. an implementation group
    4. existing management structures.

- Implementation required staff at all levels of the organisation to own the Assessment Framework and key to this was the involvement of senior managers, first-line managers, trainers and practitioners. Thirteen councils involved representatives from all four of the groups in the process of implementation. A further seven councils involved representatives from three of the groups, and three councils involved representatives from two. Only one council involved just one group in their implementation process.
- In relation to cross-boundary working councils recognised the importance of involving other agencies in the process of

implementation. At a strategic level nineteen councils involved other agencies in the implementation process. Despite this, the Assessment Framework was seen by some agencies as the sole responsibility of social services. At a practice level the Assessment Framework promoted joint working between agencies, and just under half the councils developed a joint initiative, such as an inter-agency referral record or inter-agency protocol.

- Training plays an important role in supporting the implementation of change. Where a level of attitudinal change is required, as with the Assessment Framework, training must address the 'hearts and minds' of practitioners. However, many councils underestimated the level of training required and a third of councils had no training in place when they implemented. When councils provided additional support to practitioners, such as practice mentors, workshops, or learning sets, improvements in the quality of assessments were reported.
- The number of computers within councils was generally low and councils varied in their use of paper or electronic versions of the assessment records. A quarter of the councils used only electronic versions of the records, a further thirteen (54%) councils implemented some, but not all of the records in an electronic format and five (21%) councils used only paper versions of the records.

Chapter summary

The 24 councils involved in the research varied in size, geography, and the populations they served. They included London Boroughs, Shire Counties, Metropolitan Districts and Unitary Authorities.

The ability of councils to implement a new policy is influenced by the level of change involved. The implementation of the Assessment Framework involved councils in a *developmental* change to existing assessment services; that is, an increase in the range and level of assessment services that councils provided to children. In some cases this involved councils in structural changes and 22 (92%) of the 24 councils reported that they would be modifying their existing assessment processes to implement the Assessment Framework.

The research suggests that there was a range of views among practitioners about the *legitimacy* of the Assessment Framework – that is, whether the approach to assessment set out in the Assessment Framework was appropriate for all groups of children. Some practitioners, particularly those working in specialist teams, did not consider the Assessment Framework applicable to the children they worked with. In these situations bringing about attitudinal change was a challenge to some councils and affected implementation in these teams.

The research considered councils' readiness to implement the Assessment Framework in relation to the factors identified by Hall and colleagues (1975). These factors – theoretical and technical knowledge; resources; collaborative arrangements; and administrative capacity – were considered individually to allow the impact of each factor on implementation to be considered.

Theoretical and technical knowledge referred to (a) the existence of written policies and procedures relating to the process and practice of assessment (b) the provision of information on assessments for families (c) the process of assessment within children's social services departments. Although most councils had written policies and procedures about assessments, only four routinely provided families with information *and* copies of their assessments. This suggests that implementing the Assessment Framework required not simply organisational and process change, but for some practitioners also an attitudinal change. Such attitudinal change is more difficult for councils to achieve and sustain.

The resources available to councils to implement the Assessment Framework were considered in relation to staffing, and the councils' ability to undertake core social work tasks. The research found that over a quarter (28.5%) of councils that supplied staffing information had vacancy rates of over 30 per cent. Locum practitioners were employed in over half (57%) of the councils. Staffing issues had resulted in two-thirds of the councils restricting services to looked-after children or children on child protection registers. Three-quarters of the councils reported that they had cases awaiting allocation, and practically half (46%) the councils' unallocated cases included children in need of protection and/or care or accommodation. It is anticipated that the level of staff vacancies will impact on a council's ability to implement the Assessment Framework.

The collaborative arrangements which councils had in place to support the implementation of the Assessment Framework were considered in relation to strategic planning arrangements, and joint assessment practices between councils and other agencies. The research found that there were good arrangements between councils and other agencies at a strategic level. This enabled existing strategic frameworks and relationships to be used to support the implementation of the Assessment Framework. At a practice level 19 councils (79%) reported that they were involved in joint assessments for specific groups of children. However, only three councils (12.5%) reported that they worked collaboratively with other agencies to assess the needs of all children. It is anticipated that the extent of existing collaborative working will influence the ease to which the implementation of the Assessment Framework can take place on an inter-agency basis.

The administrative arrangements of councils were considered in relation to the availability of computers to practitioners, and the structures in place for referrals and assessments. Seventeen councils had referral and assessment teams or similar structures in place. The ability to use the assessment records in an electronic format offered a number of advantages that would support practitioners in the process of implementation. However, the ability to use the records in an electronic format depended on practitioners having ready access to computers. Only in seven (29%) councils was a computer available for at least every two practitioners, while in six councils (25%) a single computer was available to four or more practitioners. The low level of access to computers suggests that few councils had either sufficient computer hardware or staff with the necessary IT skills to introduce an assessment system in an electronic format.

Social work practitioners are subjected to high levels of change. Only one council had not experienced a re-organisation of either its Children and Family Services or Social Services Department, with seven councils experiencing up to three changes, in the five years preceding implementation. Practitioners experiencing high levels of change are more likely to be resistant to further change (Bullock, 1995; Howe, 1986). It was anticipated that councils with high levels of change would have greater difficulty in implementing the Assessment Framework than other councils.

To implement the Assessment Framework councils used one of the following strategies: the employment of a specific project officer (used by two, 8.3% councils), a specific project officer supported by an implementation group (used in five, 21% councils), an implementation group (used in fifteen, 62.5% councils) and existing management structures (used in two, 8.3% councils). The most successful strategy was the appointment of a specific project officer supported by an implementation group when the officer carried sufficient authority and influence within the organisation.

To implement the Assessment Framework successfully required the commitment of staff at all levels in the council. The involvement of senior managers demonstrates a council's commitment to a new policy. Senior managers, directors or assistant directors, were involved in the implementation of the Assessment Framework in 21 (87.5%) councils. First-line managers are crucial in achieving and maintaining changes in practice. These managers were involved in the process of implementation in all but one council. The involvement of trainers in implementation ensures that training is an integral part of a council's implementation plan. Three-quarters of the councils involved trainers or training managers in the implementation of the Assessment Framework. The commitment of practitioners is essential if changes to practice are to be achieved and maintained. Eighteen councils included practitioners in the process of implementation. This strategy proved to be an important resource in informing other practitioners about the project and supporting changes to practice.

The Assessment Framework applies to all professionals working directly with children and families. The ability of councils to involve other agencies in the process of implementation affected the extent to which the Assessment Framework was perceived as a truly inter-agency guidance. Councils used different methods to involve other agencies at a strategic level. Eight established inter-agency implementation groups, a further eight used their Area Child Protection Committee, three established formal links between their internal implementation group and the Area Child Protection Committee. Only four councils implemented the Assessment Framework solely within social services.

The implementation of the Assessment Framework provided councils and other agencies with the opportunity to review current practice and develop new initiatives. Almost half of the councils developed one or more initiatives with partner agencies, such as inter-agency protocols, policies or procedures, or inter-agency referral records. It is anticipated that these developments will support the involvement of other agencies and improve the quality of assessments undertaken using the Assessment Framework.

In over half the councils (58%) training played an important role in supporting the early stages of the implementation. Initial training events and seminars were used to identify issues to be addressed during implementation, keep staff informed of proposed changes and consult on new procedures and materials.

Councils underestimated the level of training and support necessary to achieve a workforce confident in using the Assessment Framework. Most depended on short, one-off training programmes or training seminars. This may have been because councils did not appreciate:

- the level of attitudinal change required of some of their practitioners
- the impact of constant organisational changes on the ability of workers to accommodate further changes to their practice
- the problems that high vacancy rates and the use of locum staff bring.

Only five councils provided flexible training programmes and continuing support, through, for example, the use of practice mentors, action learning sets, and regular practice workshops. Where these arrangements were in place, councils reported lower resistance and improvements in the quality of assessment practice.

The number of computers to practitioners within councils was generally low. The Assessment Framework had encouraged councils to use electronic versions of some of the records. Councils varied in their use of paper or electronic versions of the assessment records. However, the decision of which version of the records to use was not always consistent with technical capacity within the council.

Chapter 3

Involving Families in the Assessment Process

> Whatever their circumstances or difficulties, the concept of partnership between State and the family, in situations where families are in need of assistance in bringing up their children, lies at the heart of child care legislation.
>
> (Department of Health *et al.*, 2000a, p.12, 1.44)

The notion of partnership between State and families is established in Part III of the Children Act 1989 and applies to both assessing the needs of a child and the provision of services. Since the introduction of the Children Act 1989 research has shown that social workers believe that working in partnership with parents is generally beneficial and most see it as a priority in their practice (Thoburn *et al.*, 1995). Research findings have validated the emphasis on working in partnership with families because of its association with better outcomes for children (Aldgate and Bradley, 1999; Cleaver, 2000; Department of Health, 1995a).

True partnership, however, depends on both parties holding equal power, a position that exists in few cases that come to the attention of social work services. Thoburn and colleagues (1995) have shown that parents and professionals can work together even when power is not equally balanced. This work developed a hierarchy of participatory practice where 'partnership' is the aim and 'keeping informed' a basic requirement. Between these two extremes lie 'participation', 'involvement' and 'consultation'.

This emphasis on partnership with families continues to underpin government policy on assessment (Department of Health *et al.*, 2000a).

Developing a co-operative working relationship with parents or caregivers is an essential part of the process of understanding what is happening to the child (Department of Health *et al.*, 2000a). However, parental involvement is only part of the assessment process. Social workers also need to work directly with children to ascertain their wishes and feelings (see, for example, the welfare checklist of the Children Act 1989). The Assessment Framework is clear that an assessment of a child in need requires that the child be seen and, subject to its age and development, listened to.

> Direct work with children is an essential part of assessment, as well as recognising their rights to be involved and consulted about matters which affect their lives. (Department of Health *et al.*, 2000a, p.43, 3.41)

These rights are enshrined in article 12 of the UN Convention on the Rights of the Child.

A key element to working in partnership with children and families is keeping them informed. In particular, the Assessment Framework stresses the value of social workers, when carrying out an assessment, explaining to family members including, when relevant, the child:

- what is happening
- why an assessment is being undertaken
- what will be the process
- what is likely to be the outcome.

The emphasis on these issues is based on the findings from a number of studies. For example, work on parents' perspectives in relation to child-protection enquiries shows that even in the most traumatic and difficult circumstances parents value professionals who give clear explanations, are open and honest and treat them with respect and dignity. They do not want to be kept in the dark, to have professionals talk about them without their knowledge and to feel patronised (Cleaver and Freeman, 1995; Freeman and Hunt, 1998; Thoburn, Wilding and Watson, 2000). Similar findings are beginning to emerge from work that explores the views of children and young people (O'Quigley, 2000).

A common parental complaint found in the studies of child protection was the lack of information about what was happening. Parents frequently reported a sense of shock and betrayal that professionals had referred them to social services without their knowledge; families felt excluded from a process that they found frightening and disempowering. They believed professionals failed to seek their views or disregarded them when decisions were made (Cleaver and Freeman, 1995; Sharland *et al.*, 1996).

These findings and guidance from Government (Department of Health, 1995b) fuelled the refocusing of children's social services in England of which the Assessment Framework is the latest element. However, changes in policy and the rewriting of practice guides do not guarantee a change in practice. This chapter explores the involvement of families in assessments carried out by social workers using the Assessment Framework and seeks to evaluate the extent to which practice has changed.

The sources of information

Information for this chapter is drawn from two sources: questionnaires returned by social work practitioners (n=216) and managers (n=93), and interviews with parents (n=50), children (n=8) and social work practitioners (n=52). The interview sample was made up of 52 cases. To qualify for inclusion in the sample, a child or young person must have been involved in a core assessment. A detailed explanation of the methods is given in Appendix I. The tables referred to in this chapter are to be found in Appendix II.

The views of social work managers and practitioners on the impact on family involvement

A larger proportion of managers than practitioners reported that the implementation of the Assessment Framework and use of the assessment records encouraged the involvement of families in the assessment process. Three-quarters of managers reported that the use of the assessment records had increased family involvement compared with 42 per cent of social work practitioners.

THE VIEWS OF MANAGERS

Managers reported that the principles underpinning the Assessment Framework and the practice of sharing what was written on the assessment records with parents or carers had improved family involvement. The reasons cited were classified under four themes:

1. a more open and honest relationship with the family
2. social workers giving a clearer explanation of their role
3. increased accountability for both social services and families

4. parents routinely consulted and whenever possible their consent gained for any actions that might be taken.

> Social workers have to share information and the completed assessment record with family. Encourages open, constructive, accountable working. I've had positive feedback from families. It helps to clarify the role of the social worker. Must cover the issue of consent, in writing etc. It's very helpful.
>
> (Team manager, locality team)

> Because social workers must be clear from the outset what the purpose and process of assessment is. This will only be successful with high quality engagement with families and high quality supervision.
>
> (Team manager, child and family team)

THE VIEWS OF SOCIAL WORK PRACTITIONERS

Forty-two per cent of social workers reported that the Assessment Framework and the use of the assessment records had increased the level of family involvement in assessments.

Kennedy and Wonnacott (2003) argue that the ecological approach promoted within the Assessment Framework should help to address the values and attitudes that allow disabled children to be more vulnerable to abuse than non-disabled children. However, social workers working with disabled children raised concerns about the relevance of the Assessment Framework and the usefulness of the assessment records for disabled children in a number of fora. For example, it was an issue frequently voiced during the familiarisation sessions, at multi-agencies conferences held by Councils with Social Services Responsibility to introduce the Assessment Framework, and at regional implementation days. The information drawn from the questionnaires supports these views. Social workers working with disabled children were less likely than their colleagues in other teams to report an increase in family involvement. Only 20 per cent reported that family involvement in the assessment process had increased.

When an assessment involved a disabled child, some social workers reflected the attitudes described by Kennedy and Wonnacott (2003) viewing parents as 'heroic carers' and the child as a passive recipient of their care. For example, they reported that the assessment records did not cover the issues about the child's health and development in sufficient detail, while collecting information about parenting capacity was generally thought to be unnecessary and insulting.

> The forms are not really appropriate for children with disabilities many of whom have parents whom one is aware cope admirably with difficult circumstances.
>
> (Social worker, disabilities team)

> Families find it intrusive. They feel they are 'entitled' to a service because they have a child with a disability and that it is insulting to have their parenting etc. assessed when they are caring 24 hours a day, 7 days a week for a child with complex needs.
>
> (Social worker, disabilities team)

Regardless of the team they were working in, social workers who reported increased levels of family involvement credited the change to practice related issues. For example, social work practitioners thought the expectation that the completed core assessment records would be shared with the family resulted in:

- a more focused approach to assessments
- an increased expectation that parents and young people's views would be recorded
- opportunities to discuss issues where the views of parents and professionals are in conflict.

> Makes involving the family easier as they can go through the document with you, and it does help to focus sessions.
>
> (Social worker, referral and assessment team)

> It gave more opportunities for the family to be involved and ensured the assessment did focus on the child rather than parents' needs.
>
> (Social worker, disability team)

> The space [on the assessment record] for parents/carers/young people's views is very positive and for them to record they have seen the assessment.
>
> (Social worker, locality team)

> Parents liked being included in the process. Parents can see the areas where professionals disagreed with parents' interpretation. Provided an arena for discussion.
>
> (Social worker, locality team)

Managers were less likely than practitioners to report neutral or negative consequences for family involvement, arising from the implementation of the Assessment Framework and the introduction of the assessment records.

Approximately a fifth (22%) of managers and a third of social workers reported that the Assessment Framework and the use of the records made little or no difference to family involvement in the assessment process. Many of the reasons given by practitioners suggest the lack of impact reflected the general difficulties they encountered in involving families in the assessment process.

> It did not – some families engage others don't. The format of assessment doesn't affect this.
>
> (Social worker, referral and assessment team)

> Directly, it appeared to be very little. The majority of families did not wish to engage and appeared uninterested in outcome, this was true of those who did engage. Helped with sharing results for planning with other professionals and foster carers but little impact upon families especially children.
>
> (Social worker, assessment team)

Very few managers (n=3) reported that the Assessment Framework and the use of the records had had a detrimental effect on family involvement, a view held by a quarter of social work practitioners.

> It prevented families and young people from free flow thinking as information is required in a specific order.
>
> (Social worker, locality team)

> I feel that some families found it intrusive and personal.
>
> (Social worker, locality team)

Confusion over the purpose of the assessment records

The issues raised by social workers in their replies suggest a degree of confusion over the purpose of the assessment records. The Department of Health's assessment records were issued with the Assessment Framework. These records were developed for social workers to record the salient information, gathered during their professional assessment, about a child's needs, parenting capacity and the family circumstances to assist in the analysis of a child and family's circumstances (Department of Health and Cleaver, 2000).

The responses from social workers suggest they used them rather differently. For example, instead of using the core records to write up a summary of an assessment, and the tick boxes to indicate professional judgement on particular issues, some workers used them as questionnaires where the tick boxes 'score' parents' answers to the questions posed by the social worker.

> Because of yes/no answers parents tend to give the one which they think we want to hear.
>
> (Social worker, long-term team)

> People feel patronised – it is like administering a census. It is time consuming and does not facilitate ease of discussion.
>
> (Social worker, children and families team)

> In a crisis a family finds it very difficult to focus on a form. This is not needs led at all – it presumes that all situations fit into the Framework. The practice reality is that they don't.
>
> (Social worker, referral and assessment team)

This impression that some social workers were using the record as a questionnaire is reinforced by the reports of some managers.

> Sometimes social workers have gone through the questions with individuals seeking their opinions but have then not expressed their own professional judgement.
>
> (Manager, locality team)

To use the Core Assessment record as a 'test paper' for families would explain why some social workers reported a negative impact on family involvement. It is sobering to find, as we shall show later in this chapter, that some families welcomed even this level of involvement and consultation.

Sharing the assessment record with the family

In order to inform families of decisions that have been made as a result of the assessment and to allow them to record their views (as stated in the Assessment Framework, 3.13), many social services departments established a policy of giving the parents a copy of the completed assessment record.

Although this was widely accepted as good practice it could result in extra work for practitioners when the family's first language is not English.

> Cultural – no facility to translate such a large document.
>
> (Social worker, referral and assessment team)

Similarly, social workers needed to spend more time when parents had poor literacy skills.

> I like the way the families are given a copy of the assessment. However it is based on an assumption of a degree of literacy.
>
> (Social worker, locality team)

Family involvement and its impact on assessments

The interviews with social workers showed that they placed considerable emphasis on ensuring parents understood what the assessment would entail. In 49 of the 52 cases included in the interview sample social workers reported that they had explained the purpose and process of the assessment to families. Ensuring that families understood the process of assessment depended on the skills of social workers. In practically every case social workers reported that their explanation covered key issues such as confidentiality, who would be involved, how long it would take, and the factors to be discussed. How effective this was will be examined later in this chapter.

The time social workers took over their explanation varied with the circumstances of the case. Explanations were in a variety of forms, some were done over the phone, others during a series of visits. For example, Case 42 involved a mother with learning difficulties where the social worker was aware that the process of assessment needed to be explained carefully to ensure that the family fully understood what was happening.

> I explained over the phone and on the visit. I told them that the initial assessment would lead to some action – referral to other agencies or allocation. I did it on several visits and kept going over it.
>
> (Social worker, referral and assessment team)

How long social workers spent on the task of explaining the assessment to families varied between two extremes – 5 minutes and an hour and a half. There were however two peaks: in 11 cases social workers reported spending half an hour, and in a further 19 cases social workers had spent an hour or more over their explanations.

> I feel that not only is it important to give the family members a copy of the core assessment but also to discuss in detail, its content and the implications of the assessment. I have found no difficulties in giving a copy to the family. The advantages are that the family are clear about what you have done with the information they have given you, the reasons for your decisions and what the child's needs are.
>
> (Social worker, long-term team)

The considerable effort and time taken by practitioners to involve families reaps its own rewards. The data suggest that the quality of social-work assessments (self-rated by social workers) is strongly associated with family involvement in the assessment process (see Table 3.1, Appendix II). Two-thirds of social workers that reported increased family involvement in the assessment process believed the quality of their assessments had improved. In comparison, less than a third (31%) of social workers who reported no increase in family involvement thought the quality of their assessments had improved.

Summary points

- Three-quarters of managers found the Assessment Framework and the use of the assessment records improved family involvement in assessments.
- Forty-two per cent of social workers reported that family involvement in the assessment process had increased.
- A fifth of managers and a third of social work practitioners reported that family involvement in the assessment process had changed very little.
- The responses of social workers that reported a negative impact on family involvement suggest considerable confusion over the purpose of the assessment records.
- Informing and involving families in the process of assessment is related to improvements in the quality of assessments.

The experiences of parents

PROFILE OF THE CASE STUDY SAMPLE (N=52)

Purposive sampling was used to ensure that the case study sample included children and young people from each of the age groups and to ensure that families of disabled children were represented. This resulted in a skewed sample with practically a quarter (n=12) of cases involving a disabled child, a much larger proportion than the 3 per cent identified in the audit of core assessments. The sampling enabled the study to examine whether practitioners' concerns over the relevance of the Assessment Framework and the assessment records for disabled children were mirrored in the experiences of families themselves.

AGE AND GENDER OF THE CHILDREN OR YOUNG PEOPLE

The case study includes similar proportion of girls (n=25, 48.1%) and boys (n=27, 51.9%). No age group dominates the sample (see Table 3.2, Appendix II).

PARENTS OR CARERS' RELATIONSHIP TO THE STUDY CHILD

The parents or carers who took part in the case study were related to the study child in different ways. Interviews were carried out with 41 mothers on their own, two mothers jointly with her husband/partner, four fathers, one step-father, a grandmother and a great aunt.

THE ROUTE TO SOCIAL SERVICES

In 30 cases the parents either approached social services themselves or were referred by another agency with their knowledge and agreement. In six cases parents knew about the referral but did not agree with it and in nine cases the parent was unaware they were being referred at all. The remaining five cases were open, and the assessment was carried out as part of the review. Two cases related to an unaccompanied asylum seeker.

REASONS FOR CONTACT WITH SOCIAL SERVICES

Parents and social workers reported a variety of reasons why the family and professionals had sought social-work help or why they had been referred to social services. In over half the cases (57.6%) child protection concerns were one of the issues reported by parents or the professional referring the case to social services.

In the majority of cases parents revealed a cluster of adversities that affected their capacity to meet the developmental needs of their child. For example, mental illness, particularly maternal depression, was identified in over a quarter of cases (26.9%), poor housing and financial difficulties, and problems with alcohol and drug use were identified in approximately a sixth of cases (17.3% and 15.3% respectively) and domestic violence in 13.4 per cent of cases. In practically a third of cases (30.7%) the parents found themselves unable to control their child's behaviour and sought professional help and advice. Table 3.3, Appendix II shows the issues identified by parents and professionals that triggered the referral to social services.

CASES INVOLVING A DISABLED CHILD

In 12 cases the referral involved a disabled child. Scrutinising the reasons why families were in contact with social services shows that in most cases the issues facing these families were complex. For example, the mother explains the family's situation in Case 11.

> C. [aged 14 years] has severe autism. His behaviour was deteriorating – he had violent and disruptive outbursts. He was becoming a danger to other children. He was on increasing medication. His brother [mildly autistic] was anxious all of the time and his sister could not bring friends around. We could not go out at all. We just could not take C. out because of his really difficult behaviour. It was affecting all of our relationships. We felt that C. needed 52-week-a-year residential schooling and care.
>
> (Mother of C.)

Similar complex issues were reported in Case 32.

> T. [aged 7 years] was having difficulties at school. Her behaviour was getting difficult at home and I needed some advice and help. I was awaiting a statement [of educational need] from the education. I needed a shoulder to cry on. I had no time for J. [4-year-old brother]. T. would throw things out of the window and telling her off did nothing. I was getting that I could not control her. I needed help.
>
> (Mother of T.)

Social workers had been concerned that the Assessment Framework and the introduction of the assessment records resulted in too much information being collected on issues that parents of disabled children saw as irrelevant. The views from the 12 parents of disabled children involved in this research would not support this premise.

- Only a quarter (n=3) thought that social workers collected too much information about their child and the family.

- Parents of disabled children were practically twice as likely as those without a disabled child, to report that the assessment definitely covered the issues they thought were important.
- Parents of disabled children reported a similar degree of involvement in the process of assessment as other parents.
- A greater proportion (83%) of parents of disabled children knew that their views were recorded in the assessment record than other parents (66%).
- A greater proportion of parents of disabled children (88%) thought the plan for their child was helpful than did other parents (68%).

CASES THAT DID NOT INVOLVE CHILD PROTECTION CONCERNS

In 22 cases the reasons for the referral did *not* involve concerns about child protection. However, because the focus of the case study was families who had been involved in a core assessment the circumstances that led to social services intervention were, nonetheless, complex and frequently required the services of a number of different agencies. For example, some families needed additional help with housing, or were experiencing difficulties in managing a disabled child's behaviour. In others the family struggled to cope with domestic violence, parental drug or alcohol use, or parental mental illness. The following two cases serve as illustrations.

The research worker describes the background in Case 11 introduced earlier.

> This is a well-to-do family living in an affluent part of S. in a large expensive house. They moved to S. from L. a few years ago and have settled well, but are separated from their extended family. They are a family with three children, two boys and a girl. Both of the boys suffer from autism, but the older brother, M. only has a mild form and is well managed within the house and community. C., 13 years, suffers from an extreme form of autism and his behaviour has deteriorated and recently became unmanageable in the home, in the school and in the community. The problems of caring for C. was putting an immense strain on the family.
>
> (Research worker)

The mother in Case 11 describes the difficulties her family was facing:

> C.'s behaviour was deteriorating – he had violent and disruptive outbursts. He was becoming a danger to other children. In respite care the staff were not feeling safe. He was on increasing medication. It was becoming very difficult for my husband and me and for his brother and sister. He was a major behaviour problem. We felt that he needed residential care and urgently.
>
> (Mother of C.)

The second set of circumstances described by the mother in Case 51 gives some insight into the impact domestic violence, parental mental illness and substance misuse have on the wellbeing of children.

> About four years ago I came to a women's refuge – my husband gave me a good hiding and I took pills and ended up in hospital – social services turned up on the doorstep. I had drink problems – they gave me practical parenting points and some support – that was OK.
>
> (Mother of Y., an 11-year-old girl)

The mother describes how the family's difficulties were compounded.

> Back in June – I contacted them [social services] and I was told I had to wait till August – and then my drugs worker made contact with them. I couldn't cope at all. My husband was beating me, I was on the drink again, not taking my anti-depressants on a regular basis. I was a mess. Y. completely freaked out to the extent that she had a CAMH worker and S. [younger daughter] went away and stayed with her dad for a while.
>
> (Mother of Y.)

These examples show that, although some 42 per cent (n=22) of cases included in the case study sample did not involve child protection concerns, families still faced a multiplicity of difficulties and in every case the social workers thought the family urgently needed professional help to cope.

CASES INVOLVING CHILD PROTECTION CONCERNS

In 30 cases the reason for referral included child protection concerns. A comparison between these cases and those featured in an earlier study of suspected child abuse (Cleaver and Freeman, 1995) reveals similarities in relation to the type of suspected abuse and the age of the child (see Tables 3.4 and 3.5, Appendix II).

Table 3.4 shows that in both samples suspected physical abuse is the most prevalent issue. In the present study the proportion of cases of suspected sexual abuse is smaller, while the proportion of cases of neglect is greater, than in the Cleaver and Freeman 1995 sample. The tendency at the time the child protection research was conducted to filter out of the system allegations concerning neglect may account for these differences (Gibbons *et al.*, 1995).

Table 3.5 shows that although children under the age of five years accounted for a somewhat larger proportion of the present interview study than the child protection study, the two sample groups show a similar overall profile in terms of the age of the children involved.

THE COMPLEXITY OF THE CASES

The 30 child protection cases included in the present study also resemble those included in the earlier child-abuse study in terms of the problems families were facing. Cleaver and Freeman (1995) studied 583 case-files and interviewed 30 families. This enabled the development of the following typology of families involved in child protection enquiries:

- multi-problem families
- specific problem families
- acutely distressed families
- families infiltrated by perpetrators of abuse
- families where the child had been abused by an outsider unknown to the family.

(See Cleaver and Freeman 1995, pp.51–53 for definitions). The present study included families representative of the first four groups.

EIGHTEEN CASES (60% OF CHILD PROTECTION REFERRALS) INVOLVED MULTI-PROBLEM FAMILIES

The reported adversities these families were experiencing were numerous, serious and long term as the following two cases show.

> Case 46. Allegations that K. was being abused by her mother and step-father. There had been a number of previous referrals about this family but not specifically about K. [aged 3 years]. The school had concerns going back some time, these were primarily school-related issues around various children from the family. There had been a murder within the family – step dad's brother had killed their father and is

> serving a life term of imprisonment. Step dad also had been in trouble with the police. Police took police protection order and child now living with maternal grand mother. No contact allowed by mum or step dad.
>
> (Social worker, long-term team)

> Case 48. I was a drug addict. I had been since I was about 14 years old. My sister and mum are addicts. I was taking coke, heroin and crack. I was shoplifting to buy the stuff but it was hard shoplifting all of the time and then selling the things for nothing. When I was about 15 my boy friend of the time said I could get more by going on the streets. I said yes and he took me out. It was easy – I could make more then I had ever had before. I was on the streets until last year when I became pregnant. He, my then boyfriend, was the father. He went back to Jamaica for some time and I found out he was going with another prostitute so I left him. I then ended up in court for prostitution and they said I was likely to get my baby taken away when it was born unless I changed, so I agreed to the social services being told. I got to a drug clinic and the social worker helped me. I am now on a methadone programme and have stopped being a prostitute. We were on the 'at risk' register before the baby was born and they said they could take him away but if I changed I would keep him. The baby had withdrawal symptoms when he was born but he is great now. The social worker was great. She was good.
>
> (17-year-old mother)

FOUR CASES (13.3% OF CHILD PROTECTION REFERRALS) INVOLVED SPECIFIC PROBLEM FAMILIES

In two cases the concerns focused only on the alleged physical abuse of a child – in one case on the alleged sexual abuse, and in the other on whether a teenage mother was able to care adequately for her new-born baby.

The following case serves as an example of a specific problem family.

> Case 4. M. [aged 2 years] got a burn between his fingers. It was cigarette burn – my cigarette. I didn't know about it. Someone reported me to the social services department. The police and a social worker turned up at my door. They said they had a report that M. had been burned. They said they had to investigate. That was the first I knew about the social services being involved.
>
> (Mother of M.)

FOUR CASES (13.3% OF CHILD PROTECTION REFERRALS) INVOLVED ACUTELY DISTRESSED FAMILIES

In these cases (all involving a single mother) problems had been building for some time and a single incident triggered the referral. The social worker explains the reason for the referral.

> Case 29. It was as a result of T.'s [boy aged 9 years] behaviour. Mum had been called to school yet again. She got to school and lashed out hitting him.

The mother discusses the difficulties she was experiencing in her relationship with T.

> We weren't getting on at all. We were getting quite distant from each other. Two years ago I just gave up, I had a nervous breakdown.

She explains the problems that led to the referral.

> T. wasn't co-operating at school. They were phoning me nearly every day to pick him up – most of the time he hadn't even done an hour at school. I'd had problems at home with him as well: verbal abuse, temper outbursts. It was also about me being frustrated with him because he was missing out on his education and the fear of him being excluded.
>
> (Mother of T.)

THREE CASES (10% OF CHILD PROTECTION REFERRALS) INVOLVED A FAMILY INFILTRATED BY A PERPETRATOR OF ABUSE

The following case is one example given from the suspected perpetrator's perspective.

> Case 1. Until they came we were not having any difficulties. Two CID men and a lady from social services came – they turned up at the front door. They said the police were investigating a paedophile ring relating to offences done up to thirty years ago. I had already had a massive stroke when the alleged offences were said to have taken place. They have made my son [A. aged 9 years] live with his grandparents. They will not let him live with me. Some woman from America said she had been abused as a girl and she gave my name. Everyone round here knows as my name was mentioned in the papers. I got beaten up the other night in my club. I am the treasurer of the local British Legion club. This young lad said I was a pervert and beat me up.
>
> (Father of A.)

In another case the mother explains the situation.

> Case 3. I saw something on television about a man we knew. He had been a friend of the family and my daughters had been round to his house. They said he had been involved in sex abuse of children. I was worried about my daughters – especially my youngest – N. [14 years] who had been going to his house since she was about 5 or 6. I contacted the police and they contacted social services who started an investigation. We were devastated – really devastated. We had never been involved in anything like this and we were terribly upset about our daughter. She had been being sexually abused for a long time. It upset us that we had never suspected him and he was coming round to our house for Sunday dinner almost every week.

This rather lengthy and detailed exploration of the cases referred for suspected child abuse in the current study shows considerable similarities in the type of families included in earlier child protection research. This parity allows us to judge whether practice, in relation to family involvement in the process of referral and assessment, has changed. The case illustrations also suggest that social workers were not systematically blocking the research team from approaching families who held negative views of social services.

PARENTAL AWARENESS OF THE REFERRAL

Findings from earlier child protection studies show that in most cases of suspected child abuse considerable discussion and decision-making between professionals from different agencies went on before parents were informed or consulted. This practice led to parents feeling very angry, resentful and powerless (Cleaver and Freeman, 1995; Farmer and Owen, 1995; Sharland *et al.*, 1996).

The current study suggests that there has been a change in practice. In the majority of cases (71.2%) parents reported that professionals talked to them about their concerns before referring them, or persuading them to approach social services themselves. This reflects the audit findings that show approximately two-thirds of referrals had been done with the parents' knowledge (see Chapter 6). Forty-six of the 52 cases resulted from a referral to social services/request for services (two cases involved unaccompanied asylum-seekers, and four were open cases subject to review). In two-thirds (n=30) of these cases parents themselves (frequently following discussion with a professional from another agency) approached social services for help or an agency made the referral with parental consent.

Nonetheless, a third (n=15) of the referrals had been done without the parents consent (n=6) or in some instances their knowledge (n=9). In most of these cases there were serious concerns about the safety of the child and little suggestion of poor practice as Case 46 shows. A description of this family was given as an example of a multi-problem family. The family was well known to social services and the police. There was a history of adult violence and numerous referrals of the older children for suspected physical abuse and neglect. The current allegation made to the police, that the 3-year-old daughter had been physically abused by both parents, resulted in a police protection order and the removal of the child.

The stepfather gives his impression of events.

> They would not say who had reported us but we know it was her [mother's] sister. She has it in for us. It was all lies but they arrested us and took the girl away. She now has to live with her [maternal] grandma and we can not see her.

Nonetheless, in a few cases the referral without parental knowledge appears to have been unnecessary.

> Case 40. There were a few referrals going back a few years – initially from the school nurse. All of a sudden the clinic kept raising issues about A.'s [12-year-old boy] weight, we had a strategy meeting and then it was given to me to do a core assessment. He wasn't putting on weight and he has been like this since he was about 3 or 4 years old, they thought it might be a case of Munchausen's by proxy.
>
> (Social worker, referral and assessment team)

> The mother reports: It wasn't our decision to go to social services it was the Clinic. We didn't know about it 'til they rang us and turned up on our doorstep. A. is a child with an eating disability. The investigation has been all around suspected abuse – it's had an impact on everybody. It's been the worst of times.
>
> (Mother of A)

Irrespective of whether the decision to refer without informing the parent was justified, the impact on parents remained the same. Parents reported that the arrival of a social worker and in many cases a police officer left them feeling angry, frightened, resentful and violated – a finding reflecting that reported in earlier studies of suspected child abuse (Cleaver and Freeman, 1995). However, subsequent involvement of parents in the assessment and planning process could change these negative perspectives.

PARENTS' UNDERSTANDING OF THE PROCESS OF ASSESSMENT

> It requires direct work with children and with family members, explaining what is happening, why an assessment is being undertaken, what will be the process and what is likely to be the outcome. (Department of Health *et al.*, 2000a, p.38, 3.32)

Regardless of how or why the case came to the attention of social services, in over three-quarters (n=40) of cases the parents reported that social workers had explained why an assessment was going to be carried out, how it would be done and what it would entail. Moreover, in the majority of cases (n=33) the parents had been shown a copy of the assessment record prior to the assessment and therefore knew the types of issues that would be explored and the sorts of information that would be recorded.

This emphasis on ensuring that parents understood what the assessment would entail was mirrored by the social workers' responses. As noted earlier in this chapter, in 49 of the 52 cases social workers reported that they had explained the purpose and process of assessment to parents. In nine cases, parents' recall of whether the processes had been explained to them differed from that of the social workers. This confusion often reflected the impact of the trauma, shock and fear of being confronted by social workers and the police over suspected child abuse. The high degree of emotion resulted in parents being unable to take things in.

Case 3 serves as an illustration. When asked if a professional had explained why the assessment was necessary and what it would involve the mother replied,

> I don't know. I was shocked. I had to have people with me as I would forget what was said. I don't really remember now.

These findings offer further evidence that practice in relation to family involvement in the assessment process has changed considerably since the time of the child protection studies. The child protection studies showed that over half the parents felt social workers had not kept them informed and involved during the enquiry (Cleaver and Freeman, 1995).

PARENTAL INVOLVEMENT IN THE PROCESS OF ASSESSMENT

The child protection studies found that well over half the parents considered the process of investigation to have been unsatisfactory (Thoburn *et al.*, 1995). In contrast, parents in the present study expressed high levels of satisfaction over the way the assessment was carried out. For example, in 44 cases parents thought that the social worker had talked to the relevant members of their family and rarely (n=3) talked to those they did not want involved.

The child protection studies also showed that little attention had been paid to keeping parents informed about the enquiry (Farmer and Owen, 1995). The present study showed that in most cases parents were kept informed. For example, in 50 cases social workers made contact with professionals from other agencies in order to assess the child's developmental needs and circumstances. In the majority of these cases (n=37) parents reported that social workers had consulted them before making contact with other agencies, and in six cases they weren't sure. In the six cases where the parent was unsure, social workers reported that they had consulted with the parent before contacting their colleagues.

Finally, the child protection studies highlighted the value parents placed in being offered some choice, control and inclusion in the planned intervention. The present research shows that the majority of parents felt involved in deciding what actions or services were needed to help their family. Thirty-seven of the 50 parents interviewed (74%), reported that social workers had discussed the possible options with them and their views had been recorded in the assessment record. Parents reported that being able to see what was written about them and their own contribution made explicit their involvement and participation in the assessment process. In 33 cases parents reported that at the end of the assessment they had been given a copy of the assessment record.

This perceived level of involvement holds true even in potentially threatening, and alienating circumstances and illustrates how involving parents in the assessment and planning process can shift initial negative attitudes. For example, Case 4, noted earlier in this chapter, came to light as a result of an anonymous referral to social services. Two-year-old M. had been reported to have a burn on his hand, was generally neglected and left with a very young baby-sitter for long periods of time. The first thing the mother knew was when:

> the police and social worker turned up at my door... I was shocked when they came.

Nonetheless, this mother reported that the social worker had explained that an assessment would be carried out and what this would entail. She was pleased that the social worker asked her what help she wanted.

> At first I did not want any help. After I got over the shock of them coming I asked for help with M. I asked for 'time out'. I wanted him to go to a nursery. Anything that would give me a break and some relief. I wanted him to change his behaviour.

The mother went on to describe how the social worker had communicated with her throughout the assessment period and reported that she had always been kept informed of everything that went on. She felt fully involved in all discussions about possible plans and services which might help her family, and although she did not always agree she clearly understood what was happening.

> I did not like registration, I disagreed with that, but I now understand it had to be done. I obviously agreed with the other services they were giving me.

CHILD IN NEED PLANS

Not all core assessments led to plans for the child and family. In six cases social workers reported that there were no plans. In three cases this was because the plan had not been completed and in the other three, social workers reported that no plan had been made. This lack of planning is also a finding from the audit of initial and core assessments (see Chapters 7 and 8 for details).

Interviews with parents suggest that they are not always aware that a plan had been developed as a result of the assessment. Thirty-two parents were aware that there was a plan. Nine parents were not sure if plans existed, although in every case the social worker reported a plan had been made and parents had been involved in its development. Examining these cases offers some insight into this disparity. For example, when Child Protection plans were made these were considered by social workers as 'the plan'. These often preceded the completion of the core assessment, and parents were confused and unsure that the assessment, which ended at a later date, had resulted in a plan. In other cases parents' uncertainty about whether plans existed cannot be so readily explained. For example, although one parent was learning-disabled, other parents in similar circumstances were aware of the plans that had been made. In eight cases parents thought there was no plan and in six of these this perception coincided with the social worker's report.

PARENTAL SATISFACTION WITH THE PLAN

The interviews with parents show high levels of satisfaction with the process of assessment, regardless of the reason for the assessment or how the case came to the attention of social services. However, parents expressed more mixed feelings over the effectiveness of the plan in meeting the needs of their child (see Table 3.6, Appendix II). Less than half the parents (45.2%) were certain the plan would help; 16.6 per cent thought the plan would be of some help; 14.2 per cent were not sure; and practically a quarter (23.8%) were certain that the plan would not be helpful.

Parents' views of the child in need plans were not related to whether they came to social services willingly or if they had been referred without their consent and/or knowledge. Nor were they related to the reason for the referral or request for services. The key factor associated with parental satisfaction with the plan is their involvement in the assessment and planning process. For example, in cases where parents reported being involved in discussions around the actions and services that might help the child and family, the parent was more likely to report positively about the impact of the plans. This finding reinforces the messages about involving families flagged up by the child protection studies (Department of Health, 1995a).

Plans are helping/will definitely help the child and family

Nineteen parents expressed very positive views about the child in need plans and the impact they had on their family. The following case serves as an example.

> Case 33. Ms G. sought the help of social service because: Me and Tom [partner] had split up. I was suffering from post natal depression – I was taking it out on L. [2 years]. I needed help and I needed support. I had just had S. [baby girl]. Tom is her dad but not L.'s. Tom had been taking drugs and was drinking. He was violent to me. He was taking most of my money. We split up and I went to live with mum… I wanted whatever help the social services could give me.
>
> (Mother of L.)

Throughout the assessment Ms G. believed she was consulted and kept informed, that the assessment covered all the important issues and the 'right amount' of information was gathered. Ms G. felt that the social worker had understood what was happening to her family, *she got to know us and what was wrong*. The plans were made with the full agreement of Ms G. and her partner Tom and they were both pleased with the outcome.

> We were pleased with them. They got us back together. The nursery [for L.] is good. We got a house and we are waiting for the counselling. I hope to go on a hairdressing course. We are happy with what happened... Things have improved with Tom. He isn't on drugs and not drinking as much. We are pleased with the help we got.
>
> (Mother of L.)

Plans will help the child and family to some extent

In seven cases parents felt what happened as a result of the plans had helped them to some extent but that many of their difficulties remained unresolved. The following case serves as an example.

> Case 19. The community midwife referred this case which involved a baby girl H. aged 10 months. Her concerns focused on the seemingly increasing domestic violence and the parents' problem drinking. The family was known to the welfare agencies and concerns had previously focused on the welfare of the children. Mr P. (father) acknowledged the impact of his drinking.
>
> > My drinking, that was the main problem all along. It does me in. It causes me to fight and get angry and the like.
>
> Mr P. understood the reason for the assessment, felt consulted and involved throughout, but was uncertain whether the social worker really understood what was happening in the family.
>
> > I think she understood it but I don't think she knew really. She can only help you a bit really.
>
> He was aware of the plans that had been made but had mixed feelings about them, acknowledging that to some extent the solutions lay within the family.
>
> > To be quite honest I haven't noticed a change in our lifestyles. I still drink. We still argue. But most couples do don't they. They have helped us out with a holiday and a crib for the baby and they have given us help with electric, gas and baby milk. I suppose they have helped us like. Problem is we still need to sort ourselves out.
> >
> > (Father of H.)

Not sure/don't know whether plans will help the child and family

In six cases parents said they were unsure or didn't know if the plans would be of benefit to their child and their family. In some cases this reflected a lack of suitable resources. Parents agreed with the plans, thought they would benefit their child and family but were still waiting for something to transpire.

Case 20 involved a Portugese mother, her English husband, their 10-year-old disabled son and their baby daughter. Mrs S. explains,

> I needed a package of care for F.... It's too much stress. Also my baby is very ill and sick because of the stress... I wanted help to make F. independent.

The family was aware that the plan was to get their son into a residential school, a plan they agreed would benefit everyone.

> It's a good plan, but still same situation, still there's no answer, no resources yet. But nothing happened, it is the system not her [the social worker]. There is no solution ever – it is frustrating.

In other cases the parent was confused and unable to recall clearly what the plans were. For example, Case 7 involved a family of the mother, father, J. (6-months-old) and his sister aged 4 years. The mother explains why social services became involved with their family.

> I was a drug addict. I was on methadone and was having a baby. The baby, J., was addicted to it. He had to be weaned off. They were worried about my care for him.

The social worker had no difficulties in involving the family in the assessment but acknowledged that the mother

> has difficulty sticking to the point as she has a very short memory span.

The aim of the assessment was to see if baby J. needed to be accommodated. A good deal of inter-agency co-operation, planning and service provision enabled the family to stay together. However, although this was the outcome the mother wanted,

> I was worried they might take him away from me, I thought they might think he was at risk,

she was only vaguely aware that there was a specific plan and was unable to comment on it.

Plans will not help the child and family

In ten cases parents did not think that the plans would benefit their child or the family. In some cases this was because the parents were at war with each other and help directed towards their child appeared irrelevant.

Case 18 involved a 3-year-old boy, M. The parents were separated and there was a long history of domestic violence and injuries to the children. The social worker found it difficult to engage with the parents.

> Both parents were pre-occupied with each other and they found it very difficult to listen. I saw them individually and whatever was discussed they would make allegations about each other.
>
> (The social worker)

The mother knew that there were plans to monitor the children's wellbeing, but thought this was unnecessary.

> They want to concentrate on those who are really at risk. The one's that die. Not me. I get punished. The system's wrong.
>
> (Mother of M.)

In others cases the solution provided by social services was at odds with what the parents wanted. In Case 25 the mother had sought the help of social services because:

> A. [15-year-old daughter] was staying out all night, going with Asians and just not going to school or doing what I wanted her to. I was absolutely p'd off – with the police coming every night. There were fights – little one seeing it – I refused to have her home.
>
> (Mother of A.)

Social services placed A. in a children's home, although the mother had asked for her to be fostered and gave the social worker the contact number of a private fostering agency. The mother was unhappy about the outcome.

> All they keep doing is having progress meetings, they say the same every time, over and over again that A. is going to go to a secure unit. I don't want that. I want my daughter to change and come home. That's all I want...they haven't done anything for her, she's got into more trouble since she got into that home. I even gave them a name of foster carers who would have had her, but they said they couldn't find one for her.
>
> (Mother of A.)

These illustrations of the degree of parental satisfaction with the outcome of assessments show satisfaction is related to:

- a shared perspective, between parents and social workers, on the difficulties families were facing
- involvement in the choice and development of the plans
- agreement with, and commitment to the plan
- the plan coming to fruition.

All these are aspects of working with families and involving them in the assessment and planning process.

PARENTS' COMMENTS ABOUT THE WHOLE ASSESSMENT PROCESS

At the end of the interview parents were asked if they wished to make any general comments on the assessment process. Parental comments highlighted aspects in the assessment process they particularly valued.

Social workers that took the time to explain why the assessment was necessary

Case 26 involved a learning disabled child.

> We were happy at the way the assessment was done. It was much longer than we expected but we did not mind that. There were certainly a lot of questions but they needed to ask them. The social worker did explain everything so we are happy with the assessment.

Case 3 shows the bewilderment of parents when social workers fail to ensure parents understood the reason for the assessment or the process. This case involved suspected sexual abuse that happened some years ago involving a friend of the family.

> They didn't really help at all. When we were upset they just added to the feeling of hurt. I am afraid. They did not explain. I did not understand why they were asking all of those questions. They should have been more helpful.

Being involved in the process

Case 11 also involved a disabled child.

> Our social worker was excellent. She worked in partnership with us as a family.

Being kept informed of what was going on during the assessment

Case 4 involved concerns of physical abuse.

> They have helped me a lot. They kept me informed. I dread to think what would have happened if they had not intervened. They have been very helpful.

Parents valued social workers that understood the difficulties facing their family

Case 33 involved concerns about the impact on the children of the mother's mental illness, the father's drinking problems and the domestic violence.

> She understood the problems we were having and helped. We felt good with her, we felt OK about the assessment. We are pleased with the help we got.

Being treated with respect

Parents deeply resented professionals who, they felt, talked down to them or did not appear to respect them. This occurred irrespective of the reason why the assessment had been carried out.

Case 25 focused on the parent's difficulties in controlling a teenage child. The mother explained:

> I don't like the way they [social workers] speak to me.

Similarly in Case 34 where there were concerns of physical abuse, the mother reported:

> I'm not happy about the core group meetings. I'm disgusted at the man running it, the way he shouts and talks down to you.

Or in Case 13 that involved a disabled child, the mother wanted the social workers to:

> speak to me with respect – like I'm not an idiot and he [disabled child] should be treated with respect as well as just costing so much.

The timeliness of social services' response

Case 6 involved concerns that the mother's depression was causing her to neglect her child.

> The best social services in the country. The court praised the social worker's report. She has been absolutely wonderful and bent over backwards. It's definitely her, but the whole department have been wonderful. They are so quick to help.

Case 36 is in contrast and involves a teenage mother experiencing difficulties over her housing.

> I just think if you don't give them a kick up the backside they don't move. I called last week to say the housing's the same and can they pay for nursery and I've had no response, nothing. They've taken the easiest way to shut me up and close the case.

Summary points

- The sampling ensured an over-representation of families with a disabled child.
- The experiences of parents of disabled children either mirrored or were more positive than other parents involved in a core assessment.
- The cases that involved child protection concerns showed considerable similarities to those included in child abuse studies undertaken before the refocusing of children's social services and the implementation of the Assessment Framework. This allowed comparisons of parental involvement in the assessment process to be made.
- The current study shows that in most cases professionals consulted parents before making a referral to social services, unless to do so would endanger the child.
- The process of assessment was routinely explained to parents.
- In the majority of cases parents expressed high levels of satisfaction over how the assessment was carried out, who was involved and their participation in the decisions taken to help their child and family.
- A comparison with the findings from the child protection studies shows that social work practice has changed considerably in relation to the level of parental participation in the process of assessment. Most parents reported being consulted, and involved

in the assessment and planning process, and that social workers sought, listened to, and recorded their views.

- Not all assessment resulted in a plan for a child in need. In six cases no plans had been made.
- Parents held varied views on the effectiveness of the child in need plan.
- Parents valued social workers who explained the reason for the assessment; who involved them in the process; who kept them informed; who treated them with respect; who understood their difficulties; and who gave a timely response.

The experiences of children and young people

> Fundamental to establishing whether a child is in need and how those needs should be best met is that the approach must be child centred. This means that the child is seen and kept in focus throughout the assessment and that account is always taken of the child's perspective. (Department of Health *et al.*, 2000a, p.10, 1.34)

We were only able to interview young people in eight cases. In 26 cases the parent was unwilling for their child to participate in the study. In another 11 cases children were below the age of 10 and in a further seven cases children were severely disabled. Any interpretation of the findings from such a small number of cases must be treated with considerable caution; they simply reflect the experiences of these eight young people who talked to members of the research team.

The eight cases involved equal numbers of boys and girls and reflected a range of different circumstances. Two cases involved young men aged 17 years, who were unaccompanied asylum seekers. Two cases involved young women aged 15 and 16 years where suspicions of sexual abuse had come to light. Two other cases involved girls aged 14 and 15 years where parents had sought help to control the behaviour of their daughters. The remaining cases involved boys, both aged 10 years, where allegations of neglect and physical abuse had been made.

Findings from the interviews with parents show that the degree of consultation and involvement in assessments has increased markedly during the past decade. The few interviews with young people suggest that the involvement of children and young people has not been as successful.

YOUNG PEOPLE'S UNDERSTANDING OF THE PROCESS OF ASSESSMENT

> Children's needs for explanations of what is happening may sometimes be overlooked. They should be informed clearly and sensitively even when they do not communicate through speech and where professionals may be unclear how much of what is being said is understood. They do not want to be kept in the dark or patronised. (Department of Health *et al.*, 2000a, p.38, 3.32)

Over three-quarters of the parents interviewed recalled that a social worker had explained the reason for the assessment and the process. However, a much smaller proportion of young people (two of the eight young people – 25%) remembered a social worker talking to them about why the assessment was to be done and what it would entail. Young people's lack of understanding was demonstrated by the finding that only one young person knew that during the assessment the social worker would collect information about themselves, other members of their family, and their circumstances. In contrast, practically all parents understood that this was an essential part of an assessment.

YOUNG PEOPLE'S INVOLVEMENT IN THE PROCESS OF ASSESSMENT

A failure to ask children and young people who should be consulted

Young people expressed less satisfaction than their parents did over the way the assessment had been conducted. For example, more than a third (n=3) of the young people thought that social workers had *not* talked to all the relevant people when carrying out the assessment.

For example, in Case 42 the mother had sought the help of social services, wanting her 15-year-old daughter, whose behaviour she could not control, fostered. As the social worker explained,

> She [mother] felt N. was out of control, she took risks and she wouldn't do anything she was told. She thought N. was born bad and was an evil child.
>
> (Social worker)

N. thought the social worker did not understand her situation and thought she should have talked to her friends:

> Friends – they know how you really are.

A similar situation is found in Case 34, where the suspicion of abuse had come to light because 10-year-old P. told his teacher that his stepfather had hit him.

> P. said George was drinking and strangled him.
>
> (Mother)

Once again the child felt there were key people the social worker should have talked to,

> my aunty Caroline and uncle James – in London,
>
> (P.)

in order to gain a full picture of what was going on.

The experience of the young woman in Case 5 also shows how important it is for social workers to tell children and young people who they are talking to during the assessment. In this case the social worker had gained the consent of the mother before talking to a number of professionals, including the school, educational welfare officer, school nurse and general practitioner. But the 15-year-old daughter S. appeared to be unaware of this and reported that,

> They should have talked to the youth centre where I go. My school teacher knew about my problems at school. They should have talked to them.

On the other hand S. believed that the social worker had approached others who she should not have done (none of whom had in fact been involved).

> They shouldn't have talked to the police. I don't think it was a good idea to go to C. [a school friend].

Although social workers routinely gained the consent of parents before talking to other professionals about their circumstances, young people were rarely consulted. In only one case, involving an unaccompanied asylum seeker, did the social worker consult the young man before approaching another professional. This young man reported that he was 'worried where to live and to eat – how to survive'. He had become depressed and said he 'needed a doctor'. As a result he was happy for the social worker to approach a doctor, 'I asked her to do that, it was important'.

Difficulties in engaging with social workers

> Engaging children: this involves developing a relationship with children so that they can be enabled to express their thoughts, concerns and opinions as part of the process of helping them make real choices, in a

> way that is age- and developmentally appropriate. (Department of Health, 2000a, p.43, 3.42)

Young people frequently found talking to social workers difficult or strange. When asked how they felt about sharing information about themselves or their family with the social worker, young people expressed views which reflected a degree of uncertainty and unease.

> A bit difficult, there were lots of questions, difficult ones.
>
> (10-year-old boy, Case 34)

> I felt strange; I was not sure who I was talking to. I did not really trust them. There were lots of questions. I could not tell them about being a Jehovah's witness. I did not know if I could trust the people I was talking to. I did not know them. I could not really trust them.
>
> (15-year-old girl, Case 5)

The importance of developing a relationship of trust is underlined by the account of 14-year-old K. in Case 2. When asked how she felt about sharing information about herself and her family with the social worker she replied,

> It depends which one. I had two social workers. One was horrible. This lady tried to put pressure on me to go back home. She said it was best to go back. The other lady was dead nice but she has now left. I don't want the other one to see me. She did not believe me what I was saying.

In other cases it appears no one was available to listen to the young person.

> I wanted to talk to someone but there was no-one to do that.
>
> (17-year-old D., asylum seeker, Case 43)

In half the cases (n=4) young people felt that the social worker had involved them in the process of the assessment.

> Yes, but not at first, but later on yes. They supported me. I got to know them a bit. I got to trust them a bit. It was better later on. She was nice.
>
> (15-year-old S., Case 5)

Involvement in the planning process

In five cases (62.5%) young people believed that the social worker had discussed actions and plans that might help themselves and their family.

For example in Case 42, 15-year-old N. recounts,

> I can only remember the foster care idea, but I got quite scared and didn't want to go, then I did and I really, really like it now.

Similarly 15-year-old S. in Case 5 recalls,

> They said counselling would help. I was not sure at first but then thought it was all right. I can't remember other things.

Although this figure (62.5%) is encouraging it still lags behind the experiences of parents where some 70 per cent reported having been involved in discussions of possible interventions.

CHILDREN'S AND YOUNG PEOPLE'S SATISFACTION WITH THE PLANS

> If teenagers do not perceive the assessment as relevant or if the services are not quickly forthcoming, they are likely to take the initiative into their own hands. (Department of Health, 1996)

Not surprising is the finding that few (n=2) young people considered that the plans that resulted from the assessment would help them.

Case 2 is a good example of what can happen when children and young people do not see the plan as relevant or helpful. This case came to light following a violent altercation between Mrs. D. and her 14-year-old daughter. The police were called to the house and contacted social services. Mrs. D. describes the circumstances.

> I had problems with K. She did what she wanted. I gave her a birthday party and said she could have a few friends in a 'stay over'. She brought 13 friends to the house to stay overnight. We had a row about that and then we had the fight. I had been drinking a lot but it did not have anything to do with drink. K. told everyone I was drinking. She did not like my boy friend. She still does not.
>
> (Mother of K.)

K. tells the same story from a different perspective.

> Mum had been drinking. She had an argument with her boyfriend. My aunt [mum's sister] then had a fight with her and I tried to stop it. Mum stamped on my toe, hit me in the face and pulled my hair. I was scared. I ran out of the house. I stayed out for a bit. I went back to the house… I came to S. [family friend] and felt safe.

K. felt she needed to live away from home.

> I wanted them to take me into care. I asked them to help my mum so she would not hit us and the kids. I was worried about the other kids. I wanted mum to stop drinking. When she was drunk we always got shouted at. The social worker did not do anything.

The resulting social services plan was for K. to return home, a plan K. was adamant that she could not comply with.

> I came to S. [family friend] and I have been here since. It was not planned by the social worker. I made the decision. The social worker wanted me to go home but I came here and I am staying here... The only thing was they said they would give me a contact number if I went home so I could ring for help if something went wrong. There were no other plans.
>
> (K.)

K. was not happy with the outcome of the plan.

> My little sisters are still at home. Nothing has changed for them. I would like them to have helped my mum stop drinking and to get rid of her boyfriend because he hit my brother and little sisters. He used to hit me. He lives there now. Sometimes we were locked in our bedroom and we had to wee in the room. We used to do it on the pillow as that was best and then we would get told off, shouted at for messing the room. I told about all this but they did not do anything. I don't think they believed me.

Neither was K.'s mother happy with the outcome.

> K. is away from home and I do not see her much. I wanted them to help me with housing and get K. to come back home. They said she should come home but did nothing about it.

Young people's comments about how the assessment process could be improved

Children and young people offered a number of suggestions that they felt would improve the assessment process. They thought that assessments would be improved if social workers listen to their side of the story and believed what they said. In Case 2, K.'s experience highlights the importance of listening to the views of children and young people when assessing their needs and formulating plans.

> I wanted them to listen to me and believe me, ask me what I wanted to happen and to get it done. Not put pressure on me to go home. They

> could have shown me what they were writing. When they were speaking to me and other people they talked to the other people in a way as if I was not there. They should have believed what I was saying.

Improved communication about what was going on during the assessment process was highlighted. For example, 16-year-old C. in Case 3 remarked that,

> I wanted more explanation about what was happening. She [the social worker] said she would ring but she didn't. I did not really know what was happening and why.

Although parents were given copies of the assessment record or the plans, young people were not. Although this may not always be appropriate for children or young people, having something to remind them of what had been said, what would happen and the plans that had been made for them, would be welcome.

> Taping what was going on would be helpful. I can't remember things.
> (15-year-old S., Case 5)

Summary points

- In only eight cases was it possible to interview the young person.
- The proportion of young people who understood the process of assessment was low.
- Young people thought that social workers did not always talk to those who they thought held important information and could make a valuable contribution to the assessment.
- Young people frequently found it strange and difficult to talk about personal issues and their family with social workers.
- Young people felt that what they said was frequently discounted or disbelieved.
- Over half the young people thought the social worker had discussed possible actions and plans with them. However, few thought that the plans would help them.
- Young people thought social work assessments could be improved.

Chapter summary

Child protection studies showed that parents involved in social work assessments and child protection enquiries found the experience traumatising and alienating. The features cited as most objectionable included: professionals discussing concerns about their family with others without first informing them; not explaining the process of assessment and the likely outcome; not keeping them informed; not discussing possible interventions (Cleaver and Freeman, 1995; Department of Health, 1995a).

The present study suggests that social work practice in relation to parental involvement in the assessment process has changed considerably. Information was drawn from questionnaires returned by social work managers (n=93) and practitioners (n=216), and interviews with parents or carers (n=50), young people (n=8) and social workers (n=52).

Three-quarters of social work managers reported that family involvement had increased since the implementation of the Assessment Framework and the introduction of the assessment records. A smaller proportion of social work practitioners (42%) thought family involvement in the assessment process had increased. Increased family involvement was attributed to:

- a more transparent and accountable relationship with the family
- a more focused approach to assessment
- increased consultation
- recording the views of family members
- discussing issues where parents and professionals disagree.

Increased involvement of the family in the assessment process was significantly associated with perceived improvements in the quality of assessments.

When social workers reported that family involvement had decreased, and those working with disabled children held particularly negative views, their responses showed that this was often due to the assessment records being used with the family as questionnaires or tests.

The reports from parents of disabled children did not support social workers' fears that the Assessment Framework and the assessment records were not appropriate for disabled children. This group of parents expressed similar or more positive experiences of the assessment process than parents whose children were not disabled.

In 30 cases suspected child abuse was the reason for the assessment. A detailed exploration of these cases showed considerable similarities with cases included in research undertaken before the refocusing of children's social services (Cleaver and Freeman, 1995). This enabled parental perspectives on their involvement in the assessment process to be compared.

A comparison with earlier research showed that social work practice in relation to parental involvement has changed. Parents reported that professionals routinely consulted them before making a referral to social services, and at the start of the assessment social workers explained the process and what it would entail. The majority of parents were very satisfied with the way social workers conducted the assessment, who was involved, and the decisions and plans that resulted from it. In cases where parents are in a state of high arousal the findings suggest more time must be devoted to ensuring they understand what will happen during the assessment.

Parents were less certain about the efficacy of the plan. In over a third (38%) of cases parents expressed uncertain or negative views about the plan. The degree of parental satisfaction with the plan is related to:

- a shared perspective between parents and social workers, on the difficulties families were facing
- involvement in the choice and development of the plans
- agreement with, and commitment to the plan
- the plan coming to fruition.

Parents valued social workers who:

- explained the reason for the assessment
- involved them in the process
- kept them informed
- treated them with respect
- understood their difficulties
- gave a timely response.

The findings from the interviews with eight young people suggest that social work practice in relation to their involvement in the assessment process has not kept pace with parental involvement. Few young people understood the process of assessment, or could remember whether a social worker had explained to them what would happen and why. They reported difficulty in talking about personal issues with social workers and felt that what they said was frequently discounted or disbelieved. Social workers did not ask young people who they should talk to to understand the young person's needs and circumstances. This resulted in young people believing that important perspectives and information about themselves failed to be considered during the assessment. Young people thought social work assessments would improve if social workers:

- listened to and respected their views and experiences
- believed what they said
- explained what was going on during the assessment
- talked to the people they thought were important
- gave them something that would remind them of what had happened and what was likely to happen in the future.

These are all issues raised by previous research that explored the children and young people's experience of social work services (see, for example, Cleaver, 2000; Department of Health, 1996; Grimshaw and Sinclair, 1997; O'Quigley, 2000; Sinclair *et al.*, 1995; Triseliotis *et al.*, 1995).

Chapter 4

The Experiences of Social Service Managers and Practitioners

Whose views are we hearing?

The councils

Separate questionnaires, designed for social workers and social work managers working in children's social services, were sent to all 25 Councils with Social Services Responsibilities that participated in the research. The councils included seven Shire Counties, three Unitary Authorities, eight London Boroughs and seven Metropolitan Districts. Twenty-one councils participated in the questionnaire survey. Two London Boroughs and two Shire Counties did not return any questionnaires. Some councils experienced particular difficulties in fulfilling their commitment to the research because at the time of the study they had high levels of staff turnover. In a few councils this resulted in the social services worker responsible for liaison with the research team being replaced and the communication link temporarily broken. In addition the high turnover meant new staff had no knowledge of the research and their potential to be involved.

In order to encourage the social workers and social work managers to complete the questionnaires these were sent to the social services worker responsible for liaison with the research team in both an electronic and paper format. The liaison worker was responsible for distributing the questionnaires to all the managers and practitioners within children's social services. This method of distribution, however, made it impossible to calculate the rate of returns. The research team were not aware either of the number of questionnaires distributed, or whether every manager and practitioner received one.

The teams

The Assessment Framework was designed to be used in the assessment and planning for all children in need and impacts on the practice of all social workers working in children's social services. The pattern of returned questionnaires shown in Table 4.1 (Appendix II) broadly reflects staffing patterns for social workers and managers employed in children's social services. In most councils the largest numbers of workers are based in *area, district or locality* teams. Given the disquiet about the Assessment Framework and the assessment records expressed during the introductory sessions by many social workers and managers working with disabled children, it was important that their views were included in this research. It is encouraging, therefore, to find one in ten of the returned questionnaires was from a social worker or manager in teams working with disabled children.

SOCIAL WORK MANAGERS

The implementation of new systems frequently generates considerable anxiety and resistance from practitioners, and the commitment and skills of first-line and middle management has been shown to be crucial to their success (see, for example, Ward, 1995).

Ninety-three social work managers responded to the questionnaire survey. As already noted in Table 4.1 these managers were responsible for supervising and managing social work practitioners based in a range of different teams. Managers represented both first-line management and middle management. Eighty-five managers described themselves as first-line managers and eight as middle managers. The Assessment Framework emphasises the importance of consistency with regard to assessment and service provision within children's social services. Such consistency does not yet apply to the job titles of social work managers. For example, at first-line manager level ten different titles were used, including: principal social worker, practice supervisor, fieldwork manager, team manager, case manager and team leader. Things were no different at the middle management level: titles included district child-care manager, service manager, deputy manager, locality manager and inter-agency link team co-ordinator. Such inconsistency must be confusing for both staff and service users who transfer from one Council with Social Services Responsibilities to another.

SOCIAL WORK PRACTITIONERS

In trying to understand social workers' perceptions and experiences of a new system for assessment it is important to take into account factors that will influence how information is sorted, prioritised and given meaning. Personality, belief and previous experience, all of which vary between individuals, and produce different responses, influence this process (Cleaver and Freeman, 1995). In the present study it was not possible to explore the personality and belief systems of social workers. However, the workers' previous experiences, in terms of how long they have been qualified and how long they have practised in child and family work, were examined.

Whether social workers are qualified and the length of time they have been qualified influences both their knowledge base and the confidence with which they approach the task of carrying out assessments consistent with the Assessment Framework. The Assessment Framework assumes a sound knowledge of child development, the factors that influence parents' capacity to meet the needs of their children and the impact of wider family and the environment: issues that should be covered in social work training courses. However, not all social workers were qualified. Table 4.2 (Appendix II) shows that 10.3 per cent of social work practitioners were not qualified, a further 32.2 per cent had been qualified for less than five years, while the remaining 57.5 per cent had been qualified for five years or more.

Because the present study sought the views of all social work practitioners employed in children's services, it was not surprising that the proportion of unqualified staff is higher, and the length of time they have been qualified lower, than would be the case in studies that sought the views of specialist groups. The returned questionnaires show that the rate of unqualified staff was twice that found in research which sought the views of social workers employed in child protection (Thoburn *et al.*, 1995). Similarly in the present study approximately a third (n=70) of the 192 qualified staff had been qualified for ten years or more, compared with half the sample involved in Thoburn and colleagues' study (1995).

Knowledge of child care and child development and confidence in one's abilities are also gained through direct experience of working with children and families. The findings show once more the generic quality of the sample of practitioners involved in this study (see Table 4.3, Appendix II). A third (34.9%) of social workers involved in the present study had been practising social work with children and families for five years or more compared with three-quarters found for social workers working in child protection (Thoburn *et al.*, 1995).

Summary points

- Of the possible 25 councils 20 contributed to the questionnaire sample.
- A total of 215 social workers and 90 managers returned questionnaires.
- Managers and practitioners represented all the different social work teams.
- The majority of managers were first-line managers.
- Social work practitioners were a generic group representing a wide range of experience and time since qualification.

Training on the Assessment Framework

The importance of training was recognised by the Department of Health when the Assessment Framework was published and launched. This emphasis on training was demonstrated in the accompanying letter signed by the Department of Health, Home Office and the Department for Education and Employment. The letter listed the actions social services departments would need to undertake to ensure successful implementation of the Assessment Framework, one of which was providing training for staff, carers and others, including administrative and reception staff; and, where appropriate, any joint training programmes.

To meet the need for training materials on the Assessment Framework, the Department of Health funded a training programme. This included the development of a training pack 'The Child's World' for trainers in social services departments (NSPCC and The University of Sheffield, 2000). Based on this work the NSPCC were funded by the Department of Health to hold a series of regional 'Training for Trainers' courses, and a training pack was distributed to every local authority social services department by the Department of Health.

Councils were then responsible for ensuring that their own social workers and managers were trained on the Assessment Framework. To deliver a programme of staff training councils applied a variety of methods. Most utilised their own resources, some also employed the services of independent training agencies, while others called on the NSPCC to deliver additional training. The bulk of staff training took place prior to the implementation of the Assessment Framework or shortly after.

In addition, each of the councils participating in the research project had at least four half-day training sessions led by members of the research team. A training pack on which these sessions were based was supplied to each council (Cleaver and Walker, 2000). The aim of these sessions was to familiarise managers and social work staff with the Assessment Framework and the use of the assessment records. In addition a session for representatives from Social Services, Education, Health and other relevant agencies was held in each council. This was used to present the principles of the Assessment Framework, explore the roles and responsibilities of different agencies in the process of assessment and planning, and explain the aims and methods of the present study.

Attendance on training courses

Despite the considerable emphasis placed on training social workers on the principles underpinning the Assessment Framework and the application of the Framework in practice, the findings from the social workers' questionnaires suggest that the extent of social workers' training needs were underestimated. Approximately a quarter (n=56) of social workers who responded to the questionnaire survey reported that they had received no training on the Assessment Framework or the assessment records.

The low numbers of returned social work questionnaires from many of the councils made it difficult to compare whether some councils were more successful than others in training their practitioners. Nonetheless, an examination of the six councils where 10 or more social work questionnaires were returned shows a wide variation in the proportion (ranging from 40% to 100%) of practitioners who reported having attended training on the Assessment Framework and the use of the assessment records.

Social workers who had been involved in training reported that in most instances (74%) their own local authority had been responsible for organising and delivering the training. In practically every case the training was a single event held over a relatively short period of time. Of the 157 social workers who attended some training:

- 32 per cent reported attending a half or single training day
- 43 per cent had attended 2 training days
- 25 per cent had attended 3 or 4 training days.

Barriers to training

The findings from the questionnaires suggest a number of reasons why the training had not reached every social worker.

THE TRAINING SCHEDULE OMITTED TEAMS THAT WERE EITHER PHYSICALLY OR STRUCTURALLY OUTSIDE SOCIAL SERVICES DEPARTMENTS

> Did not attend any – not for want of asking. Giving this social worker some training would have been a start. This team was not informed of any training opportunities.
>
> (Social worker, hospital-based team)

> Training needs to be available to all social workers – I work for an agency and have not been offered training.
>
> (Agency social worker)

A RELIANCE ON A SINGLE TRAINING EVENT

> The departmental training took place while I was on maternity leave.
>
> (Social worker, long-term children and families team)

> The planned days were cancelled and never rearranged.
>
> (Social worker, referral and assessment team)

HIGH LEVELS OF STAFF TURNOVER (INCLUDING THE USE OF AGENCY STAFF AND NEW RECRUITS)

> I missed out on the training as it was held before I arrived here.
>
> (Newly qualified social worker, referral and assessment team)

STAFF SHORTAGES MEANT INDIVIDUAL TEAMS WERE UNABLE TO RELEASE SOCIAL WORKERS TO ATTEND TRAINING COURSES

> There was never enough cover so some of us couldn't go.
>
> (Social worker, referral and assessment team)

An exploration of the characteristics of social workers that had been trained on the Assessment Framework suggested that social workers from a variety of different teams were involved. For example, staff from referral and assessment teams were no more likely to attend training on the Framework than those based in long-term teams. Similarly, unqualified or newly qualified staff were just as likely to attend a training course as those who had been qualified for longer.

Social workers' perception of the training

For those social workers that had attended training a significant proportion reported that it had not met their needs. For example, fewer than a third (30.3%) of social workers thought the training had covered most issues adequately. Just over a half (55.9%) thought it could have been better in that they would have liked more information and guidance on certain aspects of the Assessment Framework. Finally, 13.8 per cent considered the training was poor, that many key issues had been skimped and there was a general lack of clear guidance.

The degree to which social workers were satisfied with the training they received was not associated with which agency was responsible, be it social services themselves, the NSPCC or an independent training agency. Similarly, no association was found between satisfaction with training and whether social workers were unqualified or only recently qualified. The findings did suggest an association (although not statistically significant) between the type of team social workers were working in and the level of satisfaction with the training. Although the majority of social workers from every type of team thought the training could have been better, there were differences between teams in relation to more definitive opinions. For example, referral and assessment and 'Other' teams (these included disability, CAHMS, and family centre teams) were more likely to see the training as good and less likely to rate it as poor, than were area, district or locality and long-term teams (see Table 4.4, Appendix II).

Issues the training did not adequately cover

The questionnaires showed that there was considerable dissatisfaction over the content of the training. Social workers highlighted a number of issues on which they wished for further training.

HOW TO ANALYSE THE INFORMATION THEY HAD COLLECTED

> More discussion about the analysis of the information collated.
>
> (Social worker, locality team)

> Analysing information, consulting and quoting research, writing up of plans.
>
> (Social worker, locality team)

> Analysis of the information gathered. Using and interpreting tools and questionnaires.
>
> (Social worker, long-term team)

METHODS OF JOINT WORKING AND AREAS OF RESPONSIBILITY AND HOW TO CARRY OUT EFFECTIVE MULTI-AGENCY ASSESSMENTS

> Inter-agency roles and tasks were a grey area. Other agencies had no knowledge of the Framework at the time I had training and do not seem to have had training since – unless staff are trained together we will not see an improvement in taking joint responsibility.
>
> (Social worker, referral and assessment team)

PARENTAL CONSENT AND HOW TO HANDLE ISSUES OF CONFIDENTIALITY

> How to be honest and accurate in writing an assessment to be shared with a family, when there has been no time to build up a rapport with them and one does not wish to jeopardise the chances of doing so.
>
> (Social worker, disability team)

> Engaging parents/families who want a service not an assessment.
>
> (Social worker, locality team)

> Gaining the consent of parents.
>
> (Social worker, family centre)

THE IMPACT OF NEW LEGISLATION ON THE PROCESS OF ASSESSMENT

> There was some confusion over departmental policy and interpretation of the Data Protection Act and its implications for confidentiality.
>
> (Social worker, long-term team)

> The relevance of the Human Rights Act to the Assessment Framework.
>
> (Social worker, long-term team)

PRACTICAL APPLICATION – USING THE ASSESSMENT RECORDS, SCALES AND QUESTIONNAIRES

> More training with regards to the forms, 'what information to go where'.
> (Social worker, long-term team)

> More understanding of the range of items and aids that can be used in conjunction with the Framework. I have never seen the questionnaires and scales that can be used – these have not been explained.
> (Social worker, referral and assessment team)

> Relating to child protection work; use in court proceedings; use with other professionals.
> (Social worker, children and families team)

> Working with black and other ethnic minorities, also with people with a disability and mental health problems.
> (Social worker, long-term team)

The practice relevance of training

Social workers were asked to rate how useful the training had been when it came to using the assessment records in practice. A scale from 1 to 10 was used where 1 represented 'not at all useful' and 10 represented 'extremely useful'. When the middle ratings (5 and 6) are assumed to reflect broadly neutral views the findings show that only a fifth (20.3%) of social workers reported that the training had proved useful to their practice. Practically half (48.8%) thought the training was of little or no use to their practice and a further nearly a third (30.9%) expressed neutral opinions.

Social workers' perception of how useful the training was could be related to a number of factors including the content of the training courses, the type of work they were currently responsible for, how recently they qualified, and their experience of social work.

The low numbers of returned social work questionnaires from many of the councils made it difficult to compare the impact of the different training courses supplied by individual councils. It was, therefore, not possible to explore the relationship between the content of the training courses and social workers' perception of its relevance to practice. An examination of the other factors found no association between social workers' perception of how useful the training was and either the length of time they had been practising or the type of team, such as disability or referral and assessment, they were currently working in. The factor that was found to be associated with social workers' views on the usefulness of the training was the length of time since they had qualified. Those who had been qualified for less than five years were more likely to find the training useful to their practice than those who had been qualified for five years or more, and less likely to report that it had been of little or no use. For example, a third of social workers qualified for less than five years found the training of little or no use compared with nearly two-thirds (61.8%) of social workers qualified for longer.

Summary points

- Training social workers on the Assessment Framework was widely acknowledged as an essential element of successful implementation.
- Current training schedules were frequently not sufficiently flexible to ensure that all relevant staff had an opportunity to attend.
- One-off training events could not deal with all the issues on which social workers wanted information and direction.
- One-off training events were unable to address issues that arise as staff become more familiar with the Assessment Framework and new assessment practices.
- Current training courses were more successful at meeting the practice needs of practitioners who were either unqualified or qualified for less than five years.

The role of management in implementation

The consistency of implementation

Social work managers reported different levels of consistency within the teams they were responsible for, with regard to practitioners' use of the assessment records. For example, 82 per cent of managers reported that the assessment records were very or fairly consistently used in their team, while 18 per cent reported they were not consistently or extremely inconsistently used (see Figure 4.1).

The degree of consistency in the use of the assessment records varied between councils. In half the councils managers reported the records were not consistently used. However, there was considerable variability within councils and there was no case where all the managers in a particular council reported that the assessment records were not consistently used.

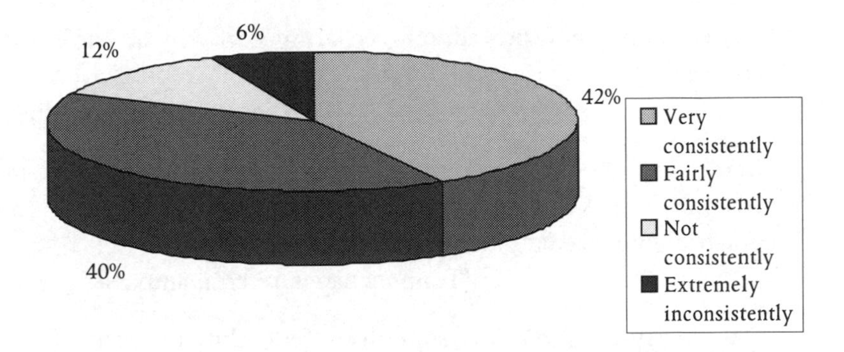

Figure 4.1 Use of the assessment records within social work teams (n=88)

Managers' reports on how consistently practitioners in their teams were using the assessment records were significantly associated with the type of team in which they worked (see Table 4.5, Appendix II). The assessment records were more likely to be consistently used in teams responsible for carrying out assessments.

Managers of long-term teams, where the majority of the work is with longer-term cases, were less likely to report consistent use of the assessment records than managers from other teams. Half the managers in long-term teams said the records were consistently used in their teams, compared with managers from any of the other teams where over 83 per cent reported consistent use of the records (see Table 4.5).

Manager workloads n=90

The majority of managers reported that the implementation of the Assessment Framework and the introduction of the assessment records had increased their workload. Nearly a fifth (18.3%) thought it had substantially increased their workload, approximately two-thirds (64.5%) considered that their workload had increased to some extent and 14 per cent felt that it had had no effect.

The implementation of the Assessment Framework and the introduction of the assessment records impacted on the workload of managers in a number of ways that reflect the findings of Rose's (2002) case study of one council's experience of implementation.

MANAGERS HAD TO SPEND TIME ENSURING THAT BOTH THEY AND PRACTITIONERS WERE FAMILIAR WITH NEW PRACTICE GUIDES AND PROCEDURES

> Understanding new procedures – ensuring staff were able to implement efficiently.
>
> (Team manager, locality team)

> Being clear about expectations, deadlines, setting up new systems and ensuring others had time to familiarise themselves with the formats, practice guidance etc., including myself.
>
> (Team manager, referral and assessment team)

> Devising systems to ensure smooth running, duty rota, etc.
>
> (Team manager, referral and assessment team)

> Initially quite demanding but now have a system in place which is kept up to date so is now more of a clerical role.
>
> (Team leader, locality team)

MANAGERS FOUND THEY NEEDED TO SPEND TIME WINNING THE HEARTS AND MINDS OF PRACTITIONERS

> Ensuring staff understood the Framework.
>
> (District child-care manager, long-term team)

> Working with the hearts and minds of the team, some of whom find new ways of working more difficult to embrace than others.
>
> (Practice manager, long-term team)

> Coping with resistance from staff.
>
> (Case manager, assessment team)

> There was resistance in relation to a different way of recording – in essence practitioners had to be reassured that nothing would be missed.
>
> (Line manager, assessment team)

> Sorting out confusion over the use of core assessments and child protection procedures.
>
> (Fieldwork manager, locality team)

> Supervision of staff in implementing the Framework. Low staffing, low morale led to significant resistance to engaging with the process.
>
> (Line manager, assessment team)

Encouraging workers to see that it replaces what they already do rather than is in addition to current practice.

(Team manager, long-term team)

TIME WAS SPENT SUPPORTING, SUPERVISING AND MONITORING PRACTITIONERS

Since its introduction it has been necessary to look at the assessment recording to ensure that all aspects have been covered and go back to the social workers if necessary. For us all there has been a period of adaptation and therefore the supervision of assessment recording has taken longer to carry out.

(Line manager, assessment team)

Workers seeking advice from me regarding the forms and the time scales.

(Line manager, long-term team)

I have to check and crosscheck the timescales of the forms, check the content and ensure they are completed correctly, keep manual records of what forms are started, ended, etc.

(Team manager, referral and assessment team)

The new Framework required extra help and support for social workers as when implementing any new process.

(Team leader, disability team)

It takes longer to supervise managers whose staff are using the materials.

(Service manager)

TIME SPENT WORKING WITH IT SYSTEMS THAT WERE NOT UP TO THE TASK

Very heavy on computer use to input – need to be computer literate, not enough computers, regularly 'crashing'.

(Care manager, assessment team)

Until the department's new computer system is up and running fully I have to record all work manually.

(Team manager, CAMHS team)

Dealing with my team's frustration with paper recording tools.

(Field manager, locality team)

> The paperwork and administration is greater. I hope in time however that this will lessen as systems become compatible.
>
> (Team manager, referral and assessment team)

TIME WAS SPENT FORGING LINKS WITH OTHER AGENCIES AND/OR DEVELOPING PROCEDURES FOR MULTI-AGENCY WORK

> Adapting the Assessment Framework for a multi-agency team. Obtaining consent from referrers has been a huge hurdle, obtaining detailed and relevant information from all agencies has been problematic.
>
> (Co-ordinator, CAMHS team)

> Taking other agencies along with SSD in implementation. Need to actively engage with local agencies which was time well spent.
>
> (Case manager, referral and assessment team)

Staff supervision

Middle and first-line managers have the responsibility for supervising, supporting and monitoring the work of practitioners in their team. The implementation of the Assessment Framework and the introduction of a more consistent and structured form of recording were expected to make this task easier. For example, in councils where case records were family-based balancing the workloads of social workers is more difficult than in councils where case records are child-based. For example, an assessment that involves a large sibling group generates more work than a similar assessment involving an individual child. The introduction of a child-based recording system should allow managers to monitor practitioner caseloads more accurately.

In addition, the introduction of the assessment records should help managers to identify gaps in social workers' practice where additional training may be needed, because to carry out and record assessments in line with the Assessment Framework requires a sound knowledge of child development.

PRACTITIONER WORKLOADS (N=90)

Practically every manager (95%) acknowledged that the implementation of the Assessment Framework and the introduction of the assessment records had increased the workloads of practitioners in their teams substantially (38%) or to some extent (57%). Three managers thought it had made little or no difference, and only a single manager reported that it had resulted in a decrease in practitioner workloads. A scrutiny of the data shows that none of the four managers who thought workloads had not increased were responsible for referral and assessment work. Two of the managers were responsible for area, district or locality teams, one for a long-term team and the other for a team working with disabled children.

Monitoring practitioners' workloads (n=88)

Over a third (39%) of managers reported that the introduction of the assessment records had improved their ability to monitor the workloads of individual practitioners. Over half (56%) considered it had made little or no difference, and four managers (5%) felt that it had to some extent hampered their ability to monitor workloads.

Identifying gaps in the practice and training of individual social workers (n=86)

Sixty-two per cent of managers reported that the assessment records had proved useful in identifying gaps in individual social workers' practice; the remaining 38 per cent had not found the records helpful. A similar proportion (56%) of managers found the records had helped them to identify the training needs of social workers; and 44 per cent had not found them useful in identifying training needs.

Managers reported that they were hampered in identifying gaps in practitioners' knowledge and training because social workers did not always record the details of their assessment.

> If there was some way of motivating some social workers to actually input the information it would help.
>
> (Care manager, assessment team)

Others considered that identifying gaps in practice and training should be dealt with during supervision.

> During the supervision process staff and managers should discuss Framework/practice issues and should identify individuals' practice/training gaps or needs.
>
> (Acting team manager, locality team)

Others thought changes to the content and layout of the assessment records would improve their task of identifying gaps in practice.

> Social workers find it difficult to understand that they [the assessment records] are a tool for recording and not the core assessment. Should be better laid out and more concise.
>
> (Team leader, locality team)

> Forms need to encourage greater emphasis on analysis of information gained.
>
> (Team manager, community child and family team)

MONITORING THE PROGRESS OF CASES (N=91)

Understanding the needs of children in individual cases

In order to support social work practitioners in monitoring the progress of children on their caseloads, managers need to understand the developmental needs and circumstances of individual children. The introduction of the assessment records had, on the whole, resulted in the majority of managers reporting improvements in their understanding of the needs of children in individual cases. Three-quarters thought the use of the assessment records had improved their understanding, while the remaining quarter felt they had made no difference.

MONITORING THE PROGRESS OF THE ASSESSMENT IN INDIVIDUAL CASES AND SUBSEQUENT SOCIAL WORK INTERVENTION (N=88)

Over two-thirds (68%) of managers reported that the use of the assessment records had enabled them to monitor the progress of an assessment in individual cases and a rather smaller proportion (59%) found it helped to monitor subsequent intervention. The extent to which managers found the assessment records were useful in monitoring assessments and subsequent intervention was related to the type of team for which managers were responsible. Managers responsible for referral and assessment teams were more likely to find the assessment records helpful in monitoring assessments and subsequent intervention than managers responsible for other teams (see Table 4.6, Appendix II).

The reports of managers responsible for teams working with disabled children reflect the uncertainty within this field of the relevance of the assessment records for their work. Professional opinion in this arena has been split. There are those who welcomed the Assessment Framework and the records because they take an ecological approach to assessment, while others believed that assessments involving disabled children should focus on their special needs and to explore the parenting capacity of parents of disabled children is unnecessarily intrusive. However, assuming that disabled children have parents with adequate capacity to meet their developmental needs may do them a disservice. Parents may need help in relation to their disabled child and, when relevant, to meet the needs of other children living at home.

MONITORING RECORDING PRACTICE (N=92)

Two-thirds of managers reported that the introduction of the assessment records had increased the amount of information recorded on children and families. A further 18 per cent considered the amount of information recorded had not changed and 15 per cent thought that it had reduced.

Although the majority of managers thought that the amount of information recorded had increased, more than a third (38%) reported benefits in relation to improvements in the quality of recording. Approximately half (49%) thought the quality of recording had not changed, and 12 per cent thought it had deteriorated. Managers suggested changes to the assessment records that would further enhance the quality of social work records. These included additions to the assessment records such as a chronology and a genogram, and deletions in order to reduce the amount of repetitive recording (many of these have been incorporated in the revised exemplars issued to support the Integrated Children's System).

There was less uncertainty amongst managers when it came to rating the impact of the assessment records on their ability to locate information on social work case files. The majority of managers (70%) found that the use of the assessment records improved their ability to find specific information on individual case files, the remaining 30 per cent reporting little change.

Summary points

- In most teams the assessment records were consistently used.
- The implementation of the Assessment Framework had increased the workload of managers.
- The assessment records improved managers' ability to monitor practitioner workloads and helped them identify gaps in training and practice.
- The use of the assessment records improved managers' understanding of the needs of individual children.

- The assessment records improved the ability of managers to monitor progress in individual cases.
- The assessment records increased the amount of information recorded during assessments but, at the same time, resulted in improvements in the quality of recording.
- The assessment records made it easier to locate information on social work files.

The impact of the Assessment Framework and use of the assessment records on the quality of assessments

Practitioner workloads

The majority (87%) of social workers reported that the use of the assessment records had increased their workload. A further 11 per cent thought it had little effect and a mere 2 per cent thought it had reduced their work. This increase in practitioners' workloads had been recognised by managers.

Social work practitioners' perception of the quality of assessments

Although practically every social worker thought the implementation of the Assessment Framework and the introduction of the assessment records had increased their workload, approximately half (54.6%) of all social workers reported that the quality of their assessments had improved.

> It gave me a very clear indication of what the child's needs are, why he was unable to return home and what needs to be done for his future to fulfil his needs.
>
> (Social worker, long-term team)

> The issues and information gathered by using the Initial Assessment record is a good tool to highlight some areas that could have been previously overlooked.
>
> (Social worker, referral and assessment team)

> Parenting skills were usefully drawn out – this was uncomfortable for some parents.
>
> (Social worker, disability team)

The last comment chimes with the views of managers of teams working with disabled children who felt the Assessment Framework resulted in a more holistic understanding of the child's needs and circumstances.

A further 32.5 per cent of social workers thought the assessment records made little or no impact on the quality of their assessments.

> The Initial Assessment record asks all the questions that would be explored anyway – they are common-sense areas to cover when assessing need. Decisions and plans for families are affected by resources and their availability not pieces of paper.
>
> (Social worker, locality team)

Finally, 12.9 per cent of social workers felt the records impaired the quality of their assessments.

> The forms do not help the assessment process, decisions or plans. They can cause barriers if filled in with some clients.
>
> (Social worker, referral and assessment team)

This report suggests the social worker used the assessment record as a questionnaire with the family, a practice not consistent with the guidance and understandably impeded the quality of the assessment.

Managers' perceptions of the quality of assessments

In contrast a larger proportion of managers (68.5%) saw an improvement in the quality of assessments. Figure 4.2 compares the perceptions of practitioners and managers.

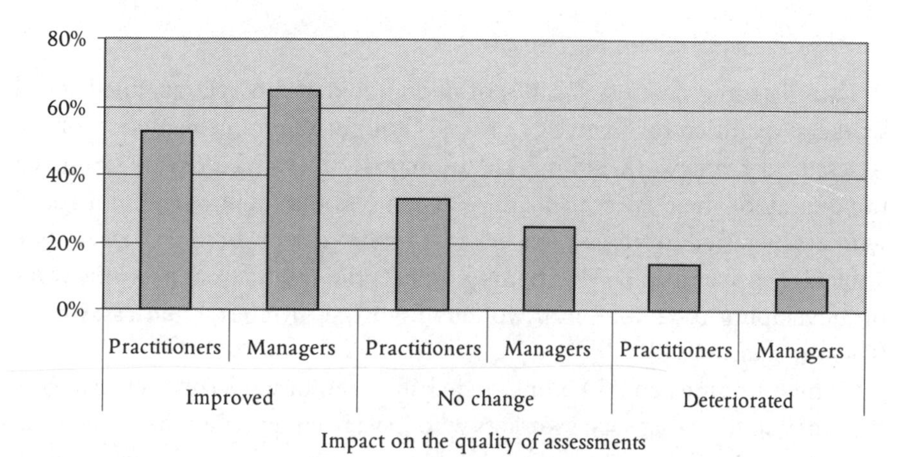

Figure 4.2 Practitioners' and managers' perception of the quality of assessments

This trend to see the impact on the quality of assessments in a more positive light may be due to a number of factors. For example, practitioners were only able to report on their own experience of carrying out assessments whilst managers reported on the assessment work of the whole team. In contrast it could be argued that practitioners have greater 'hands on' experience than managers and therefore have a more accurate understanding of how the assessment records have affected the quality of their assessments. Finally, the increased information recorded on the assessment records may enable managers to have a better understanding of the quality of the assessments in individual cases.

FACTORS THAT INFLUENCE THE SOCIAL WORKERS' PERCEPTION OF THE QUALITY OF THEIR ASSESSMENTS

A number of factors may influence social workers' perception of how the Assessment Framework and the use of the assessment records affected the quality of their assessments. For example, practice experience, qualification, training, and type of team may all influence perceptions.

An analysis of the findings shows that (a) the type of team social workers were working in and (b) the time they had been practising social work (whether qualified or not) were not significantly associated with how they thought the Assessment Framework and the assessment records affected the quality of their assessments. However, an association was found for two other factors: the period of time social workers had been qualified, and training.

The time social workers had been qualified

Practically three-quarters (72.1%) of unqualified and newly qualified social workers (qualified for two years or less) thought the implementation of the Assessment Framework and the use of the assessment records had improved the quality of their assessments. In contrast less than half (47.9%) of social workers qualified for three years or more reported such an improvement (see Table 4.7, Appendix II). This finding reflects the results from previous work on developing tools for social workers involved in referral and assessment (Cleaver *et al.*, 1998).

These findings could be interpreted in a number of ways. For example, they may suggest that social workers who have been qualified for longer (that is for three years or more) are routinely carrying out good-quality assessments, and that the introduction of the assessment records that operationalise the Assessment Framework could make little impact. Alternatively, the findings could reflect a greater reluctance among this more experienced group of practitioners to embrace change and new methods of social work practice. Indeed, until recently there has been little tradition within the social work profession of ongoing training and staff development. As a result, social workers had to depend on their own experience, team culture and working methods. The post-qualifying award in child care was introduced in 1995 (CCETSW, 1992). Consequently, social workers involved in the present study, qualified for less than five years will have entered a profession that places far greater emphasis on training.

Training

Simply attending training was not associated with whether social workers thought the assessment records had affected the quality of their assessments. However, when training addressed practical issues, such as preparing them to use the assessment records, there was a link with perceived changes to the quality of assessments (see Table 4.8, Appendix II).

The group who thought the training was 'fairly or very useful' were more likely to consider the quality of their assessments had improved as a result of the Assessment Framework and the use of assessment records than the those who rated training as 'of little or no use' (see Table 4.8). This reinforces comments made by social workers for training to place greater emphasis on the practical application of the Assessment Framework and the assessment records.

The change from family to child-based recording

The Access to Personal Files Act 1987, now replaced by the Data Protection Act 1998, gave individuals the right to see information recorded by social services about themselves. The Act also ensures that there must be a 'legitimate basis' for disclosing sensitive personal data to another party. Research following the introduction of the Access to Personal Files Act 1987 found a varied and at times confused response to the Act from practitioners and local authorities. Although many documents and records are routinely shared with service users – for example, child protection case conference reports – user access to files is still regarded with a high level of suspicion by some practitioners (Ovreveit, 1986; Shemmings, 1991).

The assessment records published by the Department of Health that accompany the Assessment Framework facilitate service users' access to files because separate forms must be completed for individual children. Furthermore, the Assessment Framework itself with its focus on the assessment of individual children underlines the value of separately recording information on each child when there is more than one child within the family. Indeed, many serious-case reviews have shown that family-based assessments can fall into the trap of focusing on the very obvious needs of one or more children within the family while failing to identify the difficulties others may be experiencing (Sinclair and Bullock, 2002).

The implementation of the Assessment Framework and the introduction of the Department of Health assessment records brought into greater clarity the need to change from family-based recording and assessment to child-based practice. Although discussions with social workers suggest that in principle they agree with the change in practice, findings from the questionnaires reveal a rather different picture. This will be examined in relation to both the referral and assessment processes.

The referral process

The Referral and Initial Information record published by the Department of Health requires information to be recorded on individual children. It was expected that a change of practice from taking family referrals to one where a separate form was completed on each child would affect both the workload of practitioners and the quality of the information gathered.

Of the 215 social workers participating in the postal questionnaire 83 had experience of taking a referral that involved several children within one family. In general, these social workers viewed this change in practice in a negative light.

The majority of these social workers (n=64, 77.1%) thought that completing separate referral forms on individual children within the same family took longer and practically two-thirds (n=55, 66.3%) thought it resulted in unnecessary duplication of information, than completing a family referral that named the individual children. Social workers are yet to be convinced that this change of practice provided many advantages at the referral stage. For example, less than a quarter (n=20, 24%) thought it provided a clear focus on the needs of individual children (see Table 4.9, Appendix II).

The assessment process

As was shown in relation to referrals, the implementation of the Assessment Framework signalled a change in practice from recording assessments in terms of the family to recording that focused on the needs of individual children.

Ninety-seven social workers had carried out an initial assessment and 95 a core assessment that involved more than one child within the same family.

RECORDING FOR INDIVIDUAL CHILDREN AND ITS IMPACT ON THE DUPLICATION OF INFORMATION

There was considerable consistency in social workers' responses to carrying out either an initial or a core assessment that involved more than one child within the same family and reflects the findings with regard to recording referrals on more than one child from the same family. The majority of social workers reported that recording separate assessments led to an unnecessary duplication of information. It is of interest to note that the proportion of social workers holding this view drops slightly for core assessments. This drop suggests that in complex cases or those where child protection issues have been raised, social workers more readily accept the need to understand the interaction and interplay of the three domains of the Assessment Framework for individual children.

The issue of duplication is one that many social services departments within the study group grappled with, particularly in terms of referrals and initial assessments. Although the majority persevered with the policy of recording separate referrals and initial assessments on individual children, a few adapted the referral and/or initial assessment record in an attempt to avoid what was seen as unnecessary duplication. For example, one department developed a single initial assessment record to use with sibling groups with a separate section to record the developmental needs of each child, but with the domains for parenting capacity and family and environmental issues being held in common. In another social services department a separate form for individual children was used, thereby ensuring social work records adhere to the Data Protection Act 1998, but information on the family and environment was simply copied from one form to another.

Such practice suggests that, although there is general agreement that the developmental needs of each child must be explored during an initial assessment, there is less understanding that parenting issues and the wider family and environment must be considered in terms of their impact on the individual child. Although some social services departments made use of their IT systems and cut and pasted the information about the family and environment onto the assessment records of more than one child within the same family, how issues impact on the individual child must still be explored. For example, an initial assessment that identifies parental mental illness cannot assume that its impact will be the same for every child within the family. Similarly, factors within wider family and environment will impact on individual children within the same family in different ways. For example, siblings may not share both parents or may belong to different racial groups. In other cases the community within which the family lives may appear hostile to a shy 9-year-old but an exciting and supportive environment for a gregarious 13-year-old.

RECORDING FOR INDIVIDUAL CHILDREN AND ITS IMPACT ON THE QUALITY OF ASSESSMENTS

When it came to considering whether recording assessments separately for individual children within the same family affected the quality of the assessment, social workers were more divided. As Table 4.10 (Appendix II) shows, approximately a third thought it impaired the quality of the assessment, just over a third held no views (in that they neither agreed nor disagreed with the statement) and just under a third did not think it impaired the quality of their assessments. There was little difference between social workers' replies in relation to initial and core assessments.

RECORDING FOR INDIVIDUAL CHILDREN AND ITS IMPACT ON THE ABILITY TO IDENTIFY THE NEEDS OF INDIVIDUAL CHILDREN

Although social workers were unsure of the advantages of separate recording for individual children in terms of the quality of their assessments, a more positive response was shown when they considered whether the practice provided a clear focus on the needs of individual children. Table 4:10 shows that the proportion that thought it provided a clear focus on the needs of individual children was twice the size of the group who thought it did not. This suggests there are real advantages for individual children when assessments shift from a family focus to a child-centred approach.

Summary points

- The introduction of the Assessment Framework and the use of the assessment records increased the workload of practitioners.
- Over half the practitioners thought the quality of their assessments had improved as a consequence. Managers saw a greater improvement.
- Social workers who were not qualified or recently qualified (less than three years) were more likely to see an improvement in the quality of their assessments than those qualified for longer.

- When social workers had attended training seen as relevant to practice this was associated with a perceived improvement in the quality of their assessments.
- Many social services departments have changed from family to child-based referrals and assessments.
- A change from family to child-based recording was seen to result in unnecessary duplication of information.
- A third of practitioners thought the change had resulted in an improvement in the quality of information recorded.
- Practically half the practitioners thought the change had resulted in a clearer focus on the needs of individual children.

Impact of the Assessment Framework and use of the assessment records on decision-making, planning, intervention and service provision

Decision-making

SOCIAL WORKERS' EXPERIENCE IN RELATION TO DECISION-MAKING IN INITIAL ASSESSMENTS

Social workers suggested a number of changes to the initial assessment record to make it a more useful tool. These suggestions have informed the revisions to the records (exemplars) published to support the Integrated Children's System. Nonetheless, a considerable proportion of social workers found the present format helped in making decisions about the information they had gathered during the assessment.

Approximately half (51%) the social workers found the initial assessment record helped them decide if the child was 'in need', 43 per cent what immediate action to take, and 39 per cent found it helped them decide if the case was sufficiently complex to warrant a core assessment (see Table 4.11, Appendix II). These figures compare favourably with the proportions (approximately a quarter for each issue) where social workers did not find the record helped them in making these decisions.

MANAGERS' EXPERIENCE IN RELATION TO DECISION-MAKING IN INITIAL ASSESSMENTS

Managers must base their decisions concerning individual children on reported information frequently gained through reading the case files or through discussions and meetings with the relevant social workers. To feel confident in making decisions, managers need good evidence-based assessments. Managers reported that the introduction of the assessment records, with their emphasis on evidence, had affected the confidence they brought to their decisions concerning individual children.

Improved managers' confidence in decision-making

Approximately half (52.4%) reported that the use of the assessment records had improved the confidence with which they are able to make decisions about children in need. Factors identified by managers that increased the level of confidence included:

- focused and evidence-based assessments
- a holistic view of the child
- increased ability to prioritise work
- safer decisions.

Focused and evidence-based assessments:

> I am presented with more focused and clearly evidenced assessments, decision-making on the foundation of tangible evidence.
>
> (Practice manager, assessment team)

A holistic view of the child:

> A clearer framework serves to evaluate the needs of the child holistically. In the past, environmental factors were not always seen as a significant feature.
>
> (Principal social worker, family support services)

Increased ability to prioritise work:

> The Framework clearly identifies the areas of need and therefore it is easier to prioritise work.
>
> (Team manager, children and families team)

Safer decisions:

> Clear information enables safer decisions.
>
> (Assistant team manager, disabled children's team)

No impact on managers' confidence in decision-making

A substantial proportion (41.3%) of managers considered that the implementation of the Assessment Framework and the introduction of the assessment records had made little or no difference to their confidence in making decisions about children in need. Managers' reports offered two explanations why their decision-making had not been affected: first, high levels of confidence in the quality of existing social workers' assessments and, second, decisions taken about children in need are not related to the findings from the assessment.

The quality of existing social workers' assessments:

> Social workers in the team have usually made appropriate decisions about the children in need with whom they have dealt.
>
> (Principal social worker, assessment team)

Decisions not related to the findings from assessments:

> Decisions are made regardless, often before core assessment is completed.
>
> (Senior social worker, locality team)

Decreased managers' confidence in decision making

Finally, five managers (6.3%) thought the Assessment Framework and the use of the assessment records had had a negative impact on their ability to make decisions. The explanations given by managers suggest this is related to:

- the quality of social workers' assessments
- the impact of introducing a new system
- a belief that existing formats were more appropriate.

The quality of social workers' assessments:

> I am having to question the validity of core assessments from the access teams as they are not backed up by evidence and I have found gaps.
>
> (Practice manager, locality team)

The impact of introducing a new system:

> I think the introduction overall has had a paralysing effect while we resolve the best way to implement in a way that fits with local circumstances.
>
> (Team manager, community child and family team)

A belief that existing formats were more appropriate:

> Internal format far more focused on needs of disabled children and user-friendly.
>
> (Project leader, disability team)

Planning and intervention

Assessments that are ecological in their focus and clearly evidence social workers' judgements should make the managers' task of planning and intervention an easier one. Over half the managers (58.4%) thought the use of the assessment records had improved the planning and subsequent social work intervention in relation to the child and family. They attributed the improvement to a number of factors.

A more focused assessment resulted in more focused plans and interventions:

> Interventions are more focused – assessment more analytical and timely.
>
> (Team manager, locality team)

> Intervention is more focused on assessed need: social workers are sharper in conducting assessments.
>
> (Team manager, child and family team)

The aims of the intervention were clearer and consequently the ability to review progress:

> Clarified aims and purpose of intervention. Allowed more accurate assessment of outcomes.
>
> (Care manager, assessment team)

> Used for more effective planning of intervention and reviewing of services.
>
> (Care manager, assessment team)

Families were more involved in the process:

> The Framework allows for families to more clearly understand the process from an early stage creating greater involvement and commitment from some families. The emphasis on needs and solutions is more positive for families.
>
> (Manager, family support team)

> Families are more involved in the assessment process and therefore more committed to the care plan.
>
> (Team manager, child and family team)

> Families are clearer regarding focus of work. Difficulty however when expectations of the assessment are not met within ongoing family support input.
>
> (Case manager, referral and assessment team)

In contrast, over a third (36.5%) of managers thought that the introduction of the assessment records had made little or no difference to social work plans and interventions with children in need and their families. Two reasons were identified.

1. Resources:

> Service provision remains the same and the quality of work of the team is largely governed by the volume of referrals (which is too high) versus the number and quality of staff (too low).
>
> (Team manager, referral and assessment team)

2. Existing good practice:

> The work and plans done previously were good.
>
> (Team leader, assessment team)

> I feel we were working to high standards before the Framework.
>
> (Team manager, referral and assessment team)

Finally, four managers thought the introduction of the assessment records had had a negative impact on social work intervention. In three of the four cases managers were responsible for teams working with disabled children. These managers thought the Assessment Framework and the required timescales for undertaking assessments were not suitable for this group of service users. These reactions reflect the views reported by some managers and practitioners (during meetings and training sessions) that the Assessment Framework was not an appropriate approach for assessing the needs of disabled children and their families.

> Families feel we're checking up on them, however hard we try and explain/sell the process.
>
> (Project leader, disability team)

> In some cases the assessment records can get in the way of building supportive relationships at a time of high stress when a child is gravely ill. Parents do not want assessment at this point, e.g. children on regional burns unit, children with neonatal intensive care problems, children with life-threatening diseases. Most parents are caring parents and want emotional support, not critical assessment.
>
> (Fieldwork manager, disabled children)

Such issues are relevant for social workers dealing with every parent. The views once again suggest confusion over the purpose of the assessment record. Some social workers appear to be under the misapprehension that the record is the assessment rather than a format to record a summary of the information gained and, using their professional judgement, to detail the plans and intervention.

Service provision

Less than half (45.8%) of managers thought the use of the assessment records had improved service provision for children in need. When managers thought service provision had been positively affected in many cases, this was attributed to an increased confidence in arguing for resources.

> Clarified needs, assessments used at meetings to gain resources.
>
> (Assistant team manager, disabled children's team)

> Clear assessment of need and accurate planning improves service provision and more cost-effective allocating of resources.
>
> (Case manager, assessment team)

Another advantage cited by managers of using the assessment records was that a holistic assessment encouraged a corporate approach to the provision of services.

> Assessment looks at holistic needs of the child – therefore other services than social services department can be utilised.
>
> (Acting team manager, locality team)

> A more corporate approach in providing the recommended services (working together).
>
> (Principal social worker, family support services)

However, a similar proportion (43.5%) of managers thought that the Assessment Framework and the use of the assessment records, although useful in identifying the needs of the child, had made little or no difference to the provision of services. This lack of impact was in all cases attributed to a lack of resources.

> Although we have plans which are child-focused, options around services available are still limited so it has made little difference. We are just clearer about why the provision is required.
>
> (Team manager, long-term team)

> The records have helped considerably in identifying need, but neither the staffing nor the resources have been available to follow through on plans. It's a major problem.
>
> (Team manager, referral and assessment team)

> If you don't have the resources you can't provide them. At least the Assessment Framework shows unmet need.
>
> (Fieldwork manager, locality team)

In nine cases (10.5%) managers felt the Assessment Framework and the assessment records had negatively impacted on service provision. In all cases managers thought the focus on recording assessments had been at a cost to service provision, although their answers also suggest that the lack of resources plays a significant part.

> The time spent on assessment in some cases is detracting from getting out there, seeing people and supporting them. Recording is important but should not become the be all and end all.
>
> (Fieldwork manager, disabled children)

> Children looked after and on Child Protection Registers now get a poor service from my team which is understaffed and expected to do detailed core assessments.
>
> (Team manager, long-term team)

Summary points

- Approximately half (between 40% and 51%) of social workers found that recording assessments using the format of the Initial Assessment record helped them in making decisions about children in need.
- Managers were more positive than social workers about the impact of the assessment records on decision-making.
- Over half the managers found the introduction of the assessment records had improved plans and interventions for children in need.
- Managers reported that the introduction of the assessment records had had less impact on service provision.

Chapter summary

The 25 Councils with Social Services Responsibilities that participated in the research were responsible for distributing the postal questionnaires (produced in an electronic and paper format) to their social workers and social work managers. A total of 215 social workers and 93 social work managers from 20 councils completed and returned questionnaires to the research team. The respondents were a diverse group that incorporated a wide range of social work experience. The practitioners and managers represented all the social work teams within children's social services, and the proportions broadly reflected the staffing patterns.

The council's own training department generally delivered the training programmes on the Assessment Framework, based on *The Child's World.* A member of the research team gave four half-day familiarisation sessions covering the use of the assessment records. A copy of the training pack used during these familiarisation sessions was supplied to each council. Social workers' exposure to this training varied. A quarter did not recall attending any form of training on the Assessment Framework or the use of the assessment records. The training courses were more successful at meeting the practice needs of practitioners who were unqualified or qualified for less than five years.

The training delivered by the council was generally a short, one-off event. This policy created a number of barriers to achieving a trained and confident staff group. The difficulties included:

- the inability to attend the event, for whatever reason, meant that the opportunity was lost
- a one-off event failed to address issues that arose as staff became more familiar with the Assessment Framework and the assessment records
- high levels of staff turnover and the use of agency staff meant that new staff could not take advantage of the training
- some councils ran training programmes that excluded particular groups of social workers (such as hospital-based teams).

The majority of managers reported that the assessment records were consistently used in the teams they were responsible for. How regularly the assessment records were used depended on the type of team. Practically every (95%) manager responsible for a referral and assessment team reported that the assessment records were routinely used.

Most managers reported that the implementation of the Assessment Framework and the introduction of the assessment records had increased their workload. Workloads increased because additional time was spent on the following tasks:

- drafting and introducing new practice guidance and procedures
- winning the hearts and minds of practitioners
- supporting, supervision and monitoring social workers
- coping with inadequate computer systems
- engaging with professionals from other agencies.

Although as a result of the Assessment Framework workloads had increased, managers also identified the following advantages:

- an improved ability to monitor practitioner workloads and identify gaps in training and practice
- improvements in the quality of recording
- increased understanding of the needs and circumstances of individual children
- better ability to monitor individual cases
- better ability to local information on social work case-files.

The majority of social workers reported that the implementation of the Assessment Framework and the introduction of the assessment records had increased their workload. Although workloads increased, so did the quality of assessments. Approximately two-thirds of managers and over half the social workers reported an improvement in the quality of assessments.

Perceived improvements in the quality of assessments were associated with the following two issues: first, social workers who were unqualified or newly qualified (less than three years) (suggesting a greater willingness to change working practices within this group) and, second, attendance on training programmes that were seen as relevant to practice.

The Assessment Framework and the assessment records predicate child-based case records rather than family records. This led to a change in practice within many social services departments. This change was seen by practitioners to have both negative and positive consequences for their practice. Most frequently voiced was the view that completing separate records for individual children within the same family resulted in unnecessary duplication of information. This suggests that social workers do not always realise the differential impact parenting issues and environmental factors have on individual children. To assume the impact is similar for all children within the family is dangerous.

Although most social workers felt that the use of the assessment records had resulted in increased recording, a third thought that the quality of their assessments had improved, and practically half felt the needs of individual children were more evident.

Chapter 4 of the *Framework for the Assessment of Children in Need and their Families* (Department of Health *et al.*, 2000a) discusses analysis, judgement and decision-making. The assessment records were designed to support this process. Approximately half the practitioners and managers reported that the assessment records had improved their ability to make decisions and plans about children in need. Finally, although the provision of services was dependent on the availability of resources, managers reported that the improved quality of the assessments had enabled them to argue more forcefully for resources, and the implementation of the Assessment Framework encouraged a more corporate approach to the provision of services.

Chapter 5

Inter-agency and Inter-professional Collaboration in Assessments of Children in Need

Little is known about the impact of inter-agency and inter-professional collaboration on outcomes for children and families (see Hallett, 1995 for a discussion of this). The notion underpinning inter-agency and inter-professional collaboration is that common goals will achieve more coherent and comprehensive services (Wigfall and Moss, 2001). The value of inter-agency and inter-professional collaboration has been strengthened by the findings from enquiry reports which supply ample evidence to show that failures of communication and collaboration contributed to numerous child deaths (Department of Health, 1991b; Owers *et al.*, 1999; Sinclair and Bullock, 2002).

Although research on outcomes has not been forthcoming, important studies exploring the effect of collaboration on administrative processes in child protection cases do exist (Birchall and Hallett, 1995; Hallett, 1995). This body of work found that in child protection enquiries inter-agency involvement is more highly developed at the early stages prior to the child protection case conference (see, for example, Hallett, 1995). Thus, inter-agency and inter-professional collaboration extends to: information sharing; a degree of joint planning to clarify the division of labour; and some shared decision-making. The level of collaboration decreases as the case progresses: for example, although the development of an inter-agency protection plan is a prerequisite for registration, in almost 40 per cent of cases the plan did not mention agencies other than social services.

A co-ordinated, multi-agency approach to child protection enquires has been emphasised by central government in Britain with a stream of circulars since 1960 culminating in Working Together (Department of Health *et al.*, 1999) and the Assessment Framework (Department of Health *et al.*, 2000a). For example, Working Together, informed by the findings from the enquiry reports, stresses the need for a co-ordinated approach between relevant agencies to safeguard children.

> Promoting children's wellbeing and safeguarding them from significant harm depends crucially upon effective information sharing, collaboration and understanding between agencies and professionals. Constructive relationships between individual workers need to be supported by a strong lead from elected or appointed authority members, and the commitment of chief officers. (Department of Health *et al.*, 1999, p.2, 1.10)

Finally, underpinning the *Framework for the Assessment of Children in Need and their Families* (Department of Health, *et al.*, 2000a) is inter-agency collaboration.

> A key principle of the Assessment Framework is that children's needs and their families' circumstances will require inter-agency collaboration to ensure full understanding of what is happening and to ensure an effective service response. (Department of Health *et al.*, 2000a, p.63, 5.1)

An important element in gaining the commitment of agencies, other than social services, to the assessment of children in need is to involve them in the implementation process. The government in the letter sent out to accompany the Assessment Framework acknowledged this. This stressed that successful implementation depended on generating ownership and commitment from senior managers and elected members and involving other agencies in their implementation plans.

The findings from this study of 24 Councils with Social Services Responsibilities in England shows that 17 established multi-agency implementation groups or delegated responsibility for implementation to their Area Child Protection Committees. In the remaining eight councils the responsibility for implementing the Assessment Framework remained with social services.

This chapter draws evidence from a number of sources to explore the impact of the Assessment Framework on inter-agency and inter-professional collaboration. The sources include the questionnaire survey (sent to social workers, social work managers and other professionals); the interview study; and the audit of case files.

The questionnaires were sent out during 2001, approximately one year after the Assessment Framework had been implemented. Each of the 24 Councils with Social Services Responsibility was responsible for distributing the questionnaires within their own area. It is likely that low or high return rates reflect distribution methods as much as the level of interest amongst potential respondents.

A total of 153 professionals from agencies other than social services returned a questionnaire from 16 councils. The number of returns varied between the councils, ranging from 1 to 29 returns, and when the averages were considered, on the whole reflected their size. For example, on average there were more questionnaires from Shire Counties (15.5%) than from Unitary Authorities (8.5%), Metropolitan Boroughs (8%) and London Boroughs (5.6%). However, there was as much variation within groups as between groups.

Profile of the other professionals n=153

Agencies represented by the professionals

The main respondents were professionals involved in health and education. Over half (61.4%, n=94) of the returned questionnaires came from health professionals. These included:

- health visitors (69)
- school nurses (10)
- community nurses (6)
- midwives (3)
- doctors (6).

Over a quarter (27.5%, n=42) came from professionals working in education, including:

- school teachers or head teachers (18)
- educational welfare officers (21)
- professional working with hearing-impaired children (1)
- child protection co-ordinator in school (1)
- school inclusion co-ordinator (1).

The remaining returns (11.1%, n=17) came from a range of professionals including police and probation officers, family centre workers, project workers in children's voluntary agencies, and women's refuges.

Time in present post

The time professionals have been in their present post may influence the confidence with which they approach the task of working with other professionals, their knowledge of inter-agency working policy and procedures, and the informal networks they have established.

Of professionals replying to the questionnaire 70 per cent had been in their present post for *over* five years: 30 per cent had been in post for less than five years (only 18, 11.8%, for 12 months or less); over a third (38%) had been working in their current job for 5–10 years; and a further 32 per cent had been in post for longer. The disciplines that the professionals represented had little impact on the length of time they had been in their current posts. For example, 29 per cent of health professionals had been in post less than five years, compared with 31 per cent of education professionals, and 35 per cent of the remaining professionals.

Familiarity with the Assessment Framework

> The familiarity of other agencies with the Assessment Framework will assist when making a referral to a social services department or contributing to an assessment of a child in need, thereby facilitating a common understanding of the child's needs within their family context. (Department of Health *et al.*, 2000a, p.29, 3.3)

The degree of familiarity with the Assessment Framework is an additional factor that will impact on the confidence and ability of professionals in other agencies to work collaboratively with social services on the assessment of children in need.

The importance of training people together to undertake the assessment of children is emphasised by both Working Together (Department of Health *et al.*, 1999) and the Assessment Framework (Department of Health *et al.*, 2000a). The social workers' questionnaires explored whether the training they had attended on the Assessment Framework had included participants from other disciplines. Social workers from 20 social services departments replied. In 12 departments one or more of the social workers reported that training had been multi-agency. However, the lack of consistency between the replies within a particular social services department, suggests a variety of training, some of which was targeted at a multi-agency audience.

When professionals, other than social services staff, attended training on the Assessment Framework (practically all of which was supplied by social services) their evaluation of it was generally positive.

> Before completing the training on the assessment of children in need, I had very limited knowledge of the way in which social services assess families. The introduction of the Assessment Framework and the training received has greatly improved my knowledge which I feel will improve working relationships between Drugline and social services.
>
> (Project worker at the children of drug users project)

However, professionals expressed frustration when training failed to materialise or was untimely.

> I am due to do the multi-agency training in a few weeks' time, many months after I was involved with the Assessment Framework.
>
> (Health visitor)

> Training which was supposed to be delivered to all child protection co-ordinators was set up but then not delivered.
>
> (School's special educational needs co-ordinator and child protection co-ordinator)

Although not every social services department held multi-agency training sessions, practically every professional who participated in the study was familiar with the Assessment Framework. Moreover, most other professionals (87%) were aware of the Department of Health's assessment records, and nearly three-quarters (73%) reported being involved in a case where the social worker had used the assessment records.

The impact of the Assessment Framework on the practice of professionals other than social workers

> The use of the Assessment Framework for assessing children in need provides a language which is common to children and their family members, as well as to professionals and other staff. (Department of Health *et al.*, 2000a, p.63, 5.4)

Impact on recording practice

Practically a third (31.4%) of the professionals reported that the Assessment Framework had affected the way they recorded information about the children for whom they had concerns. A comparison of the replies from the two main professional groups, health and education, shows that health professionals were more likely (35%) to report a positive change in their reporting practice than education professionals (24%).

When asked to elaborate on their answers, professionals' responses broadly fell into the following categories:

- structural changes
- changes in quantity
- changes in focus.

STRUCTURAL CHANGES

Professionals from agencies other than social services reported that using the domains and dimensions of the Assessment Framework had improved their recording practice. For example,

> I now consider information under the three domains. It is a useful framework to analyse information and record strengths and weaknesses.
>
> (NSPCC project manager)

> I specifically note observations under the headings on the assessment form.
>
> (Educational welfare officer)

> I have attempted to record information within the categories of the Framework, to enable me to contribute to completing the assessment.
>
> (Health visitor)

> Referrals of children in need/in need of protection, the forms now reflect the domains and dimensions of the Assessment Framework.
>
> (School nurse)

CHANGES IN QUALITY

Improvements in the quality of recording were related to more detailed and more concise record keeping.

> I keep more detailed information records and liaise regularly with schools.
>
> (School nurse)

> It has made me aware of the necessity to record all details regardless of how small and further increase my work in respect of accuracy.
>
> (Educational welfare officer)

> Briefer information, but more specific.
>
> (Educational welfare officer)

CHANGES IN FOCUS

The reports from professionals suggest the implementation of the Assessment Framework resulted in a more holistic approach to assessments of children's needs and circumstances.

> More attention to different categories. I need to think about when to record it rather than do it every time.
>
> (Health visitor)

> It has helped to ensure a holistic picture.
>
> (Health visitor)

> I include more information about environmental issues.
>
> (Health visitor)

> Reports are more expedient and organised.
>
> (Health visitor)

Impact on work with children and families

Over a quarter (27.4%) of other professionals reported that the Assessment Framework had improved their work with children and families, two-thirds (66%) that the level and quality of work had not changed, and a small proportion (6.5%) reported a negative impact.

A POSITIVE IMPACT ON WORKING WITH CHILDREN AND FAMILIES (27.4%)

A third of health professionals reported a positive impact on their work with children and families, which was twice the rate reported by education professionals (16%). A positive impact was related to the Assessment Framework affecting:

- direct work with children and families
- work with other agencies
- improved understanding of children's needs and circumstances.

Direct work with children and families

The process was more transparent for families:

> I think families see the assessment as a more positive experience – I can easily demonstrate that information gained will be used to help and gain extra support, rather than just policing them.
>
> (Health visitor)

> Our contribution to formal processes is more transparent, it has increased our ability to be more open and honest with families.
>
> (Designated nurse)

The approach was more inclusive:

> You now need to gain parental co-operation more. Whilst this can sometimes be tricky, it can also be very useful.
>
> (Head teacher)

> The opportunity is available throughout for families to contribute to social work assessments.
>
> (Health visitor)

There was a reduction in repetition:

> There is more positive input to families and reduction of overlap/repetition for those families.
>
> (Health visitor)

Work with other agencies

Professionals reported that their own work with children and families had changed because the Assessment Framework had affected their relationship with social services. They cited a number of effects including better communication, a clearer understanding of roles and responsibilities, and increased ability to advocate for children.

Better communication:

> Improved communication with other agencies.
>
> (Health visitor)

> Encourages more inter agency collaboration in assessing and developing strategies.
>
> (Health visitor)

Understanding the roles and responsibilities:

> Roles more clearly defined. We are all working 'from the same hymn sheet'.
>
> (Health visitor)

> The health staff feel that the quality of work has improved it has allowed us to be clearer about the legislative basis of referrals and our duty to assist with children and families.
>
> (Designated nurse)

Advocating for children:

> The Framework provides greater leverage on which to advocate for children with social services departments and more shared understanding of the components of an assessment.
>
> (Project manager NSPCC)

> I am now able to identify children who are vulnerable but who have not necessarily suffered significant harm. Hence I can begin to try and access help in a preventative framework/model rather than purely reactive.
>
> (Health visitor)

Improved understanding of children's needs and circumstances

Professionals reported that the Assessment Framework had impacted on their work with children and families because the conceptual framework encouraged more holistic assessments that ensured that issues related to children's safety were identified.

> More informed by the assessment – wider focus on three domains, less individualising.
>
> (Project manager NSPCC)

> It is very useful to have a broad conceptual framework to use and I think it reduces the subjectivity of judgement.
>
> (Health visitor)

> It has enabled me to undertake work with people outside of our usual client group and has consolidated my ways of working with families and looking at the wider picture within a multi-disciplinary framework.
>
> (Practitioner in an under-5s and family support centre)

> Easier to identify areas of concern and areas where intervention may help.
>
> (Health visitor)

> I am asking more direct questions regarding child protection.
>
> (Health visitor)

NO IMPACT ON WORKING WITH CHILDREN AND FAMILIES (66%)

The majority of professionals reported that the Assessment Framework had no impact on their work with children and families. The lack of impact did not reflect any shortcomings in the Assessment Framework but was attributed to:

- social services operating a high threshold for services – services being restricted to children in need of protection
- a failure in communication.

In some cases professionals reported that families felt disappointed and disillusioned when assessments failed to result in any services.

High thresholds for services

> We have a high referral rate for children involved in domestic violence. Our longer-term involvement with our more difficult cases highlights that very little service provision is given to these children until or unless they are injured in the situation.
>
> (Police)

> It feels like there is no support for these families until it becomes a child protection issue.
>
> (Health visitor)

A failure in communication

In other cases a failure to communicate the outcome of assessments left professionals feeling ineffectual and powerless.

> Often we have informed families about the referral to social services and there is often no response from them. This makes us appear ineffectual to families.
>
> (Health visitor)

> I have completed the forms in partnership with families which has been beneficial in opening other discussions. However, families have still not received much needed resources and this has had a negative/demoralising effect on some of them. In other cases where neither I or the family have any response from social services I feel it has led to mistrust from families towards me and not been helpful in my working relationship.
>
> (Health visitor)

A NEGATIVE IMPACT ON WORKING WITH CHILDREN AND FAMILIES (6.5%)

Only nine professionals reported that the Assessment Framework had had a negative impact on the work with children and families. The reasons for the negative impact centred on three issues:

- misunderstanding the purpose of the assessment records
- a failure in communication
- increased paperwork.

Misunderstanding the purpose of the assessment records

Social workers employed by voluntary bodies mirrored the misunderstandings cited by social services practitioners; the core assessment record was seen as a questionnaire rather than a format to record the summary of the assessment.

> Core assessments have led to a lot of frustration and feeling by parents that professionals do not understand their situation, because the questions are so much geared towards children without disabilities and where child protection is an issue. The questions and guidance suggest that disability is an add-on. This is insulting to parents and children who have severe impairments.
>
> (Social worker employed with Barnardos)

This report also reflects the views expressed by some social workers, that the Assessment Framework is not relevant for assessing disabled children and their families.

A failure to communicate

We are not aware if work is being undertaken by social services and feel unable to refer our clients to access the resources.

(Educational welfare officer)

Total failure to advise referrer of decisions or response to referral can lead to lengthy gaps in case work. Lack of credibility with families when referrals made with consent then no contact made by social services. On the rare occasions when notified of a decision not to take action, no rationale is offered.

(Educational welfare officer)

Increased paperwork

Lots of time spent doing reports to inform the documentation which does not cater for complex health needs. In turn the hours available for visiting families are reduced.

(Community children's nurse)

An awful lot of paperwork for all parties involved – when at the end of it all there are few resources to call upon – no matter what issues were raised by the assessment.

(Health visitor)

Such duplication of paperwork is being addressed by the Integrated Children's System.

The impact of the Assessment Framework on the professionals' understanding of the roles and responsibilities of social services

Making referrals

Part III of the Children Act 1989 lays a legal obligation on councils with social services responsibility to provide services to children in need. The criteria for defining who is a child in need are set out in Section 17(10) of the Children Act. However, in order to know how to respond to children for whom they have concerns professionals from agencies other than social services need to understand the criteria for defining 'a child in need'. Understanding the criteria will enable them to decide whether to refer to social services, refer to another agency, or respond to the needs of the child and family with their own resources. To facilitate this understanding,

> The framework for assessment provides that common language based on explicit values about children, knowledge about what children need to ensure their successful development, and the factors in their lives which may positively or negatively influence their upbringing. (Department of Health *et al.*, 1999, p.x)

Eleven councils had developed an inter-agency referral form. Although these differed from one council to another, all the forms incorporated a section for information to be recorded on each of the three domains of the Assessment Framework: children's developmental needs, parenting capacity, and family and environmental factors. The inter-agency referral form was developed and introduced through the multi-agency groups established to implement the Assessment Framework. It was anticipated that this work would have a number of benefits for professionals making referrals to social services:

- Professionals would be more aware of whether the criteria for a child in need applied to the child in question.
- The professional would have a better understanding of the needs of the child and family and whether these could be met by their own agency or an agency other than social services.
- Referrals to social services would include all the information known to the referrer in a format consistent with the Initial Assessment record, thus reducing the need for follow-up communication.

Practically half (47.6%) the professionals involved in the questionnaire survey reported that the Assessment Framework had improved their understanding of when to refer a child to social services. In particular, the findings reinforce those of Ward and Peel (2002) that when professionals structure the information they have on cases it improves the quality of their own assessments and results in a reduction in referrals to social services.

> It has been very helpful to use the dimensions of the Framework for detailed referrals to ensure concerns and information given is concise and tight. Helps to create focused and better referrals.
>
> (Health visitor)

> Appears to make/encourage schools to take more responsibility than previously.
>
> (Health visitor)

> A more thorough assessment is done by myself. This is good as it gives me more information to work with.
>
> (Education welfare officer)

A slightly smaller proportion (41%) of other professionals reported that their understanding had not changed. Of those who reported no change half said that their understanding had always been good and half that they had little understanding and this had not improved. Professionals only expanded on their replies when their understanding remained poor.

> Other than the new referral form for social services, the introduction of the Assessment Framework has had no impact on my practice or relationship with social services. Communication remains very poor and I am unable to understand their threshold criteria which do not appear to be consistent.
>
> (Health visitor)

> Unaware of the Assessment Framework and the use of the assessment forms.
>
> (Teacher special educational needs)

Seventeen other professionals (11.4%) reported that their understanding of what constitutes a child in need had deteriorated. Confusion was not confined to a particular professional group: for example, 12 per cent of health professionals and 9.5 per cent of education professionals reported increased confusion. Their answers suggest the increased confusion was linked to the process of establishing new systems rather than the Assessment Framework itself.

> I find the whole Assessment Framework confusing and would appreciate further courses with dialogue.
>
> (Head teacher)

Roles and responsibilities of social services

> Inter-agency, inter-disciplinary assessment practice requires an additional set of knowledge and skills to that required for working within a single agency or independently. It requires that all staff understand the

> roles and responsibilities of staff working in contexts different to their own. (Department of Health *et al.*, 2000a, p.63, 5.4)

Research into child protection practice suggests that to make inter-agency and inter-professional work a reality an understanding of the respective roles in assessment and intervention is essential (Stevenson, 2000).

Practically half (47.7%) the professionals reported that the Assessment Framework had improved their understanding of the roles and responsibilities of social services. A similar proportion (42%) reported that it had not affected their understanding. Of those that reported no change, practically three-quarters (71%) noted that this was because their understanding had been good prior to the implementation of the Assessment Framework, and the remaining proportion (29%) because their understanding had been poor and this had not changed. A further 10 per cent of professionals reported that they were now more confused about the roles and responsibilities of social services.

Putting these findings together with those relating to professionals' understanding of the criteria for a child in need, shows that two-thirds (67%) of professionals understood when to refer a child to social services (it had either improved or had always been good) and more than three-quarters (79%) understood the roles and responsibilities of social services.

The impact of the Assessment Framework on the level and quality of communication with social services

> Social services departments have lead responsibility for undertaking assessments of children in need. In order to arrive at well-balanced judgements about the needs of children, practitioners and their managers may benefit from the expertise and experience of professionals in other disciplines. These professionals can act as consultants or advisers to assist and contribute to the assessment processes, which includes analysis of information gathered. (Department of Health *et al.*, 1999, p.57, 4.18)

Failures in communication have been shown to contribute to numerous child deaths (Department of Health, 1991b). Working Together (Department of Health *et al.*, 1999, p.3, 1.13) affirms that co-operation across disciplines and agencies is vital if children are to be protected.

The findings from the audit of social work files show that in practically three-quarters (72.3%) of social workers had involved at least one other agency in the initial assessment process. In 42 per cent of cases two or more other agencies had been involved (see Chapter 7 for more details). The questionnaires returned by professionals from agencies other than social services reinforce the impression that in the majority of initial assessments agencies are working together. Practically three-quarters of other professionals reported that, since the implementation of the Assessment Framework, the level and quality of communication had improved or remained good.

Improvements in communication

A third of other professionals reported that the level (32%) and the quality (33%) of communication with social services had improved since the implementation of the Assessment Framework.

> The quality of communication has improved. More focused, based on normative data not just feelings.
>
> (Teacher)

> There does appear to be greater inter-agency working relationships between social workers and school nurses which is of great benefit to the child and family.
>
> (School nurse)

> We have always found co-operation excellent but now it is more focused and I feel that we are more in tune. We recognise each other's strengths and areas of involvement.
>
> (Health visitor)

No change in communication

Some 60 per cent of other professionals reported that the level (58%) and quality (60%) of communication had not changed. Of these two-thirds reported that communication had always been good.

> Always worked with colleagues to provide high level of quality support.
>
> (Practitioner for service for hearing impaired children)

> We generally have a good exchange of information between child protection team and social services.
>
> (Police)

When professionals reported that communication remained poor the reasons they gave suggested that this was related to:

- lack of agreement over the definition of a child in need
- poor practice
- restricted resources
- teething problems when introducing a new system.

LACK OF AGREEMENT OVER THE DEFINITION OF A CHILD IN NEED

> Continued poor communication. Constant management changes. At field level there is no agreement about definition of a child in need.
>
> (Health visitor)

POOR PRACTICE

> In the past referrals done by letter were not answered, we always had to phone up and follow up our letters. This does not seem to have changed with the new forms, we are still having to chase up referrals.
>
> (Project worker at Home-Start)

RESTRICTED RESOURCES

> Unfortunately there have been significant cutbacks in services here (provided by social services) due to financial difficulties. This has inevitably affected all aspects of social services service delivery and inter-agency liaison.
>
> (Community paediatrician)

TEETHING PROBLEMS WHEN INTRODUCING A NEW SYSTEM

> Would have changed if totally implemented, in early stages yet.
>
> (Health visitor)

Decreased communication

Less than 10 per cent of professionals found that the level (9.8%) or quality (7%) of communication with social services had deteriorated since the implementation of the Assessment Framework.

> It gave me higher expectations that children in need could be supported in a more appropriate way. I have not seen evidence of this.
>
> (Health visitor)

The illustrations suggest that this was attributed to:

- restricted resources
- possible poor practice.

RESTRICTED RESOURCES

> Communication seems to be worse. Department seems to have fewer resources than ever. Only children with child protection needs are given priority because of lack of financial resources.
>
> (Health visitor)

> If anything there has been less involvement because social workers are not available so much as they used to be.
>
> (Head teacher)

POSSIBLE POOR PRACTICE

> It is a waste of time referring clients when social services fail abysmally to even initiate the first stage, i.e. professionals' meeting. I find it very alarming that one has to write an official letter of complaint before a key worker is allocated.
>
> (Community midwife)

> The main effect has been on the relationship and communication with the initial assessment team. Health visitor and school nurse information, concerns or views are not sought if the referral comes from another agency. Referrals from health visitors and school nurses are not respected. Children in need of protection are not even assessed as children in need.
>
> (Health visitor)

The impact of the Assessment Framework on the inter-agency and inter-professional collaboration in the assessment, plans and delivery of services for children in need

> In order to ensure optimal outcomes for children, whilst at the same time avoiding duplication of services or children receiving no service at all, it is important for all disciplines and agencies to work in a co-ordinated way to an agreed plan. (Department of Health *et al.*, 2000a, p.63, 5.2)

The social workers' perspective on assessments and plans

The social workers' questionnaires asked for their views on the impact of the Assessment Framework on the collaboration of other agencies in assessments of children in need. Less than a third (29%) of social work practitioners reported that collaboration on assessments had increased, two-thirds (66%) considered that it had not changed and 5 per cent thought that inter-agency collaboration had been reduced.

AN INCREASE IN THE DEGREE OF COLLABORATION OVER ASSESSMENTS

The reasons cited by social workers as to why collaboration had increased related to:

- the structured way information is given
- greater clarity in the roles and responsibilities of agencies
- a greater willingness to share information.

The structured way information is given

> Other agencies can be asked to provide assessment information and this does happen.
>
> (Social worker, hospital team)

> More joint working together as other agencies assisted in completing the records with social workers.
>
> (Social worker in a locality team)

Greater clarity in the roles and responsibilities of agencies

> Core assessment record has increased the level of responsibility being shared.
>
> (Social worker, locality team)

> When other agencies are involved it makes it clear that they have a role in assessing the needs of a family.
>
> (Social worker, initial assessment team)

> Places greater expectation on other agencies to do their bit in terms of contributing to the assessment. Positive response to date from other agencies.
>
> (Social worker, long-term team)

A greater willingness to share information

> Agencies appeared more co-operative in giving up time to contribute, i.e. by meeting face to face rather than talking on telephone, hence areas explored in more depth.
>
> (Social worker, locality team)

NO CHANGE IN THE DEGREE OF COLLABORATION OVER ASSESSMENTS

Two-thirds of social work practitioners thought that the Assessment Framework had not affected the degree of collaboration between agencies in the assessment of children in need. In many cases the explanations given by social workers suggest that, in some councils, assessment was not perceived as a shared responsibility by other agencies.

> Other agencies feel that it is social services department's duty to complete [assessments] and often fail to give or share information.
>
> (Social worker, locality team)

> No significant change. Inter-agency working in R. is not well developed re: Assessment Framework. Other agencies think it is social services-led not multi-agency ownership.
>
> (Social worker, locality team)

In some cases the impact on collaborative work appears to depend on the agency in question.

> More co-operation with education. Some resistance from other agencies.
>
> (Social worker, disability team)

> Health visitors and schools have become more involved and are happy to take part. Most doctors are reluctant.
>
> (Social worker, locality team)

A DECREASE IN THE DEGREE OF COLLABORATION OVER ASSESSMENTS

In a few instances social workers reported that collaboration over the assessment of children in need had decreased.

> Almost nil [collaboration], they don't understand what it is or see why they should take part.
>
> (Social worker, locality team)

> It has caused friction with GPs asking for fees and refusing to give information unless they receive them. Information from schools of very limited use and below standard of that collected previously; the same applies to health records.
>
> (Social worker, assessment team)

The other professionals' perspectives on assessments and plans

AN INCREASE IN COLLABORATION OVER ASSESSMENTS AND PLANS

The proportion of professionals from agencies other than social services who reported that the implementation of the Assessment Framework had increased their collaboration with social services in the assessment of children in need was similar to that reported by social work practitioners. Approximately a third of other professionals reported that collaboration in the assessment (32%) and planning (32%) for children in need had improved.

Comments of professionals on individual cases illustrate the satisfaction when collaboration is successful.

> I think there has been a lot of co-operation between social services and education in this case.
>
> (Head teacher)

> I don't think it could be improved. The liaison was excellent. Plans were put forward very quickly. I couldn't fault it really.
>
> (Midwife)

> In this case I've been particularly pleased. The consultation between me and social services department has been very good.
>
> (Health visitor)

> It has improved communication. The joint planning involved is very good. The assessment process reinforces joint working.
>
> (Head teacher)

NO CHANGE IN COLLABORATION OVER ASSESSMENTS AND PLANS

Practically two-thirds (64%) of other professionals reported that collaboration in the assessment and planning for children in need had not changed with the implementation of the Assessment Framework, and 4 per cent felt it had declined. In many cases, as has been noted previously, the lack of improvement or the decline in collaborative work was attributed to:

- restricted resources
- poor practice
- inappropriate use of the assessment records.

Restricted resources

The reports of professionals show considerable understanding and sympathy for the restricted budgets and staffing problems facing social services.

> Where there have been difficulties it hasn't been a lack of willingness as much as a lack of availability of resources. Overall I think we work well together within the constraints of time which we are all working with.
>
> (Head teacher)

Poor practice

The inadequacy of feedback following referrals has been found in previous studies of inter-agency co-operation in child protection (Hallett, 1995). Both Working Together and the Assessment Framework give robust guidance on keeping referrers and the family informed of the decisions that have been taken.

> The family, the original referrer and other professionals and services involved in the assessment, should as far as possible be told what action has been taken, consistent with respecting the confidentiality of the child and family concerned, and not jeopardising further action in respect of child protection concerns (which may include police investigations). (Department of Health *et al.*, 1999, p.43, 5.17)
>
> Agencies and individuals involved in the assessment should also be informed of the decisions, with reasons for these made clear. (Department of Health *et al.*, 2000a, p.32, 3.13)

The findings from the current study suggest this issue has not yet been fully addressed. Professionals reported that social services failed to keep them informed about the progress or outcome of assessments.

> Health visitors give information to social services but get no response. They decide what to do without consulting the health visitor.
>
> (Health visitor)

> The lack of communication is common. I found out more about what was happening about my original concerns from the mother than I did from the social services department.
>
> (Health visitor)

> They never inform us of the outcome of assessments. We find out by repeated calls to social workers.
>
> (Health visitor)

> We frequently have to chase up after one month requests of parents who had had no communication from social services.
>
> (Head teacher)

Inappropriate use of the assessment records

In some cases professionals reported that they were expected to complete parts of the core assessment themselves, a job they felt quite rightly was not appropriate.

> They sent me the health section of the form to complete. This is not useful as a way of me contributing my knowledge of the family or of their problems.
>
> (School nurse)

> The first request that I had was to receive a blank copy of the health section of the Core Assessment record. I had no training and did not feel comfortable doing this. I asked my manager and she agreed that I needn't complete this.
>
> (Health visitor)

As has been discussed in previous chapters, many social workers did not fully understand the purpose of the assessment records. When the research was taking place the implementation of the Assessment Framework was still in its infancy. At this stage the training and supervision had not always been successful in ensuring that practitioners understood that the assessment records were designed to support social workers in recording and analysing all the relevant information gathered during an assessment, including that gained from other agencies.

The delivery of services

> At the strategic level, agencies and professionals need to work in partnership with each other and with service users, to plan comprehensive and co-ordinated children's services. (Department of Health *et al.*, 1999, p.3, 1.11)

The Assessment Framework is seen to have had less impact on inter-agency and inter-professional service delivery to children in need than on the earlier stages of assessment and planning – a finding that reflects previous research on child protection (Hallett, 1995).

Only a fifth (22%) of other professionals reported that collaboration in the delivery of services had increased, three-quarters (76%) reported the degree of collaboration had not changed, and 3 per cent thought it had decreased.

FACTORS ASSOCIATED WITH THE DEGREE OF COLLABORATION

The factors that other professionals cited as relating to the degree of collaboration included:

- the planning process
- common definitions
- the level of resources.

The planning process

Involvement in the planning process was pivotal to collaboration in service provision. When collaboration in service provision was perceived to have improved, this was attributed to a greater degree of involvement in the planning process.

> It has often made my input much more specific – detailed minutes with action points specifically named to dovetail input in appropriate areas.
>
> (Community nurse – learning disabilities)

The reverse was also true. A lack of involvement in the planning process was seen to hamper collaboration in the delivery of services.

> I think it would have been nice to have had a Core Group Meeting involving agencies or recommended by Case Conference. For the plan to have been agreed between all relevant agencies.
>
> (Health visitor)

> I would have liked to have been involved in the planning meetings. I think my knowledge would have been useful.
>
> (Community nurse)

Indeed, some professionals expressed a willingness to shoulder greater responsibility for working with children in need.

> It made me concerned and aware of how little contact we have with these vulnerable children. We just seem to be a referral agency. I would like us to have more impact may be with some counselling and training to back us.
>
> (School nurse)

> There seems to be a huge re-assessment of what agencies have to offer.
>
> (Health visitor)

When not involved professionals expressed considerable frustration.

> I am asked to sign off assessments without a chance to read/digest or comment on them, and sometimes I'm not even told the outcome.
>
> (Health visitor)

Common definitions

Collaboration in the delivery of services for children in need was hampered because professionals from different disciplines used different criteria for defining a child in need.

> Health and social services are working to different thresholds. Therefore, health visitors are left with a case of great need and concern with no support from social services due to lack of staff. The children are de-registered straight back to the care of the health visitor and no clarification of the social services input at all.
>
> (Health visitor)

The level of resources

Finally, changes in the level of resources available, and the structure of services were also cited as responsible for impeding inter-agency collaboration in the delivery of services.

> We feel that the delivery of services and co-operation between agencies has deteriorated perhaps due to change in delivery of services, i.e. initial assessment team being based further away and low staffing levels in both initial assessment team and family support team. Both changes took place at same time and service delivery and response time was affected.
>
> (Health visitor)

> Service reductions cause anxiety as to whether we can really provide a comprehensive multi-agency response to vulnerable children's needs.
>
> (Consultant community paediatrician)

Chapter summary

Inter-agency and inter-professional collaboration is a key principle underpinning the Assessment Framework and Working Together. Questionnaires were sent approximately one year after the Assessment Framework had been implemented. Each social services department had responsibility for distributing the questionnaires to other relevant agencies within their own area. A total of 153 professionals from agencies other than social services responded to the questionnaire survey. Over half (61.4%) were health professionals, over a quarter (27.5%) were education professionals and the remaining 11.1per cent included professionals from a variety of other agencies.

Over three-quarters of professionals from agencies other than social services had been in their present post for over five years. This suggests that many professionals will have established informal relationships with social work practitioners.

Training on the Assessment Framework was generally seen as the responsibility of social services. Other professionals welcomed and valued the training sessions they attended.

Practically a third (31.4%) of professionals from agencies other than social services reported that the Assessment Framework had resulted in them changing the way they recorded information about vulnerable children. The use of the domains and dimension of the Assessment Framework was found to make recording more detailed and focused.

Over a quarter (27.4%) of professionals from agencies other than social services reported that the Assessment Framework had improved their work with children and families, two-thirds (66%) reported no change, and 6.5 per cent reported that their work had deteriorated. Improvements resulted from: a more transparent and inclusive approach to children and families, increased understanding of the needs and circumstances of children, and improved working relationships with other agencies.

Since the implementation of the Assessment Framework two-thirds (67%) of professionals from agencies other than social services reported that their understanding of the criteria used to define a child in need had either improved or remained good. A slightly higher proportion (79%) reported that their understanding of the roles and responsibilities of social services had increased or remained at a high level.

Practically three-quarters (73.9%) of professionals from agencies other than social services reported that collaboration in the process of assessment and plans had either improved or remained at a high level. (Approximately a third had reported that collaboration had improved, two-thirds reported no change and 4 per cent felt that it had declined.) These perceptions mirror those of social work practitioners. However, collaboration in the delivery of services was not at this high level, reflecting the findings from child protection studies (Hallett, 1995). In less than half (48%) of cases professionals from agencies other than social services reported that collaboration with social services over the provision of services had increased or remained at a high level.

Issues reported by professionals as related to improved inter-agency and inter-professional collaboration in assessment, planning, and delivery of services for children in need include:

- a more structured way to record information about vulnerable children and families
- a more holistic picture of the child's needs and circumstances
- increased clarity in the roles and responsibilities of individual agencies
- greater willingness to share information
- greater involvement in the planning process.

Issues reported as related to hampering collaborative work include:

- lack of agreements over definitions, including the criteria to define a child in need
- poor social work practice, particularly a failure to communicate the outcome of referrals and assessments and inappropriate use of the assessment records
- restricted resources
- increased paperwork
- teething difficulties in the introduction of a new assessment system.

Chapter 6

Referrals

Findings from the Audit

The sample (n=2248)

The audit was carried out during the autumn of 2001, approximately one year after Councils with Social Services Responsibilities had implemented the Assessment Framework and introduced the recording forms. The audit aimed to include a 100 consecutive referrals to children's social services from each participating council and follow their progress through the system. The objective was to provide information on the types of case referred to social services, and the proportion and characteristics of referrals that led to an initial assessment and to a core assessment. It would also enable the quality of social work recording to be examined (see Appendix I for detailed information about the audit sample).

The findings of the audit reflect information recorded on the referral and assessment records. It cannot be assumed that where information was missing from the records it had not been recorded elsewhere in the case-file.

Twenty-four councils were involved in the audit, resulting in 2248 referrals. The 2248 referrals led to 866 initial assessments (38.5%), and 68 (3.0%) core assessments.

The purpose of the Referral and Initial Information record

> The Referral and Initial Information Record gathers together the essential information about the child including ethnicity, household composition, parental responsibility and agencies currently involved with the child and family. (Department of Health, 2000a, p.1)

The Referral and Initial Information record provides social workers with a format to record the reason the referral or request for services was made and how the social service department responded to it. It therefore has two purposes:

- to record essential information about the child and family
- to record the social service department's and other agencies' response to the referral.

The referral and assessment records were developed as a single-entry system, and information to be recorded on the Referral and Initial Information record, such as the child's ethnicity or religion, are *not* entered on the assessment records. Thus, it is important that social workers note essential information about the child and family on the Referral and Initial Information record either at the point of referral or at a later date when this information becomes available.

Recording patterns for the Referral and Initial Information record

For the Referral and Initial Information record to serve the purpose for which it was designed, social workers need to record systematically all the essential information available at the time of referral. However, not all the Councils with Social Services Responsibilities that participated in the research used the Department of Health's Referral and Information record. Fifteen councils used it (some with additional sections to capture data needed for their own information systems). The remaining nine councils used a locally derived referral format that (although it collected much of the information) was not entirely consistent with the Referral and Information record. For the purpose of the research all the various types of referral forms were included in audit.

The information recorded on the referral form can be divided into information relating to the characteristics of the case and information recorded for administrative purposes.

Case-related information (see Table 6.1, Appendix II)

The reason for and source of the referral, and the action taken had been recorded on practically every referral form (90.7%). Information relating to the child was also recorded in most cases. For example, in practically every case the social worker had recorded the child's name, address, age and gender, and in practically three-quarters of cases, the child's ethnicity.

Thoburn *et al.*'s (2000) research suggests councils with a substantial proportion of their population from black or other minority ethnic communities consistently record information related to the ethnicity of the child. No such association was found within the present study. For example, four London Boroughs had between a third and 45 per cent of their population from black and ethnic minority communities, but the average rate of recording information on the child's ethnicity for these boroughs was 67 per cent. In contrast, in 13 councils (five Shire Counties, four Metropolitan Boroughs, three Unitary Authorities, and one Outer London Borough) 95 per cent of the population was white British and the average rate of recording information on ethnicity was 73 per cent.

Although the Children Act 1989 requires councils to 'give due consideration to...the child's religious persuasion', the child's religion was rarely recorded at the point of referral (noted in only 29.1% of cases). The findings reinforce earlier studies and suggest the importance of religion or spirituality for children and families is still not always recognised by social workers (Dutt and Phillips, 2000; Seden, 1995, 2001). In today's multicultural society knowledge of the religious festivals and customs followed by a particular family will enable social workers to approach contact more sensitively.

Recording practice in relation to the identity of the child's carers and relatives was variable. Although social workers noted the identity of the principal carer and who lived in the household in approximately 70 per cent of cases, information about key family members who were not part of the household had been recorded in only a quarter of cases. This information can be key to ensuring the child's safety particularly in cases of suspected child sexual abuse (Cleaver and Freeman, 1996).

Administrative information (see Table 6.1, Appendix II)

Some aspects of administrative data were recorded in a more consistent manner than others. For example, in most cases (95.1%) social workers had signed the referral form, and in 80.9 per cent the signature of the manager was also evident. The absence of a signature may not always signify a lack of managerial scrutiny. When councils with Social Services Responsibilities kept their referral records on computer, the format did not always enable managers to note their involvement and a paper copy was not systematically included in the paper-based case-file.

In order to calculate the proportion of referrals completed within the required time, social workers need to record the start and end date on the referral form. This had been done in 80 per cent of cases.

Finally, whether the parent was aware of the referral had been recorded in less than two-thirds of cases (62.5%). Recording whether parents are aware of the referral is important because it will influence the social workers' approach to the family.

Summary points

- The audit consists of 2248 referrals from 24 councils.
- Social workers routinely recorded key information about the source and reason for the referral, the characteristics of the child and the identity of the principal carer. Other information, such as the child's religion and significant relatives who were not part of the household, was considered less relevant and recording was poor.

Time taken to complete the referral

(Information available on 1800 referrals)

> There is an expectation that within one working day of a referral being received or new information coming to or from within a social services department about an open case, there will be a decision about what response is required. (Department of Health *et al.*, 2000a, p.31, 3.8)

In practically two-thirds of cases (61.2%) social workers completed the referral (recorded a decision about what response was required) within the required timescale. In a further 13.2 per cent of cases social workers completed the referral within four working days, and in a quarter of cases (25.6%) social workers took more than four working days to complete the referral.

The ability to complete referrals within time may be associated with factors related to the structure of the social services departments, and the case characteristics.

Structure of the social services departments

There was a wide variation between the Councils with Social Services Responsibilities in the rate of referrals completed on time. For example, one social services department completed only 9.8 per cent of referrals on time; at the other extreme one authority completed every referral within the required time. The average completion rate was 60.8 per cent. Eight councils completed less than half of their referrals on time; nine completed between 50 and 70 per cent on time, and six had been able to complete over 70 per cent of their referrals on time.

A scrutiny of the type of council shows that Metropolitan Districts as a group were more likely to complete referrals within the required time, Shire Counties fell within the middle range, and Unitary Authorities and London Boroughs completed the lowest proportion of referrals on time.

The ability to complete referrals on time was also related to the quality of the collaborative arrangements that existed prior to implementation. Councils that involved other agencies in their strategic plans prior to implementation were more likely to complete referrals on time than councils that had not.

Table 6.1 Councils completing referrals on time

Type of Council	*Within time limit*
7 London Boroughs	42.3%
3 Unitary Authorities	46.5%
6 Shire Counties	58.9%

Fifty-seven per cent of councils with good collaborative arrangements prior to implementation completed over 60 per cent of referrals on time, compared with 25 per cent of those that had less well-established collaborative arrangements.

No association was found with other organisational issues concerning the councils. For example, a central point for all referrals, staffing levels in children and family services, the appointment of a dedicated project manager to implement the Assessment Framework were not related to referrals being completed on time.

Case-related factors

Similarly, no association was found between case-related factors and referrals being completed on time. For example, there was no link between referrals completed on time and the reason for, or source of, the referral. It might be expected that referrals without parental knowledge might be delayed because, in cases where this would not place the child at increased risk of significant harm, social workers might request the referrer to consult the parent prior to accepting the referral. However, no association was found between parental awareness of the referral and referrals being completed on time.

Summary points

- Practically two-thirds of referrals were completed within the required timescale.
- Shire Counties and Metropolitan Districts completed a higher proportion of referrals on time than London Boroughs and Unitary Authorities.
- Councils which had established good collaborative arrangements between relevant agencies prior to implementation completed a higher proportion of referrals on time.

The characteristics of the referrals

Re-referrals

> A re-referral is defined as a referral about the same child/young person within a twelve-month period from when the child's case was last closed. (Department of Health, 2000a, p.2)

The referral form offers a single tick box to record that the referral is a re-referral. As a result, when the box is not ticked this may reflect either that the referral is the first referral or that the social worker failed to record this information. The revised Referral and Initial Information record issued to support the Integrated Children's System, resolves this problem. In 369 (16.4%) cases social workers had recorded that the referral was a re-referral.

THE ASSOCIATION BETWEEN RE-REFERRALS AND THE CHARACTERISTICS OF THE CHILD

Re-referrals were not associated with the age or gender of the child. However, re-referrals were associated with the ethnicity of the child. Black (27.9%) and mixed-race (26.1%) children were more likely to be re-referrals than Asian (14.3%) and white (16.1%) children.

THE ASSOCIATION BETWEEN RE-REFERRALS AND PROCESS ISSUES

Re-referrals were associated with the source of the referral. Referrals from the school or non-professionals were more likely to be re-referrals than referrals from any other sources ($\chi^2(5) = 17.341$. $p<.004$).

Summary points

- 16.4 per cent of referrals were re-referrals.
- Black and mixed-race children were more likely than other ethnic groups to be re-referrals.
- Schools and non-professionals were more likely to re-refer cases than other sources of referral.

Parental awareness of the referral

(Information available on 1405 referrals)

There are few opportunities for the parent or carer to be involved at the referral stage. A good starting point for future work with the family is to inform the parent or carer that a referral will be made unless to do so would place the child at risk of significant harm.

> While professionals should seek, in general, to discuss any concerns with the family and, where possible, seek their agreement to making referrals to social services, *this should only be done where such discussion and agreement-seeking will not place a child at increased risk of significant harm.* (Department of Health *et al.*, 1999, p.40, 5.6)

In practically two-thirds of cases (64.1%) the parent was aware of the referral.

The association between parental awareness of the referral and the type of council

Councils differed considerably in the levels of parental consultation prior to referral. They range from those where less than a half (46%) of parents were aware that a referral has been made, to those where 80 per cent of parents were aware of the referral.

Categorising the councils into the four types shows that professionals in Shire Counties and Unitary Authorities were more likely to seek parental agreement prior to referring to social services (71% of parents were aware of the referral in both types of council) than those in London Boroughs and Metropolitan Districts (63% and 56% respectively).

The association between parental awareness of the referral and the reason for referral

In cases where it could be argued that agreement-seeking could place the child at risk of increased significant harm, parents were less likely to be aware of the referral than in other cases. For example, (see Table 6.2, Appendix II) parents were aware of the referral in less than half the cases where the main reason for the referral was child protection concerns (49.6%), or parental alcohol/drug misuse (41.7%). In contrast, over three-quarters of parents were aware of the referral in cases involving a disabled child (95.5%), a child beyond parental control (85.4%), financial (82.1%), or housing problems (76.7%).

A focus on referrals solely from professionals (that is, separating them from referrals from non-professionals) shows some similarities (see Table 6.3, Appendix II). Parents were least likely to have been informed of the referral when it related to parental alcohol/drug use (42.1%) or domestic violence (48.4%) and most likely when it related to a disabled child or financial problems (>90% of cases). The findings suggest that professionals' willingness to seek parental agreement prior to making a referral is inversely related to the degree of perceived parental culpability in the reason for referral.

The association between parental awareness of the referral and the source of the referral

Practically three-quarters (73.8%) of referrals made by non-professionals (parents, children/young people, relatives, friends and neighbours) were done with parental knowledge. Of interest are the differences found between professionals making referrals. Over three-quarters of referrals made by health were done with parental knowledge. This contrasts with the pattern found for education, the police and 'other sources' where approximately half or less than half of the referrals they made to social services were with parental knowledge (see Table 6.4, Appendix II). However, the differences between the professional groups disappears when the reason for the referral is held constant except for those related to child protection concerns.

In child protection referrals health and the police generally informed the parents before referring them (parents were aware of the referral in respectively, 71.2% and 68.2% of cases). Parents were aware of referrals in approximately half the cases when referrals came from other social services departments (48.7%) or from non-professionals (49.3%). In contrast schools or 'other' sources rarely informed parents before making the referral to social services (parents were aware of the referral in respectively, 33.3 and 20.3% of cases).

The low level of agreement-seeking by schools reflects the finding that practically half (44.8%) of their referrals related to child protection concerns. Local education authorities have a duty to ensure that schools safeguard and promote the welfare of children (Education Act 2002, Part II, 175:1). However, there is no expectation that school staff will inform parents of their concerns about possible child abuse prior to making a referral to social services (Department of Education and Science circular 4/88; Hallett, 1995). In addition, secondary schools have little day-to-day contact with parents, and informing them of their concerns prior to referring the case to social services may have resource implications and result in delay, because a specific meeting would have to be convened (Farmer and Owen, 1995). Finally, some teachers in primary schools are reluctant to jeopardise their relationship with parents by raising the issue of possible child abuse.

The association between parental awareness of the referral and factors related to communication

Professionals may be more reluctant to seek parental agreement to make a referral to social services when communication is more difficult. For example, research suggests that welfare professionals, such as health, education and social services, are more at ease in communicating with mothers than with fathers. Similar difficulties in language or culture may create a barrier to communication. A scrutiny of the data, however, showed no significant association between parental awareness of a referral being made to social services and the gender of the main carer, the ethnicity of the child, or whether an interpreter was required.

Summary points

- Practically two-thirds of parents were aware of the referral.
- Shire Counties and Unitary Authorities were more likely to alert parents to the referral than London Boroughs and Metropolitan Districts.
- The reason for the referral was related to parents' awareness that it had been made.
- Health professionals were more likely to inform parents before making a referral to social services than other professionals.

Profile of the referrals

Age of child

(Information available on 2162 referrals)

Children under the age of 5 years accounted for a larger proportion of referrals than older age groups. Approximately a third of all referrals involved a child younger than 5 years, half were equally distributed between children aged 5 to 9 years and young people aged 10 and 14 years. Young people 15 years and older accounted for 14 per cent of all referrals (see Table 6.5, Appendix II).

Gender of the child

(Information available on 2023 referrals)

Similar proportions of girls (48.3%) and boys (51.7%) were referred to social services. No significant relationship was found between the age group and gender of the child.

Ethnicity of the child

(Information available on1530 referrals)

Although the census categories were used to collect this data, numbers in many categories were very small. Consequently, for analysis purposes the 16 categories have been collapsed into five: black, Asian, white, mixed race, and other (see Table 6.6, Appendix II).

White children account for 80.2 per cent of referrals. There were similar proportions of black (7.2%) and Asian (6.4%) children referred to social services. The proportion of children from black or other ethnic minority communities varied greatly between the participating councils and reflected the populations they served. For example, in the four London Boroughs where between a third and 45 per cent of the population they served is from a black or other minority ethnic community, children from black or other minority ethnic groups accounted for between 40 per cent and 74 per cent of referrals (averaged at 60%). In contrast children from black or other minority ethnic groups averaged 11 per cent for the 13 councils where 5 per cent or less of the population is from black or other minority ethnic communities.

The child's ethnicity was not found to be associated with either age or gender.

Child's main carer

(Information available on 1634 referrals)

In the majority of cases (83.7%) the mother was the main carer. The father had been recorded as the main carer in 13 per cent of cases and in a further 54 cases (3.3%) the main carer was someone other than the mother or father, in most cases a relative.

Source of the referral

(Information available on 2162 referrals)

Table 6.7, Appendix II shows non-professionals, such as parents, children, relatives, friends and neighbours, were responsible for the largest proportion of referrals (29.5%). Parents accounted for more than two-thirds (68.7%) of the non-professional group. Children and young people made up 9.9 per cent of the group, and the remaining 21.3 per cent were relatives, friends and neighbours.

Health and the police were the most frequent sources of professional referrals. They accounted for 17.8 per cent and 17.2 per cent respectively. Social services departments referred a further 13.2 per cent of cases. Education (10.5%) and other sources (11.8%) accounted for the remaining referrals.

THE ASSOCIATION BETWEEN THE SOURCES OF THE REFERRAL AND THE CHILD'S AGE GROUP

(Information available on 2088 referrals)

The source of the referral was associated with the age of the child (see Table 6.8, Appendix II).

Non-professionals were the most frequent source of referrals for all age groups except children under 5 years, when health professionals were the main source. When agencies were responsible for referrals the involvement of the major professionals groups (health, police, school and other social services) varied with the age of the child.

- Health accounted for 29.2 per cent of referrals of children under 5 years.
- Referrals for children aged 5 to 9 years came equally from all the major professional groups.
- The police (21%) and schools (14.6%) were key sources of referrals for young people 10 to 14 years.

- The police (17.4%) and health (13.5%) were major sources of referrals for young people 15 years or more.

The findings reflect the particular age groups of children that professionals have most contact with. For example, the work of health visitors brings them into regular contact with children under the age of 5 years, and again with teenage mothers. Schools have daily contact with children between the age of 5 years and 16 years. Finally, the police are most likely to be involved with children because of anti-social behaviour, bringing them frequently into contact with children over the age of 10 years.

THE ASSOCIATION BETWEEN THE SOURCE OF THE REFERRAL AND THE ETHNICITY OF THE CHILD

(Information available on 1458 referrals)

Interesting differences were identified when the source of the referral and the child's ethnicity were explored (see Table 6.9, Appendix II). Previous research offers explanations to help understand some of these differences.

Although non-professionals were shown to be the main source of referrals involving white (accounting for 32.8% of referrals) or black (accounting for 29.9% of referrals) children they were not the main source of referrals for Asian children. Social services referred a higher proportion of Asian children than any other ethnic group. Research has found that families from South Asian communities are frequently unaware of what social work services were available (Qureshi *et al.*, 2000).

Health was the main source of referrals for Asian (26.6%) and mixed-race (29.4%) children. A study of the health of Britain's ethnic minority groups offers some insight into this anomaly. Black and minority ethnic people experience poorer health than the white community, with Pakistani and Bangladeshi people reporting the poorest health (Nazroo, 1997).

Education referred a larger proportion of black children than any other ethnic group. This bias towards black children reflects the considerable evidence that suggests black children are perceived more negatively by teachers than other children (Kundnani, 1989, quoted in Department of Health, 2000b, p.42).

Reasons for the referrals

(Information available on 2190 referrals)

The Assessment Framework is relevant for all agencies involved in assessments that concern the welfare of children. The Guidance implies that an awareness of the Assessment Framework should assist the process of referral. Indeed, some councils involved in the research developed inter-agency referral forms that allowed the referring agency to record the information within the domains and dimensions of the Assessment Framework. However, in most cases the reason for the referral noted on the social services' referral form focused on a single issue or incident. These frequently related to the third domain of the Assessment Framework, 'Family and Environmental Factors'. For example, the referral might show that the police reported an incidence of domestic violence, a health visitor reported concern about a mother's alcohol or drug use, or a parent sought help with housing or financial problems. In other cases the report gave information about the child's developmental needs. For example, a health visitor had reported a young mother as having difficulty in relating to her new baby, or a school reported an unexplained bruise on a child.

However, the information about the reason for referral available on the referral form was frequently scant and did not allow cases to be categorised using the domains and dimensions of the Assessment Framework. Consequently, the reason for referral has been classified in the more traditional way, that is, in terms of the concerns raised by the referrer.

THE LARGEST PROPORTION OF REFERRALS WAS RELATED TO CHILD PROTECTION CONCERNS (SEE TABLE 6.10, APPENDIX II).

This predominance of child protection referrals reflects findings from other studies (see, for example, Thoburn *et al.*, 2000).

- Child protection concerns accounted for practically a third (30.3%) of all referrals.
- Other parenting issues accounted for a further 15.4 per cent of referrals.
- Approximately 10 per cent of referrals were because a child/young person was beyond parental control (10.9%) and a further 10 per cent because of concerns about domestic violence (9.8%).
- Approximately a fifth (22.5%) of referrals related to issues such as parental mental illness, parental alcohol and drug misuse, disabled children, asylum seekers (see Table 6.10, Appendix II for details).
- Referrals classified as 'other' (11.2%) referred to a rag-bag of reasons that ranged from requests that a child be accommodated,

to neighbours reporting that a 10-year-old child had been left alone in the house.

THE ASSOCIATION BETWEEN THE REASON FOR REFERRAL AND THE TYPE OF COUNCIL WITH SOCIAL SERVICES RESPONSIBILITY

The findings are based on 22 of the 23 councils because two councils had to be discounted (see Appendix I for details). Child protection referrals made up 30.3 per cent of referrals from all the 22 councils. However, the findings indicate considerable variation in the patterns of referrals between the 22 councils.

- Thirteen councils clustered around the mean (that is, the proportion of referrals that were for child protection concerns amounted to some 10 per cent more or less than the average of 30.3%).
- In five councils child protection referrals accounted for a higher proportion of referrals, including one council where 63 per cent of referrals were for child protection concerns.
- In four councils child protection referrals accounted for a small proportion of the referrals: in two councils 18.8 per cent and in a further two councils 10.3 per cent.

These wide discrepancies may reflect the threshold for services or eligibility criteria developed by Councils with Social Services Responsibilities. When eligibility criteria are used as a way of gate-keeping services, referring agencies may present their concerns about a child and family in terms of child protection (Department of Health, 1995a).

A scrutiny of the 'outlying' councils (those that do not cluster around the mean) provides evidence to support this notion. Councils with low levels of child protection referrals had high levels of referrals for reasons that in other councils may have been classified as child protection concerns. For example, the council where child protection concerns accounted for 63 per cent of referrals had a very low level of referrals for domestic violence (2%) and other parenting issues (5%). The reverse situation was found for councils with low levels of child protection referrals. In the two councils where child protection referrals accounted for 10.3 per cent of referrals, those for domestic violence (27.3% in the first council and 15.4% in the second) and other parenting issues (20.8% in the first council and 26.5% in the second) accounted for a high proportion of referrals.

THE ASSOCIATION BETWEEN THE REASON FOR REFERRAL AND THE AGE GROUP OF THE CHILD

The proportion of referrals for child protection concerns decreased as the age group of the child increased. Children under 5 years accounted for approximately a third of child protection referrals (34.1%), children aged 5 to 9 years and 10 to 14 years accounted for a further 27.7 per cent and 28 per cent respectively, and young people 15 years and over, accounted for 10.2 per cent. This pattern was also found in referrals relating to domestic violence, parental alcohol/drug use, parental mental illness, and other parenting issues (see Table 6.11, Appendix II).

Referrals for other reasons showed a rather different pattern. For example, referrals relating to a disabled child were fairly evenly distributed across the age bands, except for young people aged 15 years and over, who accounted for only 11.1 per cent of these referrals. Older children dominated referrals relating to a child or young person being beyond parental control. Indeed, children aged 10 years and over accounted for 77.4 per cent of such referrals. The youngest and oldest age group dominated referrals for financial or housing problems. This suggests that professionals were particularly aware of the impact of poverty and poor housing on the development of children under 5 years, and on the health and circumstances of young people living independently.

THE ASSOCIATION BETWEEN THE REASON FOR REFERRAL AND THE GENDER OF THE CHILD

(Information available on 1947 referrals)

The reason for the referral was linked to the gender of the child or young person (see Table 6.12, Appendix II). Some findings reflect research evidence of how particular issues impact differentially on boys and girls; others are less easy to understand.

- A larger proportion of girls than boys was referred for parental mental illness (58.3%). Research on depressed mothers found girls more likely to show symptoms of depression than boys (Goodyer *et al.*, 1993).
- A larger proportion of boys than girls was referred because the young person was beyond parental control (61.4%), or because the child was disabled (66.3%). Boys are more prevalent than girls in the population of disabled children (Bee, 2000) and those who display conduct problems (Farrington, 1987).

- Similar proportions of girls and boys were referred because of child protection concerns, domestic violence, and 'other' reasons.

Less easy to understand are the following findings.

- A larger proportion of girls than boys were referred for parental alcohol or drug misuse (59.3%). Research, however, suggests the reverse should be true; boys fare much worse than girls in households where one or more parent has such problems (Rydelius, 1983).
- Girls were more likely than boys to feature in referrals relating to financial problems (59.4%) and boys were more likely than girls to be the focus of referrals relating to housing problems (59.1%).

THE ASSOCIATION BETWEEN THE REASON FOR REFERRAL AND THE ETHNICITY OF THE CHILD

There was no association between the ethnicity of the child and the reason for referral.

THE ASSOCIATION BETWEEN THE REASON FOR REFERRAL AND THE SOURCE OF THE REFERRAL

A scrutiny of the reason for referral and its source shows expected links between particular professional groups and the types of referral. Professionals tended to refer issues with which their work brought them in contact. For example, police generally referred cases relating to domestic violence and child protection. Health professionals referred cases related to parental alcohol or drug use, parental mental illness, and disabled children. Education professionals referred child protection cases. Similarly, non-professionals sought the help of social services for issues that were important to them, such as seeking help over a child beyond their control, financial or housing problems, and help with a disabled child. Child protection referrals were fairly equally distributed across the various sources of referral (see Table 6.13, Appendix II).

Referrals from the police

It is good practice for the police to notify the social services department when they have responded to an incident of domestic violence and it is known that a child is a member of the household. If the police have specific concerns about the safety or welfare of a child, they should make a referral to the social services department citing the basis for their concerns. (Department of Health *et al.*, 1999, p.73, 6.39)

Over half (57.2%) of domestic violence referrals came from the police.

Referrals from health

Health is the primary source of referrals involving parental alcohol/drug misuse (39%) and those related to parental mental illness (47.2%). Health is the source of practically a third (32.2%) of all referrals involving a disabled child.

Referrals from non-professional sources (of which the parents accounted for 69%)

Non-professionals were the main source of referrals involving disabled children (43.3%), children beyond parental control (55.1%), other parenting issues (30.4%), financial (71.3%) and housing (52%) problems.

Further action arising from the referral

(Information available on 2034 referrals)

The section on the Referral and Initial Information record that indicates the further action provides options for the social worker to tick, and space for other actions to be described.

In practically half (46.2%) of all referrals social workers had recorded that the case would progress to an initial assessment. There was considerable variation between the 24 participating councils. At one extreme an initial assessment was the recorded action in 11.9 per cent of cases in one Shire County and 12.7 per cent in one London Borough. At the other extreme, it was the recorded action in 83.6 per cent of referrals in one Shire County and 95.5 per cent of referrals in one Metropolitan District.

A high rate of child protection referrals did not always translate into a high rate of initial assessments being the action recorded on the referral form. For example, of the five councils with high rates of child protection referrals, only three had high (10% above the mean) rates of initial assessment being the recorded action. This finding gives some support to the notion that strict gate-keeping may result in professionals from other agencies referring cases inappropriately in terms of child protection concerns.

- In 16.8 per cent of cases the recorded action was information being provided to the family.

- In 6.8 per cent of cases the recorded action was a referral to another agency.
- In 15.5 per cent of cases the recorded action was some other action.
- In nearly a quarter of cases (23.8%) the only recorded action was no further action.

(See Table 6.14, Appendix II)

The figures do not add up to 100 per cent because in some cases social workers had recorded more than one further action. For example, in some cases an initial assessment was recommended and a referral to another agency.

THE RELATIONSHIP BETWEEN THE FURTHER ACTION RECORDED ON THE REFERRAL AND THE AGE GROUP OF THE CHILD

Similar proportions of referrals for children aged less than 5 years, 5 to 9 years, and 10 to 14 years resulted in an initial assessment or the provision of information being the recorded action. In approximately half the cases the recorded action was an initial assessment, and between 13 and 18 per cent of referrals for these age groups, the recorded action was the provision of information.

Young people aged 15 years and over were dealt with in a different way from younger children. The recorded action for referrals involving this age group was less likely (36.6%) to be an initial assessment, and more likely (26.3%) to be the provision of information (see Tables 6.15 and 6.16, Appendix II).

There was no significant association between the age group of the children and the recorded outcome being a referral to another agency, other action, or no further action.

THE RELATIONSHIP BETWEEN THE FURTHER ACTION RECORDED ON THE REFERRAL AND THE GENDER OF THE CHILD

No association was found between the gender of the child and the recorded further action.

THE RELATIONSHIP BETWEEN THE FURTHER ACTION RECORDED ON THE REFERRAL AND THE ETHNICITY OF THE CHILD

Table 6.17 (Appendix II) shows a significant association between the recorded action being an initial assessment and the ethnicity of the child.

White or mixed-race children are significantly more likely to have an initial assessment as the recorded action than black or Asian children. Other recorded outcomes were not significantly associated with the ethnicity of the child. Chapter 7 will show that these discrepancies disappear when the data on cases that actually progress to an initial assessment are examined.

THE RELATIONSHIP BETWEEN THE FURTHER ACTION RECORDED ON THE REFERRAL AND THE REASON FOR THE REFERRAL

Recorded action was an initial assessment

Practically half (46.4%) of the referrals resulted in an initial assessment being the recorded action. The reason for referral was significantly associated with the recorded action being an initial assessment (see Table 6.18, Appendix II). In 55.8 per cent of child protection referrals the action recorded was an initial assessment.

Previous research suggests that there is little agreement between social work practitioners as to how 'a child in need' should be defined (Colton *et al.*, 1995). The current findings show that some types of referral were more likely to lead to an initial assessment being the recorded action. For example, in practically three-quarters (73.7%) of referrals for parental alcohol or drug use the recorded action was an initial assessment. An initial assessment was also frequently recorded as the action when referrals involved a disabled child; occurring in 56.8 per cent of cases.

In other cases an initial assessment was rarely the recorded action. For example, referrals related to financial problems (18.3%), other issues (30.8%), housing problems (33.3%), and domestic violence (36.6%) were less likely to have an initial assessment recorded as the recommended further action. This reinforces the findings from both research and inspections which found social services departments tend to focus on children at risk of significant harm rather than on family support (Aldgate and Tunstill, 1995; Colton *et al.*, 1995; Social Services Inspectorate, 1996). Indeed, Aldgate and Tunstill (1995) showed that few authorities defined children as 'in need' because they were living in substandard housing, or in low-income families.

Recorded action was a referral to another agency

In 6.8 per cent of cases (n=139) the recorded action was a referral to another agency. In 24 of these an initial assessment had also been the recorded action. The reason for referral was related to the recorded action being referral to another agency (omitting those that also had an initial assessment as a recorded action, see Table 6.19, Appendix II).

Referrals related to parental alcohol/drug use (no cases); child protection cases (2.2%) and domestic violence (4%) were least likely to have as the recorded action referral to another agency.

Cases most likely to have referral to another agency as the recorded action were those where the referral involved a disabled child (13.6%) or a child or young person beyond parental control (12.5%).

Recorded action was the provision of information

In 17 per cent of cases (n=340) the recorded action was the provision of information to the young person or family. In 17 of these cases an initial assessment was also a recorded action, and in a further 41 cases the recorded further action included referral to another agency. Thus, in 14.1 per cent of cases (n=282) the sole recorded action was the provision of information.

There was a significant relationship between the reason for referral and the sole recorded action being the provision of information (see Table 6.20, Appendix II). For example, cases least likely to have the provision of information as the sole recorded action were referrals involving a disabled child (6.8%), child protection referrals (6.9%), and parental mental illness (7.3%). Cases most likely to have the provision of information as the sole recorded action include referrals relating to housing issues (32.2%), financial problems (27.9%) and domestic violence (22.8%).

Recorded action was some other further action

In 279 cases social workers had not ticked any of the further action boxes but recorded free text under the further action box. This could include actions such as a child protection conference or accommodation for the child. Referrals relating to financial problems (26.9%), other issues (21.3%), and child protection concerns (17.2%) accounted for the largest proportion of cases where this was the only recorded action (see Table 6.21, Appendix II).

Recorded action was no further action

Practically a quarter (23.6%) of cases resulted in no further action being the sole recorded outcome. This is a much greater proportion than the 9 per cent found by Thoburn *et al.* (2000) in their study of neglect. However, Thoburn and colleagues suggest that their figure may be an underestimation because parents reported that visits to the 'reception' or 'customer service' teams often went unrecorded.

The findings show a significant relationship between the reason for referral and no further action being recorded on the referral form (see Table 6.22, Appendix II). Referrals most likely to result in no further action being the only action recorded were those for financial difficulties (36.5%) and domestic violence (30.8%). Referrals least likely to result in no further action being recorded were referrals relating to a disabled child (10.2%), and those for parental alcohol or drug use (10.5%).

Links between the type of referral and the recorded action

This exploration of the association between the reason for referral and the action recorded on the referral form has shown a number of interesting patterns.

An initial assessment was the recorded action in the majority of referrals for parental alcohol and drug use, and those involving a disabled child. The recorded action for referrals for child protection, parental mental illness, and child/young person beyond parental control, was varied. For example, in approximately half the child protection referrals an initial assessment was recorded, a further fifth had no further action recorded and the remaining proportion was distributed between the other options. Referrals relating to financial problems, housing, and domestic violence were most likely to result in social workers recording the action as the provision of information or no further action.

This low level of intervention for referrals related to poverty or domestic violence suggests that messages from research have not fully influenced practice. For example, there is a considerable body of research on domestic violence that shows its negative impact on children's health and development (see, for example, Brandon and Lewis, 1996; Cleaver *et al.*, 1999; Jaffe *et al.*, 1990; Morley and Mullender, 1994). Similarly, much has been written on the impact of poverty and poor housing on children's health and development (see, for example, Gregg *et al.*, 1999; Hague and Malos, 1994; Jack, 2001; Malos and Hague, 1997).

RELATIONSHIP BETWEEN THE SOURCE OF THE REFERRAL AND RECORDED ACTION

Holding the reason for the referral constant shows no association between the source of the referral and the recorded action.

Summary points

- Younger children accounted for proportionately more referrals than older children.
- An equal proportion of boys and girls were referred to social services.
- In the majority of cases the mother was the main carer.
- Non-professionals, parents, young people, relatives, friends and neighbours, were responsible for the largest proportion of referrals.
- The source of the referral was associated with the age and ethnicity of the child. Professionals generally referred the type of children with which they had most contact.
- The source of the referral was linked to the ethnicity of the child.
- Child protection concerns accounted for practically a third of all referrals.
- The reason for referral was related to the age group of the children.
- The associations between the reason for referral and the gender of the child generally reflect the higher levels of need within the general population identified by previous research.
- The association between the reason for the referral and the source of the referral reflects the focus of the professional groups.
- The recorded action in practically half (46.2%) the referrals was an initial assessment, in 16.8 per cent to provide information to the family, in 6.9 per cent a referral to another agency, and in nearly a quarter (23.9%) no further action.

Chapter summary

Twenty-four Councils with Social Services Responsibilities participated in the audit. Referrals were identified sequentially from a given date. The audit consisted of 2248 referrals.

The expectation had been that councils participating in the research would use the Department of Health's referral and assessment records, adding sections to collect additional information necessary for local systems. However, nine social services departments continued to use locally designed referral forms that were not consistent with the Referral and Initial Information record. Although this affected how and what information was recorded, they were sufficiently similar to allow the data to be included in the audit.

At the point of referral, recording for both administrative and case related information was generally of a high standard. However, social workers did not routinely record information about the child's religion (noted in only 29% of cases). Unpublished research suggests that religion is not routinely recorded for black children (Department of Health, 2000b). The findings from the present study suggest that in today's multicultural society greater attention needs to be paid to recording the religious persuasion of every child. The other issue not routinely recorded (noted in only a quarter of cases) was the identity of relatives not living in the child's household. Although this may not be significant in every case, it can be key to ensuring the safety of children in cases of sexual abuse that involve wider family and friends (Cleaver and Freeman, 1996).

Approximately two-thirds of referrals were completed on time. The ability to complete referrals on time was associated with the type of council, and the collaborative arrangements with other agencies that were in place prior to implementation. Shire Counties and Metropolitan Boroughs were more likely than London Boroughs and Unitary Authorities to complete referrals on time.

Re-referrals accounted for 16.4 per cent of all referrals. Black and mixed-race children were over-represented in the re-referral group. It will be seen in Chapter 8 that proportionately, cases involving black and mixed-race children were less likely to progress to a core assessment than any other ethnic group. This suggests greater attention may need to be paid to assessing children from these communities to ensure that interventions fully address their needs.

Referrals from the school and non-professionals were more likely to be re-referrals than referrals from other sources. Chapters 7 and 8 will show that proportionately fewer cases referred by non-professionals progressed to either an initial or a core assessment than cases that emanated from other sources (this did not hold true for referrals from the school). More attention may need to be paid to referrals coming from non-professionals to ensure that parents, children, relatives and neighbours do not have to make numerous referrals before they are acted on.

The referral sample included equal proportions of boys and girls. This balance between the genders continued through initial assessment and core assessment. Children under 5 years accounted for the largest proportion of referrals (approximately a third). Approximately a quarter of referrals related to children 5 to 9 years and a similar proportion to young people 10 to 14 years. Young people aged 15 years and over, accounted for the fewest (14%) referrals.

Non-professionals – that is, young people, parents, relatives, friends and neighbours – were the main source of referrals and accounted for 29.5 per cent of all referrals. Health and the police were the most frequent source of professional referrals, followed by other social services departments and education.

The source of the referral was associated with the type of case and generally reflected the groups of children with which they had most contact. For example, non-professionals accounted for the largest proportion of referrals for practically every age group of children, and those from both the black and white communities. Children under 5 years were more likely to be referred by health. Referrals from health related predominantly to infants and young people aged 15 years and over. Health was also responsible for referring the largest proportion of children from Asian communities and children of mixed race. This may reflect the poor health experienced by Pakistani and Bangladeshi communities (Nazroo, 1997) and the ignorance of what social work services have to offer within Asian communities (Qureshi *et al.*, 2000). Referrals from education tended to involve young people aged 10 to 14 years and black pupils, reinforcing earlier evidence that black boys of this age group experience greater difficulties in school than their peers (Kundnani, 1998).

Child protection concerns accounted for practically a third (30.3%) of all referrals. The remaining referrals were distributed in the following way. Other parenting issues made up 15.4 per cent, 20 per cent were evenly distributed between child/young person beyond parental control and domestic violence, and a further 22.5 per cent were made up of issues such as parental mental illness, parental drug and alcohol use, and disabled children. The remaining referrals, classified as 'other', were a medley of reasons that did not fit the specified categories.

The profile of referrals varied considerably between the participating councils. When the proportion of child protection referrals was low this was balanced by high rates of referrals for domestic violence and other parenting issues. This suggests that the thresholds for accepting referrals operated by different councils are mirrored in the ways professionals make their referrals.

The reason for the referral was associated with the age and gender of the child. The relationship with the child's age followed an expected pattern. For example, the proportion of child protection referrals decreased as the age group of the children increased, disabled children fell equally between most age bands, and issues around parental control generally featured older children. The older and the youngest age groups dominated referrals for financial and housing problems, those arguably most at risk from the effects of poverty and poor housing. The association between the reason for referral and the gender of the child reflected the gender most vulnerable to the issue. For example, boys are over-represented in the population of disabled children and accounted for a larger proportion of referrals relating to a disabled child.

The further action recorded on the referral form suggests that in practically half (46.2%) the cases the decision was to progress to an initial assessment. In 16.8 per cent of cases information was provided to the families, and in a further 6.9 per cent of cases the decision was to refer the family to another agency, and in 15.4 per cent of cases the social worker had recorded some other action. For practically a quarter of referrals (23.9%) no further action had been the recorded outcome.

Case factors were associated with the action recorded by social workers at the end of the referral. When the recorded action was an initial assessment a positive association was related to cases involving white or mixed-race children, and referrals for parental alcohol/drug use and disabled children. Black and Asian children, young people over the age of 15 years, and referrals for financial or housing problems or domestic violence were negatively associated with the decision to undertake an initial assessment. When the recorded decision was no further action, this was positively associated with referrals for financial difficulties, domestic violence, and negatively associated with referrals involving a disabled child and those for parental alcohol/drug use.

Chapter 7

Initial Assessments

Findings from the Audit

The sample (n=866)

> An initial assessment is defined as a brief assessment of each child referred to social services with a request for services to be provided.
>
> (Department of Health *et al.*, 2000a, p.31, 3.9)

Of the 2248 referrals audited 866 (38.5%) progressed to an initial assessment.

Inconsistencies between the action recorded on the referral form and the documentation found on the case-file

A scrutiny of the case-file showed considerable inconsistency between the outcome recorded on the referral form and the documentation found on file. For example, although social workers had recorded an initial assessment as the recommended action in 939 cases, for only three-quarters of these referrals (n=707) was an initial assessment found on the file. Furthermore, in 159 cases an initial assessment was found on the case-file when this had *not* been the recorded action on the referral form.

CASES THAT SHOULD HAVE PROGRESSED TO AN INITIAL ASSESSMENT (N=707)

The level of consistency for different types of referral ranged between 70.0 per cent and 86.7 per cent (see Table 7.1, Appendix II). Referrals for parental mental illness (86.7%), child beyond parental control (82.7%), and financial problems (84.2%) showed higher rates of consistency between the recorded action and the case proceeding to an initial assessment than other types of referral.

Three-quarters of referrals for child protection showed a consistency between the recorded action and the case proceeding to an initial assessment (reflecting the mean for all types of referral). The greatest degree of inconsistency was found for referrals for disabled children and housing problems: in only 70 per cent of cases did the recorded action synchronise with an initial assessment being found on the file.

A comparison of the sources of the referral showed most cluster around the mean rate in relation to cases progressing to an initial assessment (see Table 7.2, Appendix II). However, referrals from health (79.6%) were most likely to proceed to an initial assessment when this had been recorded as the action on the referral. In contrast, those from the police (65.5%) were least likely to proceed.

CASES THAT UNEXPECTEDLY PROGRESSED TO AN INITIAL ASSESSMENT (N=159)

In 159 cases an initial assessment was found on the case-file when this had not been the recorded action at the time of referral. In 45.9 per cent of these cases (n=73) the social worker had not recorded any information under the further-action section of the referral form. When information had been recorded (n=86), this showed a range of different recommended actions. In 52 cases the social worker had noted information in the 'other' section of the record, of which 16 specified child protection enquiries. For the remaining cases where an initial assessment was unexpectedly found on the case-file, the recorded action in 13 cases had been the provision of information, in 9 referral to another agency, and in 12 no further action.

The source of referral was linked to cases that unexpectedly proceeded to an initial assessment. Ten per cent of referrals from health were reassigned to an initial assessment compared with only 5 per cent of referrals from the police or the non-professionals, that is, parents, children/young people, relatives, friends and neighbours.

Possible reasons for the mismatch

There are a number of reasons that could explain the inconsistencies between the action recorded on the referral form and the documentation found on the case-file.

POOR RECORDING PRACTICE

The finding that social workers had failed to record the further action on the referral form in 45.9 per cent of cases suggests that practice issues account for a considerable proportion of the inconsistencies. In addition, inconsistencies may be due to managers not making the decision about what action to take at the time of referral. Checking whether the managers' signatures were found on the referral form would evidence this. Unfortunately, this was not possible because the computer format that some social services departments used for their referrals did not always indicate whether managers had signed them and paper copies were not consistently held of the case-file.

THE SOURCE OF THE REFERRAL

The source of referral is related to the degree of consistency between the action recorded on the referral form, and an Initial Assessment record being found on the case-file. When referrals came from health professionals, there was greater consistency than referrals from the police. This suggests professionals, such as health visitors, who have an ongoing relationship with the family are more likely to take responsibility for following up referrals than those who do not (such as the police).

For example, a police constable's responsibility for the case ends once the required form had been completed and processed. Indeed, in one social services department staff reported that referrals from the police involving incidents of domestic violence came to them in 'batches', suggesting this is procedurally led rather than focusing on the needs of individual children. No distinction appears to have been made between police contacts following a response to an incidence of domestic violence where there are specific concerns about the safety or welfare of a child (that should form a referral), and those that were simply notifications to social services (Department of Health *et al.*, 1999 p.73, 6.39).

ORGANISATIONAL DIFFICULTIES

The inconsistencies may also be related to the way different Councils with Social Services Responsibilities organise their work. For example, when the team responsible for referrals is not responsible for the initial assessments, the assessment team may reassess the decisions taken by the team taking the referral. There was considerable variation in the rate of inconsistency between the social services departments. Amalgamating the inconsistencies (referrals that indicated an initial assessment but no initial assessment found on the case-file, and those where no initial assessment had been indicated but an initial assessment found on the file), shows an average rate of inconsistencies for all the research councils of 17.7 per cent. The rate of inconsistency ranged between 0.9 and 32.8 per cent. Six departments had inconsistency rates at least 10 per cent greater than the average. The rate of inconsistency was associated with the council's theoretical and technical knowledge (i.e. written guidance for practitioners on assessment, information for families, and an approach to assessment that was consistent with the Assessment Framework). Councils with poor theoretical and technical knowledge prior to implementation tended to have above-average rates of inconsistency in their recording practice. The converse was true for councils with good theoretical and technical knowledge.

RESOURCE ISSUES

Information gained during discussions with social services managers and practitioners suggests that when departments have limited resources, referrals may be prioritised and those not considered urgent left to linger in 'social work baskets' before being weeded out.

NEW INFORMATION COMING INTO THE DEPARTMENT RESULTS IN A CHANGE IN THE DECISION

Further information coming into the department may result in the decision made at the time of the referral being reviewed, but not recorded. However, irrespective of whether the inconsistencies were due to organisational or resource issues or because new information about the case was received, the reasons why the decision had been changed should be recorded on the referral form.

Summary points

- There was considerable inconsistency between the outcome recorded on the referral form and the documentation found on the file.
- Inconsistencies between recording on the referral form and the documentation found on the case-file may result from either organisational or practice issues.

The profile of referrals that did progress to an initial assessment (n=866)

This section explores whether particular types of referral are more likely to progress to an initial assessment than others.

Re-referrals

In 128 cases the initial assessment was carried out on a case that had been re-referred to social services. There was no association between the case being a re-referral and progression to an initial assessment. Approximately a third (34.7%) of re-referrals progressed to an initial assessment compared with 39.3 per cent of first-time referrals.

Age of the child

Very similar proportions of referrals relating to the following age groups progressed to an initial assessment:

- under 5 years, 39.7 per cent
- 5 to 9 years, 39.9 per cent
- 10 to 14 years, 41.6 per cent.

However, a significantly smaller proportion (28.2%) of referrals relating to young people aged 15 years and over progressed to an initial assessment ($\chi^2(3) = 16.579$. $p<.001$).

Gender and ethnicity of the child

There was no association between either the gender or the ethnicity of the child and whether the referral progressed to an initial assessment.

The reason for the referral

Over a third (38.8%) of all initial assessments were done on cases where the referral indicated child protection concerns. Referrals for child protection concerns accounted for a higher proportion of the initial assessments than any other reason for referral. Nonetheless, less than half (46.5%) of child protection referrals progressed to an initial assessment. This reflects the findings in Thoburn and colleagues' study of neglect (2000).

The reason for referral was significantly associated with the case progressing to an initial assessment. Referrals related to parental alcohol/drug misuse (57.4%), and parental mental illness (51.6%) were significantly more likely to progress to an initial assessment than other types of referral. In contrast referrals for financial (14.3%) or housing (29.5%) problems were less likely to progress to an initial assessment (see Table 7.3, Appendix II). The low rates of referrals for financial or housing problems progressing to an initial assessment reflect the findings from Aldgate and Tunstill's study (1995). Children living in families that experience problems related to poverty and poor housing are least likely to be categorised as children in need.

The source of the referral

Referrals from health (48.1%) and education (43.2%) were significantly more likely to result in an initial assessment than referrals from other sources. Less than a third of referrals from the police (31.2%) progressed to an initial assessment (see Table 7.4, Appendix II). This relationship, however, is rarely independent of the reason for the referral. For example, the source of the referral does not differentiate between child protection referrals that progressed to an initial assessment and those that did not.

The only type of referral where the source remained significant was referrals for domestic violence. Domestic violence referrals emanating from health (72.7%) or education (66.7%) were significantly more likely ($\chi^2(7) = 26.555$. $p<.000$) to progress to an initial assessment than those from the police (26.1%) or from non-professionals (18.8%). This may reflect the degree of flexibility social services can apply in responding to police notifications relating to incidents of domestic violence.

> Normally, one serious incident or several lesser incidents of domestic violence where there is a child in the household would indicate that the social services department should carry out an initial assessment of the child and family, including consulting existing records. (Department of Health *et al.*, 1999, p.72, 6.40)

Indeed, consultation meetings with line managers suggest that social services departments feel 'swamped' by police notifications relating to incidents of domestic violence where there are children living in the household. Consequently, some departments have developed a policy of not reacting to such notifications until three or more have been received concerning a particular family. This practice may be acceptable if, when the police have specific concerns about the safety or welfare of the child, they make a referral citing the basis for their concerns. However, if no distinction is made between police notifications and referrals, a policy of allowing referrals to accumulate before responding may place some children at risk of significant harm.

Summary points

Those referrals most likely to result in an initial assessment were:

- child under the age of 15 years
- reason for the referral was related to parental alcohol/drug misuse (57.4%) or parental mental illness (51.6%)
- domestic violence referrals made by health (48.1%) or education (43.2%).

Those referrals least likely to result in an initial assessment were:

- young person aged 15 years or older (28.2%)
- reason for the referral was related to financial (14.3%) or housing (29.5%) problems
- domestic violence referrals made by the police (26.1%) or the non-professionals (18.8%). The category 'non-professionals' includes parents, children/young people, relatives, friends and neighbours.

Cases undergoing an initial assessment (n=866)

Recording patterns for the Initial Assessment record

> The Initial Assessment record continues the process of systematic information gathering, commenced in the Referral and Initial Information record, and the analysis of this material. (Department of Health, 2000a, p.4)

When undertaking an initial assessment it is essential that social workers record relevant information on the three domains of children's developmental needs, parenting capacity and family and environmental factors, because it makes decisions about the action taken transparent and evidence-based.

The type of information recorded on the Initial Assessment record can be divided into case-related and administrative information.

CASE-RELATED INFORMATION (SEE TABLE 7.5, APPENDIX II)

Information about the case was consistently recorded. For example, the reason for the initial assessment was recorded in practically every case (96.3%).

Social workers recorded information on the individual dimensions of child's developmental needs in over 80 per cent of cases, about parenting capacity and issues that affect it, in over three-quarters of cases, and on family and environmental factors in over 80 per cent of cases. Social workers also routinely summarised the information they collected (found on 90.1% of the records) and recorded the further action that was to be taken in 86.8 per cent of cases.

ADMINISTRATIVE INFORMATION (SEE TABLE 7.5)

In general, information for administrative purposes had also been recorded. For example, the time taken to complete the assessment was noted in 80 per cent of cases, and the social worker and manager had signed the Initial Assessment record in over 82.0 per cent of cases. However, social workers did not routinely record whether a copy of the Initial Assessment record had been given to the family: this had been noted in only 60.2 per cent of cases.

Time taken to complete initial assessments

(Information available on 710 initial assessments)

The Assessment Framework states that an initial assessment:

> should be undertaken *within a maximum of 7 working days* but could be very brief depending on the child's circumstances.

Moreover, there is clear guidance over how to calculate the time taken.

> An initial assessment is deemed to have commenced at the point of referral to the social services department or when new information on an open case indicates an initial assessment should be repeated. (Department of Health *et al.*, 2000a, p.32, 3.9)

Two-thirds (66.4%) of initial assessments were undertaken within seven working days – rather higher than the rate of 60.8 per cent found for referrals completed on time.

Structure of the social services departments

The councils showed considerable variation in their ability to undertake initial assessments within the required time. The proportion completed on time ranged between 41.2 per cent and 91.7 per cent. For example, four councils completed over 80 per cent of their initial assessments within the required time; 11 councils completed between 60 and 80 per cent, and seven completed less than 60 per cent on time.

The rates of completion within the required time were linked to the type of council. It is interesting to note that the link between the type of council and the ability to complete initial assessments on time did not altogether mirror the findings for referrals done on time. London Boroughs and Unitary Authorities continued to show poorer rates while Shire Counties and Metropolitan Districts completed a larger proportion of referrals and initial assessments on time.

The collaborative arrangements in place prior to implementation

Table 7.1 Councils completing initial assessments and referrals on time

Type of Council	*Initial assessments completed on time*	*Referrals completed on time*
7 London Boroughs	58.5%	42.3%
3 Unitary Authorities	60.6%	46.5%
6 Shire Counties	72.1%	58.9%
6 Metropolitan Districts	76.5%	63.9%

Councils that reported having good collaborative arrangements between social services and other relevant agencies in place prior to implementation were more likely to complete initial assessments on time than councils that did not. Seventy-one per cent of councils with good collaborative arrangements in place completed over 60 per cent of initial assessments on time compared with 56 per cent of councils that had less well-established collaborative arrangements.

Case-related factors

The reason for carrying out the initial assessment was linked to whether it was completed on time. Table 7.6 (Appendix II) shows over two-thirds (67.3%) of initial assessments carried out because of child protection concerns were completed on time (mirroring the rate for all types of initial assessments). However, only half (50.9%) of initial assessments carried out because of domestic violence were done on time. In contrast, over 80 per cent of initial assessments related to housing problems (80.8%) or an unaccompanied asylum seeker (87.5%) were completed on time. The findings suggest that social workers may be trying to assess complex cases during an initial assessment and are unable therefore to complete them within the required time.

Summary points

- Social workers routinely recorded case-related information. Administrative information was less likely to be routinely recorded.
- Two-thirds of initial assessments were undertaken within seven working days.

The profile of initial assessment cases

Reason for the initial assessment

The major reasons for referrals is reflected by the major reasons for initial assessments (see Table 7.7, Appendix II). The following reasons accounted for the largest proportion of initial assessments:

- child protection concerns accounted for over a third of initial assessments
- parenting issues other than drug/alcohol misuse and mental illness for 14.9 per cent
- child/young person beyond parental control for 12.1 per cent.

Although the overall distribution is similar, the proportions of some types of case have increased while others have decreased. For example, the child protection concerns accounted for 30.3 per cent of referrals and 38.8 per cent of initial assessments (an increase of 8 percentage points). Minor increases were also found for concerns around parental mental illness (increased from 2.8% to 4.0%), parental alcohol/drug use (increased from 2.8% to 4.8%), and child/young person being beyond parental control (increased from 10.9% to 12.1%). In contrast, the proportion of other types of cases decreased. Domestic violence cases dropped from 9.8 to 7.1 per cent, financial problems from 5.4 to 2.0 per cent, and housing problems from 4.8 to 3.7 per cent.

The involvement of other agencies in the assessment process

> Agencies should be consulted and involved as appropriate as part of the initial assessment. (Department of Health, 2000a, p.5)

In practically three-quarters of cases (n=626, 72.3%) at least one other agency was involved in the initial assessment. In 42 per cent of cases social workers had involved two or more agencies in the assessment (see Chapter 5 for a detailed discussion of inter-agency involvement).

The children

Initial assessments included different proportions of children for the various age groups. For example, over a third (35.8%) of initial assessments were carried out on children less than 5 years of age. A further quarter were done on children aged 5 to 9 years, while 28.9 per cent were done on young people aged 10 to 14 years. In contrast only 10.2 per cent of initial assessments related to young people aged 15 years or more (see Table 7.8, Appendix II).

GENDER OF THE CHILD

Information was missing from 73 cases (only 19 of whom were unborn children). Initial assessments were just as likely to relate to girls (n=386, 48.7%) as to boys (n= 407, 51.3%).

ETHNICITY OF THE CHILD

The distribution of children from different ethnic groups involved in an initial assessment reflected that found at the time of referral. Some 80 per cent of initial assessments involved white children. Approximately 6 per cent involved black children, and 6 per cent children of Asian background, a further 5 per cent involved children of mixed race, and around 1 per cent involved children of other races (see Table 7.9, Appendix II).

The level of needs identified by the initial assessment

The Initial Assessment record provides individual sections for social workers to record information on the three domains of: children's developmental needs, parenting capacity, and family and environmental factors. Each section is subdivided to allow workers to detail information for each dimension within the domain. For example, with regard to the child's developmental needs social workers are able to record the identified strengths and areas of developmental need affecting the child's health, education, emotional and behavioural development and self-care skills, identity and social presentation, and family and social relations. Similar structures are in place with regard to the other two domains of parenting capacity, and family and environmental factors.

CHILDREN'S DEVELOPMENTAL NEEDS

Social workers did not systematically record information for each developmental dimension. For example, in one case there was an excellent description of the child's health but nothing recorded in the section for identity and social presentation, and no explanation of why this had not been completed. As a result of this inconsistency in recording, the number of cases where information was available varied between the individual dimensions (see Table 7.10, Appendix II).

The dimension for which social workers had identified the greatest level of developmental need for children was in relation to their family and social relationships. Developmental needs had been recorded in half the cases (49.7%). In approximately 40 per cent of cases developmental needs were recorded in relation to children's emotional and behavioural development, and in a third of cases (34.4%) in relation to children's educational (cognitive) development. The lowest level of developmental needs was recorded in relation to children's health, identity and social presentation. Developmental needs had been recorded in a quarter of cases in relation to these developmental dimensions (Table 7.10).

In a quarter of cases (24.8%) social workers identified developmental needs in three or more of the following five child development dimensions: health, education, emotional and behavioural development and self-care skills, identity and social presentation, and family and social relationships. These cases have been classified by the research team as having severe needs in relation to children's development.

PARENTING CAPACITY

Social workers identified lower levels of difficulties in relation to parenting capacity than to the child's developmental needs. The parenting dimension most frequently identified as causing concern was the capacity to ensure the child's safety and to provide stability. In a third of cases (33.8%) difficulties in ensuring safety had been recorded, and in 30.2 per cent of cases in relation to stability. In approximately a fifth of cases parenting difficulties in relation to emotional warmth (20.2%) and in providing guidance and boundaries (23%) were recorded. Basic care and stimulation were the parenting dimensions where least difficulties were noted. In 16.9 per cent cases social workers recorded parents as experiencing difficulty in meeting the child's needs for stimulation, and in 11.5 per cent of cases in meeting the child's needs for basic care (Table 7.11, Appendix II).

In a fifth (19.3%) of cases social workers identified difficulties in relation to parenting capacity in three or more of the following six parenting dimensions: basic care, ensuring safety, emotional warmth, stimulation, guidance and boundaries, and stability. These cases have been classified by the research team as having severe difficulties in relation to parenting capacity.

ISSUES AFFECTING PARENTS'/CARERS' CAPACITIES TO RESPOND APPROPRIATELY TO THE CHILD/YOUNG PERSON'S NEEDS

Research shows that certain issues are likely to have a detrimental impact on parents' capacity to respond appropriately to children's developmental needs. These include: physical and mental illness, learning disability, substance use, domestic violence, childhood abuse, a history of violence or child abuse, and having been in care during childhood. The initial assessment provides a designated section for social workers to record information about these issues, or to note that they don't apply to the particular family involved in the assessment. Unfortunately, in a quarter of cases (n=220) no information had been recorded.

The information available showed that in approximately three-quarters of cases (72.9%) social workers noted that families were experiencing difficulties with one or more of these issues. The issues families experienced the most difficulties related to parental mental illness (16.9% of cases), a history of violence/domestic violence (16.6% of cases), parental alcohol or drug problems (11.6% of cases) and physical illness (7.4% of cases). Any one of the other issues likely to affect parenting capacity impacted on less than 5 per cent of cases (Table 7.12, Appendix II).

FAMILY AND ENVIRONMENTAL FACTORS

Social workers recorded the highest level of needs in relation to the domain of family and environmental factors. Family history and functioning affected practically two-thirds (65.2%) of cases. Difficulties had been recorded for the dimension of social resources in 40.3 per cent of cases, in relation to housing in 30 per cent of cases, and in relation to employment and income in 27.6 per cent of cases (Table 7.13, Appendix II).

Social workers identified difficulties in relation to this domain in two or more of the four family and environmental dimensions, for more than a third (37%) of the children involved in initial assessments. These cases were classified by the research team as having severe difficulties in relation to family and environmental factors.

The salience of the domain of family and environmental factors should not be underestimated. The findings suggest severe difficulties in this domain impact on a larger proportion of children in need (37%) than either the domain of children's needs (24.8%) or parenting capacity (19.3%).

MULTIPLE-PROBLEM CASES (N=61, ACCOUNTING FOR 2.7% OF ALL REFERRALS)

Cases have been rated as having multiple problems when severe difficulties were identified in all three domains: children's development, parenting capacity, and family and environmental factors. Sixty-one cases were thus classified. Problems were compounded (see Table 7.14, Appendix II) because many of these families were also experiencing issues that affected parenting capacity, such as parental mental illness (11 cases), learning disabilities (6 cases), domestic violence (9 cases), and alcohol or drug abuse (6 cases).

A PROFILE OF MULTIPLE-PROBLEM CASES

A higher proportion of cases involving children under the age of 5 years (11.6%) and those 15 years and over (9.4%) were categorised as multiple-problem cases. Only 8.1 per cent of children aged 5 to 9 years and 7 per cent of young people aged 10 to 14 years fell into the multiple-problem group. A rather higher proportion of boys (8.8%) than girls (6.2%) was categorised as multiple-problem cases.

Cases involving Asian children were more likely to be categorised as multiple-problem cases than those involving children of other backgrounds. Ten per cent of cases involving an Asian child were thus classified compared with 7.3 per cent of cases involving white children, and 6.5 per cent of cases involving children of mixed race. No case involving a black child was classified as a multiple-problem case.

The reason for the assessment was linked to whether cases were classified as multiple-problem cases. Cases where the initial assessment was carried out because the child/young person was beyond parental control were more likely to be categorised as multiple-problem cases (16.8%), than assessments done for other reasons. In approximately 10 per cent of cases, where the initial assessment had been carried out because of parental mental illness, other parenting issues, or housing problems, were classified as multiple-problem cases. In other types of cases the proportion classified as multiple-problem cases was smaller (see Table 7.15, Appendix II for more details). Multiple-problem cases accounted for only 4.6 per cent of initial assessment carried out because of child protection concerns.

Decisions recorded on the Initial Assessment Record

The guidance issued with the recording forms (Department of Health, 2000a) informs social workers that the *Further action* section should be used to record any actions taken during or on completion of the initial assessment. The record allows social workers to record more than one action when this is appropriate. For example, when a core assessment is planned, during the process the child and family may receive a service.

In 45 per cent of cases the initial assessment resulted in no further action being recorded. The most frequently recorded action was to provide a service to the child and family. In 29 per cent of cases providing a service was the recorded action. In a quarter of cases the recorded action was a referral to another agency. In 14.5 per cent of cases the child and family were allocated a social worker, and in 9.1 per cent of cases the recorded action was a core assessment (Table 7.16, Appendix II).

THE RECORDED FURTHER ACTION IN MULTIPLE-PROBLEM CASES

Multiple-problem cases are significantly more likely to result in some action being recorded than other cases (Table 7.17, Appendix II). In over three-quarters of multiple-problem cases (82.5%) some further action was recorded compared to approximately half (52.7%) when this was not the case.

Although this high rate of intervention is to be commended, it is of some concern that in 17.5 per cent of multiple-problem cases (n=10) no further action had been the recorded outcome. Furthermore, a scrutiny of the case-file showed that in none of these ten cases had the decision been reviewed and a core assessment subsequently undertaken.

RELATIONSHIP BETWEEN TYPE OF RECORDED FURTHER ACTION AND COMPLEXITY OF THE CASE

Multiple-problem cases were significantly more likely to result in a recommendation for services than less complex cases. Sixty-three per cent of multiple-problem cases led to such a recommended outcome, compared with 26.6 per cent of less complex cases ($\chi^2(1)=34.048.\ p<.000$).

Although there were no other associations found between the complexity of cases and the recorded outcome, a trend was identified in relation to core assessments. A greater proportion of multiple-problem cases (14.5%) led to a core assessment being the recorded action than less complex cases (8.5%). The trend was not statistically significant.

As already noted, in the ten cases categorised as having multiple problems the recorded decision was no further action.

INFORMING FAMILIES OF THE DECISIONS MADE FOLLOWING AN INITIAL ASSESSMENT

One way of informing families of the decisions that have been made as a result of the initial assessment is to provide the family with a copy of the completed record. The Initial Assessment record provides social workers with the opportunity to record whether and when this was done.

The audit showed that social workers do not systematically record whether a copy of the completed Initial Assessment record is given to the family. Information about this issue had been noted in only 60.2 per cent of cases (n=521).

The available data suggests that in less than a third of cases (31.7%, n=165) social workers had given families a copy of the completed Initial Assessment record. Supplying parents with a copy of the completed record was related to the reason for the assessment and the recorded further action. When the initial assessment had been carried out because of parental alcohol or drug use, a copy of the completed record was rarely given to parents (given in only 9% of cases). In cases where the initial assessment led to no further action only a quarter of parents had been given a copy of the completed record.

Summary points

- Only 10 per cent of initial assessments were carried out on young people aged 15 years and older.
- The reason for the initial assessments reflected that found for referrals. Child protection concerns was the most frequent reason for an initial assessment.
- In practically three-quarters of cases social workers had involved at least one other agency in the assessment.

- In 27 per cent of cases children were living in families where there was domestic violence, parental mental illness, or problem alcohol or drug use.
- Sixty-one cases were rated by the research team as having multiple problems (severe difficulties in all three domains).
- In practically half (45%) of all cases the initial assessment resulted in no further action being recorded.
- The most frequently recorded action was the provision of a service (noted in 29% of cases).
- Cases rated as having multiple problems were more likely to lead to the provision of services being the recorded action. Nonetheless, in ten (17.5%) multiple-problem cases the assessment resulted in no further action.
- Social workers gave parents a copy of the completed initial assessment was recorded in only a third of cases.

Chapter summary

Twenty-four Councils with Social Services Responsibilities participated in the audit. The audit consisted of 2248 referrals of which over a third (n=866, 38.5%) progressed to an initial assessment.

There was considerable inconsistency between the action recorded on the referral form and the documentation found on the case-file. Inconsistencies resulted from organisational issues, such as the type of council and the degree of theoretical and technical knowledge that existed prior to implementation. Inconsistencies also resulted from practice issues, such as poor recording practice, and the referring agency's degree of continued involvement in the case.

Referrals most likely to progress to an initial assessment included those where:

- the child was under the age of 15 years
- the reason for referral was related to parental alcohol/drug misuse or parental mental illness
- health or education made a referral for domestic violence.

Referrals for financial or housing problems were least likely to result in an initial assessment.

At the initial assessment stage case recording was at a very high standard, the only information not routinely recorded at this point being whether a copy of the Initial Assessment record was given to the family. Approximately two-thirds of initial assessments were completed on time. Carrying out initial assessments on time was linked to the type of council, the degree of collaborative arrangements prior to implementation, and the reason for the initial assessment.

The reason for the initial assessments reflected the reason for referral. Child protection concerns accounted for the largest proportion of initial assessments, followed by other parenting issues, and children or young people being beyond parental control. The initial assessments involved equal proportions of girls and boys. Children under the age of 5 years were most likely to be involved in an initial assessment (accounting for over a third of all assessments) than middle-year children. Young people aged 15 years and older featured in 10 per cent of cases. In practically three-quarters of cases social workers had involved at least one other agency in the assessment, and in 42 per cent of cases two or more agencies.

A number of factors were identified with whether referrals progressed to an initial assessment:

- Cases most likely to progress to an initial assessment involved children under the age of 15 years, and those relating to parental alcohol/drug use, and parental mental illness.
- Cases least likely to progress to an initial assessment involved young people aged 15 years or older, those that related to financial or housing problems, and police referrals relating to domestic violence.

The low rates of referrals for financial and housing problems progressing to an initial assessment reflects the earlier findings that these issues are least likely to result in children being categorised as children in need (Aldgate and Tunstill, 1995). The resulting profile of the reason for initial assessments reflects that found for referrals, with slight increases in some categories and decreases in others.

Social workers identified the child as having developmental needs in half (49.7%) the cases, with the greatest degree of developmental need being in relation to family and social relationships. In a quarter of cases the research team categorised the child's developmental needs as severe. In a third (33.8%) of cases social workers identified difficulties in parenting capacity; ensuring the child's safety was the most common. In a fifth of cases the research team categorised the parenting difficulties as severe. The domain where difficulties were most frequently identified was family and environmental factors. In over a third (37%) of cases the research team categorised the difficulties in relation to the family and environmental factors as severe.

In two-thirds of cases (65.2%) difficulties had been recorded, with issues around family history and functioning being most prevalent. In over a quarter of cases (27%) the child was living in a family where there was domestic violence, parental mental illness, or problem alcohol or drug use. When social workers had noted difficulties in three or more of the dimensions in each of the domains, the case was categorised at having multiple problems. Sixty-one cases were categorised as having multiple problems.

The Initial Assessment record enabled social workers to record a number of recommended further actions. For practically half (45%) of the initial assessments the recorded outcome was no further action. In over a quarter (29%) the social worker had recorded that services should be provided to the child and family. In a quarter the social workers had recorded that the family was to be referred to another agency, and in 9.1 per cent (n=70) of cases the recommendation was for a core assessment. A social worker had been allocated to 14.5 per cent of cases.

Chapter 8

Core Assessments

Findings from the Audit

The sample (n=68)

> A core assessment is defined as an in-depth assessment which addresses the central or most important aspects of the needs of a child and the capacity of his or her parents or caregivers to response appropriately to these needs within the wider family and community context.
>
> (Department of Health *et al.*, 2000a, p.32, 3.11)

Of the 2248 referrals audited 866 (38.5%) progressed to an initial assessment and 68 (3%) to a core assessment.

It was anticipated that in the majority of cases the decision of how best to respond to concerns about the child's development and circumstances would be made on the basis of information gathered during an initial assessment. Nonetheless, the finding that only 3 per cent of referrals progressed to a core assessment was unexpected. Before discussing the characteristics of cases that did progress to a core assessment, it is important to explore why so few Core Assessment records were found on the case-files. Discussions with managers suggest this was related to a number of factors of which two are particularly relevant:

- Teams working with disabled children and child protection cases continued to use existing assessment frameworks and documentation.
- The implementation of the Assessment Framework and the introduction of the records had not yet fully bedded in. As a result, although there was considerable confidence in completing

> initial assessments, some line managers and practitioners were wary of embarking on core assessments. One method of coping, found in a number of councils, was for information on detailed assessments to be recorded on Initial Assessment records (as one manager explained there were initial assessments and super initial assessments). This practice led to difficulties in completing initial assessments within the required time.

Inconsistencies between the further action recorded on the Initial Assessment record and the documentation found on the case-file

The issue of inconsistencies between the recorded further action and the documentation found on the case-file, identified at the point of transfer from referral to initial assessment, was also apparent at the transfer between initial and core assessment. For example, in 70 cases social workers had recorded a core assessment as the further action on the Initial Assessment record, but a scrutiny of the documentation revealed a Core Assessment record in only 31 cases. In a further 37 cases a Core Assessment record was found on the case-file when this had not been recorded as the further action on the Initial Assessment record. Focusing on the identity of the Councils with Social Services Responsibilities showed inconsistencies existed in all of them.

CASES THAT SHOULD HAVE PROGRESSED TO A CORE ASSESSMENT (N=39)

The source of the referral was linked to the consistency between the action recorded on the Initial Assessment record and the documentation found on the case-files. Referrals from health and education, where the Initial Assessment record recommended a core assessment, were more likely to result in a core assessment being undertaken than referrals from other sources. There was consistency between the recorded action and the documentation on the case-file in two-thirds of initial assessments referred by health or education compared with 45 per cent from non-professionals, 41 per cent from other social services, and 25 per cent of referrals from the police. Non-professionals include parents, children and young people, relatives, friends and neighbours. This pattern reflected that found in relation to the transfer between the point of referral and initial assessment.

The numbers are small and no links can be safely made between the reason for referral and the consistency between the recorded further action and the documentation of a core assessment found on the case-file. Nonetheless, it is of some concern to find that in less than half (48.1%) the child protection referrals, where the social worker had recorded a core assessment as the recommended further action on Initial Assessment record, was the Core Assessment record found on the case-file (see Table 8.1, Appendix II). Moreover, cases referred for parental mental illness, housing problems, other parenting issues, and 'other' reasons were unlikely to proceed to a core assessment even when this was the further action recommended on the Initial Assessment record.

Families categorised as multiple-problem cases accounted for six of the 39 cases where no Core Assessment record was found on the case-file, when this had been the recorded action on the Initial Assessment record.

CASES THAT UNEXPECTEDLY PROCEEDED TO A CORE ASSESSMENT (N=37)

Cases that unexpectedly proceeded to a core assessment fell into two groups. First, cases where no initial assessment had been undertaken, i.e. referrals led directly to a core assessment (n=19). Second, cases where an initial assessment had been carried out but a core assessment had *not* been the recorded further action (n=18). These included six cases where the further action was a strategy meeting, three where it was to provide services or refer to another agency, and six where the outcome was no further action. Finally, in three cases the social worker had not recorded any further action.

Referrals from other social services departments that fell into either of these two groups were most likely to have been reassigned, accounting for 37.8 per cent (n=14) of the 37 cases. The police accounted for seven reassigned cases (four of which arose from a strategy discussion), health for five, schools and non-professionals each accounted for three cases and other sources for the remaining four cases. The source of the referral had not been recorded in one case.

Of the cases that unexpectedly proceeded to a core assessment 84 per cent involved child protection referrals. The reason for the referral in 37 core assessments were as follows:

- 31 child protection concerns
- 2 domestic violence
- 1 parental alcohol/drugs problems
- 1 other parenting issues
- 1 disabled child
- 1 reason for referral not recorded.

One multiple-problem case unexpectedly proceeded to a core assessment.

Possible reasons for the mismatch

There are a number of explanations why the information recorded on the Initial Assessment record and the documentation found in the case-file are inconsistent. Although some reflect good practice, others do not.

GOOD PRACTICE

> A core assessment is deemed to have commenced at the point the initial assessment ended, or a strategy discussion decided to initiate enquiries under s47, or new information obtained on an open case indicates a core assessment should be undertaken. (Department of Health *et al.*, 2000a, p.32, 3.13)

The data throw considerable insight onto the reasons why cases unexpectedly progressed to a core assessment. In some cases the action reflected good practice. A detailed scrutiny of the findings reveals that in six cases a strategy discussion/meeting had been the recommended further action and the decision to undertake a core assessment arose from this, a process consistent with the Assessment Framework.

In 11 of the 19 cases where the decision to undertake a core assessment had been made at the point of referral, the referral came from another social services department. Further exploration of these data reveals that these were open cases, and therefore carrying out a core assessment was consistent with the Assessment Framework.

A FAILURE TO FOLLOW GOVERNMENT GUIDANCE

The remaining seven cases, where referrals led directly to core assessments, were child protection referrals. This suggests that in 11.8 per cent of core assessments (eight out of the 68 core assessments audited) social work practice may not be in line with the Assessment Framework. Both Working Together to Safeguard Children and recent supplementary guidance specify the importance of carrying out an initial assessment for child protection cases, however brief.

> Although initial assessment is the next stage after referral the time taken to complete the initial assessment may be very brief if it quickly becomes clear that there is reasonable cause to suspect the child is suffering or is

likely to suffer significant harm. (Department of Health *et al.*, 2001, p.22, 3.16)

THE SOURCE OF THE REFERRAL

The source of referral was linked to the degree of consistency between the action recorded on the Initial Assessment record, and a Core Assessment record being found on the case-file. The same association was found at the point of transfer between referral and initial assessment. Professionals who continue to have contact with families are more likely to follow up their cases than professionals who do not, and this appears to have influenced how cases are handled by social services. There was greater consistency between the action recorded on the Initial Assessment record and a Core Assessment record being found on the case-file when the case had been referred by health or education than cases referred by the police or non-professionals.

POOR RECORDING

In a further six cases that unexpectedly progressed to a core assessment, the recorded action on the Initial Assessment record was 'no further action' and in three cases the provision of services or a referral to another agency had been recommended. The original decision recorded on the Initial Assessment record may have been revised in the light of further information coming into the department. However, this had not been recorded and there was no evidence to show why these cases had been reassigned. Finally, in the remaining three cases where a core assessment had been undertaken unexpectedly, the social worker had left blank the further action section of the Initial Assessment record.

Summary points

- The audit included 68 Core Assessment records – 3 per cent of all referrals.
- There was considerable inconsistency between the outcome recorded on the Initial Assessment record and the documentation found on the file.

Profile of referrals that did progress to a core assessment (n=68)

The data have shown that referrals relating to parental drug or alcohol abuse or mental illness that involve children under that age of 15 years are more likely to progress to an *initial assessment* than other types of referral. This section examines whether there are links between the type of referral and whether cases progress to a *core assessment.*

Age of child

Although a slightly larger proportion of referrals involving younger children progressed to a core assessment this difference was minimal. The data show that 3.5 per cent of referrals involving children under 5 years and children aged 5 to 9 years progressed to a core assessment, compared with 2.3 per cent of the older age groups.

Gender of the child

The gender of the child or young person was not associated with whether the case progressed to a core assessment. Of all referrals involving boys, 3.3 per cent progressed to a core assessment compared with 2.8 per cent of referrals involving girls.

Ethnicity of the child

The small numbers of cases that progressed to a core assessment and the paucity of recording in relation to ethnicity have resulted in poor data. Nonetheless, it of interest to note that referrals involving black children were least likely to progress to a core assessment (0.7%), while those where the social worker had recorded the child's ethnicity as 'any other ethnic group' (8.6%) were most likely to progress. Some 5 per cent of referrals involving Asian children, 3.4 per cent of referrals involving white children and 2.5 per cent of those involving mixed-race children, progressed to a core assessment.

The reason for the referral

The reason for the referral was linked to whether cases progressed to a core assessment. Child protection referrals and referrals relating to parental alcohol or drug misuse were more likely to progress to a core assessment than referrals for other reasons (see Table 8.2, Appendix II). No referrals relating to parental mental illness, financial or housing problems progressed to a core assessment.

The source of the referral

Social services departments referred a third (33.8%) of all cases that progressed to a core assessment (7.2% of referrals from social services departments progressed to a core assessment). This reflects the finding that a considerable proportion of core assessments was carried out on open cases that have been transferred from one authority to another.

Health referred a fifth (20%) of all cases that led to a core assessment (3.2% of referrals from health progressed to a core assessment). Police referred 16.9 per cent of all referrals that progressed to a core assessment, schools 10.8 per cent and non-professionals 12.3 per cent. Referrals from non-professionals were least likely to progress to a core assessment, only 1.2 per cent of these referrals leading to a core assessment (see Table 8.3, Appendix II).

Summary points

Those referrals most likely to progress to a core assessment were:

- child protection referrals and those for parental alcohol/drug misuse
- referrals from social services departments.

Those referrals least likely to progress to a core assessment were:

- referrals relating to parental mental illness, financial and housing problems
- referrals that come from non-professionals (parents, children and young people, relatives, friends and neighbours).

Cases undergoing a core assessment n=68

Recording patterns for the Core Assessment record

PARALLEL RECORDING SYSTEMS

There was considerable variation in the quality of recording information on the Core Assessment record. In approximately a third of cases the Core Assessment record provided a clear picture of the findings from the assessment. The social worker had identified the agencies consulted during the assessment and recorded the contribution of the family. Information about the child's needs, parenting capacity, and family and environmental factors had been noted, using both the tick boxes to demonstrate the social worker's professional judgement, and free script to elaborate or establish the context. The analysis of the information was evidenced and the recorded objectives and plans reflected the findings from the assessment.

In other cases either very little information had been recorded or it was inconsistently recorded. In some cases social workers recorded only brief details identifying the case. For example, in one case the social worker had simply recorded his/her name on the record – all the rest was left blank. In others the social workers' name and the agencies consulted were the only information found on the record. In others social workers had included the reason for the assessment before abandoning any further recording on the record; or information about the child's needs and circumstances but no analysis, objectives and plan had been recorded. Finally, in a few cases the social worker had recorded their name, the reason for the assessment, and then jumped to the plan for the child and family.

A possible explanation for information only being recorded in the early sections of the record is that social workers are in the process of carrying out the assessment and, therefore, the record was as yet incomplete. However, a scrutiny of the case-file and checks with the relevant managers did not support this notion. What became evident was that in a number of councils, referrals involving child protection concerns were routed through a different system and information recorded on child protection formats. Very basic data and/or the decisions of the Child Protection Conference would be the only information recorded on the Core Assessment record. This is not consistent with the Assessment Framework or Working Together.

> The Framework for the Assessment of Children in Need and their Families provides a structure for helping to collect and analyse information obtained in the course of s47 enquiries. (Department of Health *et al.*, 1999, p.48, 5.33)

The practice led to considerable confusion among social workers and left some feeling frustrated as parallel systems led to duplication in recording.

> We did not do the plan on the core assessment record. We did it as part of the child protection recording. The core assessment was like an extra piece of work, like an additional document.
>
> (Social worker's response to the questionnaire in authority W)

> I really have mixed feelings about the Core Assessment form. I don't think it is an assessment. It's an information-gathering exercise. I'm still doing risk assessments.
>
> (Social worker's response to the questionnaire in authority D)

The rate of recording administrative and management information

Recording administrative or management information has three purposes. First, it enables the progress of individual cases to be monitored. Second, the information will inform local management data collection and enable appropriate service planning. Third, authorities will be able to supply the required information for national data collection.

Administrative and management data includes:

- the identity of the social worker and other professionals consulted during the assessment
- key dates, such as the timing of the assessment, when family members were seen, and the date for the review
- specific information about children's health, education and offending behaviour.

THE IDENTITY OF THE SOCIAL WORKER AND OTHER KEY PROFESSIONALS

In order to identify who is responsible for a particular case the social worker should record his or her name on the front page of the record. In most cases, (n=60, 88.2%) social workers had noted their name on the Core Assessment record. Nonetheless, it is of some concern that in eight cases this information was missing.

In the majority of cases (n=56, 82.4%) social workers recorded the identity of other agencies consulted during the assessment.

DATES

> The timescale for completion of the core assessment is a *maximum of 35 working days.* (Department of Health *et al.*, 2000a, p.32, 3.11)

In the majority of cases (n=48, 70.6%) social workers had recorded the start date of the assessment. However, recording the end date was more unusual and had been noted in only half the cases (n=34, 50%). As a result, information on the time taken to carry out core assessments is restricted to half the cases.

To understand the perspectives of different family members, including the child, requires the social worker to carry out direct work with the individuals concerned.

> Gathering information and making sense of a family's situation are key phases in the process of assessment. It is not possible to do this without the knowledge and involvement of the family. (Department of Health *et al.*, 2000a, p.38, 3.32)

One way of monitoring the work done by social workers in specific cases is to record the times the child and family are seen. Social workers did not systematically record when they saw the family. The dates when the social worker saw the child and other members of the family had been recorded in less than half the cases (n=42, 61.8%).

The Assessment Framework notes that when work is being carried out with a child in need living with their family it is good practice to review the plan at least every six months.

> There should also be a clear recorded statement on the plan about when and how it will be reviewed. (Department of Health *et al.*, 2000a, p.61, 4.36)

The Core Assessment record provides a space for social workers to record the date when the plan will be reviewed and when it will be reviewed in supervision. Dates when the plan would be reviewed were rarely recorded. In only five cases (7.4%) had social workers noted the agreed date for the review, although twice as many had noted the date for the plan to be reviewed in supervision (n=10, 14.7%).

SPECIFIC INFORMATION ABOUT THE CHILD OR YOUNG PERSON

Local authorities are required to supply information on key indicators for national data collection. The Core Assessment record enables this data to be identified.

Details relating to the child's health included information about immunisations (recorded in 31 cases, 45.6%), and for young people information about childbirth (recorded in 16 out of a possible 23 cases, 69.6%). Information relating to education was not routinely recorded. For example, in only seven of a possible 39 cases (17.9%) had the social worker recorded SATS results, and whether the child had been excluded from school was noted in only two cases (5.1%). Finally, information relating to the courts was also sparse. Possible court orders relating to the child had been noted in eight cases (11.8%), but information on offending behaviour such as the number of cautions and/or convictions within the past year had not been recorded on any Core Assessment record.

The rate of recording information relating to the assessment process

> ...careful and systematic gathering of information, and its summary and analysis according to the framework can assist professionals in making sound evidence based judgements. (Department of Health *et al.*, 2000a, p.56, 4.16)

Information relating to the assessment process includes:

- the reason for the assessment
- information gathered during the assessment
- summaries of the data
- analysis
- objectives and plans.

THE REASON FOR THE ASSESSMENT

The reason for the core assessment had been recorded in the majority of cases (n=61, 89.7%). In the seven cases where this had not been recorded, a scrutiny of the documentation showed no consistency in relation to the type of referral. These cases included three referred because of domestic violence, two related to possible child abuse, one to concerns about the overall parenting, and one because the child's behaviour was beyond parental control.

INFORMATION GATHERED DURING THE ASSESSMENT

It is particularly important to record information about the child's development and circumstances, because a lack of information has been consistently cited by inquiry reports to have adversely affected the way cases are handled (Munro, 1998). The Core Assessment record enables social workers to record their professional judgements about key aspects of children's developmental needs, parenting capacity and family and environmental issues through the use of tick boxes. In addition, the record enables social workers to clarify or contextualise their decisions and judgements through the use of free text. To record information and judgements using these two methods was originally introduced in the Looking After Children materials more than ten years ago. Nonetheless, this joint approach was new to social workers that had not worked with looked-after children. The introduction of new ways of recording assessments caused considerable confusion, anxiety and resistance. For example, many social workers perceived the Core Assessment record as a questionnaire that was the assessment itself (see Chapter 4 for more details).

> The core assessment is too complex and difficult to use in practice. The process does not work. The requirement to ask specific questions leads to people lying for fear of giving the answer wrong. It tries to bypass social work skills for eliciting information through guided discussion or other well-tried methods. It is orientated to literate families and alienates the less academic.
>
> (Social worker's response to the questionnaire, authority W2)

> It is not so much the issues although these are affected but the style. The tick box approach is not client-centred and is very mechanistic – you have to avoid making the information fit the questions – it definitely narrows the focus rather than a holistic data-gathering exercise.
>
> (Social worker's response to the questionnaire, authority C)

Children's developmental needs

In fifty-five per cent of cases social workers recorded their decisions about at least one aspect of the child's development through the use of the tick boxes. A somewhat smaller proportion of social workers recorded information through the use of free text. The rate of recording depended on the developmental dimension being assessed. Social workers were more likely to record information about the child's health, and behavioural and emotional development than about other areas of development (see Table 8.4, Appendix II).

Parenting capacity

A similar pattern of recording was found in relation to information about the parents' capacity to meet the child's needs. Once again, social workers were slightly more likely to use tick boxes to record decisions about parental capacity, than free text.

For all of the dimensions within the *Child's Developmental Needs* domain (some data recorded in 48.5% of cases), and *Parental Capacity to Respond* (some data recorded in 45.6% of cases) the pattern was similar. Decisions were recorded in approximately half the cases.

However, when information was recorded it was generally done well. Social workers clearly evidenced the child's needs and parenting capacity. In cases where recording was scant, it could be argued that social workers were making a professional decision that information was not required within a particular dimension. However, the pattern of recording did not support this premise. In 26 cases (38.2%) no information had been recorded for any of the child developmental needs or parents' capacity to meet them.

The summary sections at the end of each developmental dimension, are designed for social workers to summarise the information recorded about the child's developmental needs and the extent to which parents are responding appropriately. The short summary sections are the first stage in the process of analysis. These summaries should reflect the evidence presented by the social workers through the use of tick boxes to record professionals' judgements and free text to expand or record further information (see Table 8.6, Appendix II).

In a small proportion of cases social workers only used the short summary section to record information gathered during the assessment of the child's developmental needs and parenting capacity. For example, although social workers had used the tick boxes to record decisions about the child's health in 33 cases and parenting capacity in 30 cases, a summary of the child's health and parenting capacity had been noted in 41 cases. That social workers complete the summary section without recording detailed information relating to the developmental needs themselves, raises questions about the evidence on which the summary has been based.

The rate of completed summary sections varied between developmental dimensions, reflecting the findings noted earlier on recording practice for the individual developmental dimensions. Social workers were more likely to complete a summary section for health, and behavioural and emotional development (60% of cases) than for other dimensions (see Table 8.6).

Issues affecting parenting capacity

Research has shown that issues such as physical or mental illness, domestic violence, problem substance use, childhood abuse, and a history of child abuse can affect a parent's capacity to respond appropriately to their child's needs. The Core Assessment record includes a section for social workers to record any information gathered during the assessment that relates to these issues. The audit shows a consistent pattern in the recording practice. In practically half the cases (n=32, 47.1%) social workers recorded information relating to issues affecting parenting capacity.

Family and environmental factors

The core assessment also expects social workers to explore the impact on the child and parents or carers of factors within the wider family and environment. These include issues such as family history and functioning, housing, employment and income, and their degree of social integration and community support. In two-thirds (n=46) of cases social workers had recorded information on this domain (see Table 8.7, Appendix II). A summary section at the end of this domain enables information about the various issues to be brought together. Social workers had summarised the information in this section in 28 cases (39.7%).

Summaries

The Core Assessment record contains three main summary sections. These enable social workers to bring together all the information gathered and recorded throughout the record on the needs and strengths relating to the child's development, parenting capacity and relevant factors within the wider family and environment. In some 60 per cent of cases social workers used each of the three main summary sections to record information (see Table 8.8, Appendix II). When the summary sections had been completed, in most cases social workers were appropriately identifying both strengths and needs within each domain. Nonetheless, in approximately 13 per cent of cases the summary section had been used to record additional information about a case rather than to summarise detailed information recorded earlier in the record.

Recording practice was not always logical. First, in some cases the main summary sections were used in isolation to the rest of the document. For example, in relation to the summary of the child's developmental needs, completed in 29 cases, in ten cases this did not relate to information recorded in the sections on the child's developmental needs because these had been left blank. Second, in other cases the summary sections were not completed when information was available. For example, in 16 of the 39 cases where the child's summary had not been completed, information on the child's developmental needs had been evidenced in the individual sections.

The analysis

At the conclusion of this phase of assessment, there should be an analysis of the findings in order to understand the child's needs and circumstances and inform planning, case objectives and the nature of service provision (see Department of Health *et al.*, 2000a, p.32, 3.11).

In the analysis section social workers are expected to weigh up how the identified needs and strengths within the child, parents, wider family and environment inter-relate and affect the child's health and development. The ability to do this depends on social workers using relevant theories to make sense of the information they have gathered. Previous research suggests many social workers lack such a knowledge base or the required skills (Munro, 1998).

The responses contained in the social workers' questionnaires (described in Chapter 4) reinforce these earlier research findings and may have affected the quality of core assessments. Many social workers reported feeling anxious, ill-prepared and poorly equipped for the task of analysis. Moreover, it was an aspect of assessment which social workers and managers felt that training had failed to address adequately (see Chapter 4).

The findings from the audit support social workers' concerns about their competence in analysing the findings from their assessments. Once again the completion rate was poor; some recording had been made in this section in 61.8 per cent (n=42) cases. In 38.2 per cent (n=26) of cases the analysis section of the record had *not* been completed.

When information was recorded in the analysis section of the record, in approximately half the cases (42.9%, n=18) social workers had noted additional descriptive information about the child and family – it was not an analysis of the information about the child's developmental needs and circumstances. In the remaining cases (n=24) social workers had demonstrated competent analysis skills and utilised the information noted in the record. The analysis was categorised as competent when it identified the child's needs and circumstances, and the service provision to address the issues (see Table 8.9, Appendix II).

The analysis of the assessment should be based on the information recorded in the summary sections. Once again there appeared to be little logic in recording practices. For example, of the 42 cases where the analysis had been done, in 20 cases there was no summary of the child's developmental needs or parenting capacity found on the Core Assessment record. Furthermore, for the 26 cases where the analysis section had been left blank, in seven cases the social worker had recorded a full summary of child's developmental needs and parenting capacity.

The objectives and plans

> The details of the plan are bench marks against which the progress of the family and commitment of workers are measured, and therefore it is important that they should be realistic and not vague statements of good intent. (Department of Health, 1995b, p.80, 8.27)

The final key section within the Core Assessment record relates to the objectives and plans. While there is no current requirement for a formal plan except in child protection cases and for looked-after children, the Assessment Framework nevertheless contains the principle that services should only be provided with a plan to support them and that this plan should be based on an assessment.

The completion rate for the objectives and plans section of the Core Assessment record was poor (see Table 8.10, Appendix II). In only a third of cases (n=23) was a plan completed to meet the child's developmental needs. Given the importance of the plan in making and reviewing decisions about children and families, this is of considerable concern.

When Core Assessments records included a plan, the quality was variable. For example, in 20 cases the plan related to the needs identified and recorded in relation to the child's development, but in only four of these cases did it relate to all the child's identified developmental needs (see Table 8.10).

In three cases the plan failed to address the needs in one or more domain, and in one of these cases the plan appeared completely unrelated to the needs identified in any of the three dimensions.

The audit has shown that in a number of cases social workers' recording was erratic. Information was recorded in some sections and not in others and there was little evidence to suggest that the pattern of information gathering, summary, analysis and plans was a practice every social worker was following.

The rate of recording information relating to family participation

There is some data that social workers should record on the Core Assessment record that relates to family participation. This includes:

- whether information leaflets and documents have been given to the family

- issues related to the communication needs of individual family members
- the views of family members in relation to the assessment
- signatures and comments.

INFORMATION LEAFLETS AND DOCUMENTS

> Local authorities are required by section 26 of the Children Act 1989 to establish complaints procedures, and children and parents should be provided with information about these. (Department of Health *et al.*, 2000a, p.32, 3.13)

In approximately a fifth (n=15, 22%) of cases social workers recorded whether a copy of the complaints procedures or access to records had been given to the family. Such a low rate suggests social workers rarely provide this sort of information to the family when carrying out a core assessment.

After the core assessment had been completed the parents and child, if appropriate, should be informed of the outcome. One way of doing this is to give the family a copy of the assessment record or of the plan. In only eight cases (11.8%) had the social worker recorded whether a copy of the assessment record had been given to relevant family members, suggesting families are rarely given a copy of the Core Assessment record. The difficulties that many authorities experience in producing a duplicate of the record (reported in Chapter 4) may account for this.

INFORMATION TO ASSIST COMMUNICATION WITH THE FAMILY

Effective assessment depends on both parties feeling confident and at ease with the method of communication used. Social workers, therefore, need to explore and record whether there are any specific communication needs for the child, parent or carer and if so what action has been taken to address them. In approximately half the cases (n=33, 48.5%) social workers recorded whether there were any communication needs for either the child or a parent.

THE VIEWS OF FAMILY MEMBERS

Parents and older children have the opportunity to have their views about the child's developmental needs, parenting capacity, and family and environmental issues, noted on the core assessment record.

Parents included in the interview sample (discussed in Chapter 3) valued social workers seeking their views and believed these had been recorded; however, the audit suggests this is not routine practice. In only a fifth of the audited cases had the social worker recorded the views of individual family members about the child's needs and circumstances.

SIGNATURES OF FAMILY MEMBERS AND COMMENTS ON THE ASSESSMENT

> There are some general principles about plans for working with children and families, whatever the circumstances in which they have been drawn up. First that, wherever possible, they should be drawn up in agreement with the child/young person and key family members and their commitment to the plan should have been secured. (Department of Health *et al.*, 2000a, p.61, 4.34)

It was rare to find the signatures or comments from either the child/young person or key family members on the Core Assessment record. In only four cases (5.9%) was the signature of a parent found on the core assessment record. In only six cases (8.8%) had parents' comments on the process of the assessment been recorded; the comments of young people had not been recorded on any Core Assessment record.

Summary points

- This audit was restricted the Department of Health's referral and assessment records and it would be misleading to assume that where information was missing from this documentation it is also missing from the case-file. Nonetheless, the councils that participated in this study had undertaken to introduce these records and use them to record all the relevant data.
- The audit of the Core Assessment records showed that in most cases social workers recorded information relating to the identity of the professionals involved in the assessment (noted in over 80% of cases).
- Dates relating to the process of assessment, such as the time taken (recorded in 50% of cases) and when the child and family were seen (noted in 61.8% of cases) were more likely to be recorded than dates relating to the review (noted in 8.2% of cases).
- The information on key indicators for national data collection varied. Information on health indicators was supplied in

practically half the cases, while information on educational standards was noted in less than a fifth of cases, and court orders relating to the child noted in only 11.8 per cent of cases.

- The reason for the core assessment was recorded in 89.7 per cent of cases.
- Information had been recorded in approximately half the cases in relation to the child's developmental needs (48.5% of cases) and parenting capacity (45.6% of cases) and family and environmental factors (55.9% of cases).
- In 60 per cent of cases social workers recorded information in the three main summary sections.
- The analysis section of the record was poorly completed. Information had been recorded in 42 (61.8%) cases. In many cases the social worker had used this section to record additional descriptive information rather than to analyse information recorded earlier in the record. In only 24 cases (35.3%) was a competent analysis of the data found on the Core Assessment record.
- In only a third of cases did the Core Assessment record contain a plan. The quality of the plans was variable and rarely related to all the child's identified needs and circumstances.
- Recording practice was not always systematic. In some cases there was little evidence to suggest social workers followed a logical process of information gathering, summary and analysis, on which objectives and plans were based.
- Recording information about communicating with the family was poor. Social workers rarely recorded whether a copy of the assessment or plan had been given to the family.
- In only a fifth of cases had the family's views about their situation been recorded. In less than 10 per cent of cases did family members sign or record their view about the process of assessment. Although it must not be assumed the rate of recording families' views was equated with how frequently they were sought, this does suggest that social workers did not see this as an important element in the recording of assessments.

Profile of the core assessment cases (n=68)

Sixty-eight referrals (3.0%) progressed to a core assessment. This rate is much lower than many social services departments expected. Some insights as to why the rate was so low are offered from the findings from the interviews, questionnaires, and audit of the Initial Assessment records. For example, the reports from social work managers and practitioners (described in Chapter 4) indicate there was considerable reluctance on the part of social workers to progress from an initial assessment to a core assessment. Moreover, many practitioners reported that they were still unfamiliar with the Core Assessment records and felt unprepared and ill-equipped in using them. They perceived core assessments as arduous and time-consuming. Evidence from the audit suggests social workers were carrying out detailed initial assessments, frequently running well beyond the timescales, on cases where the circumstances would suggest a core assessment would have been more appropriate. Substantiating these reports is the finding that six multiple-problem cases recommended for a core assessment did not progress to a core assessment.

Time taken to carry out the core assessment

Social workers are required to note on the Core Assessment record the start and end date of the assessment. Social workers did not consistently record both dates. In 20 cases the start date was missing and in a further 14 cases the end date had not been recorded. As a result, information on the time taken to carry out the core assessment was available in only 34 cases.

In 25 (73.5%) of the 34 cases where information was available had been completed within the required time. However, this rate may be misleading as the failure to record the end date may indicate that social workers had overrun the required time. Assuming that all core assessments where the information on the end date was missing were not done within the required time would reduce the proportion of core assessments completed within the required time to approximately a third (36.8%). This figure is more in line with the messages received from social workers during interviews, from the questionnaires and during the numerous feedback sessions and conferences.

The average time taken to undertake a core assessment for complex cases was 36 hours (see Chapter 9), suggesting that organisational and structural issues are affecting social workers' ability to complete assessments on time rather than case-related factors.

Reason for the Core Assessment

(Information available in 61 cases)

In the majority of cases social workers carried out core assessments because of child protection concerns. In over three-quarters (n=48, 78.7%) of cases the main reason for the core assessment was a concern that the child was in need of protection. Social workers cited a variety of reasons for the remaining 13 cases. In three cases the reason was parental alcohol or drug misuse. Social workers had carried out a core assessment in two cases for each of the following reasons: domestic violence, 'other parenting issues', a disabled child, the child or young person was beyond parental control. Finally, one core assessment involved an unaccompanied asylum seeker and one fell into the category of 'other'.

The complexity of the case

The analysis of the initial assessments enabled cases where difficulties had been identified in more than two or three dimensions in all three domains to be categorised as multiple-problem cases. Sixty-one cases were categorised as multiple-problem cases. It would be expected that every one of these cases would result in a core assessment. It is of some concern that a quarter of the multiple-problem cases (n=15) did not progress to a core assessment.

Sources of information (other than the family)

> Information may be gathered from a variety of sources, using methods which will be determined by the purpose of the assessment and the particular circumstances of each child and family. (Department of Health *et al.*, 2000a, p.54, 4.6)

Agencies consulted during a core assessment

> While this assessment is led by social services, it will invariably involve other agencies or independent professionals, who will either provide advice to social services or undertake specialist assessments. (Department of Health *et al.*, 2000a, p.32, 3.11)

In undertaking the majority (86.7%) of core assessments social workers had consulted professionals working in other agencies. In 70.6 per cent of cases two or more professionals from other agencies had been consulted, and in over a third of cases (38.2%) professionals from three or more agencies had been involved.

The agency most frequently consulted by social workers undertaking a core assessment was the police (see Table 8.11, Appendix II). Social workers noted that the police had been consulted in 58.8 per cent (n=40) of the core assessments. This is consistent with the finding that the majority of core assessments were carried out because of child protection concerns.

In approximately half the cases (51.5%, n=35) social workers consulted other groups of professionals. These included, for example, family centre workers, practitioners from drug or alcohol units, psychiatric nurses, and educational psychologists. In 42.6 per cent of cases social workers had consulted health visitors' and in approximately a third of cases the general practitioner (n=22) or the school (n=24) had been consulted.

Scales and Questionnaires

A set of questionnaires and scales accompanied the publication of the Assessment Framework.

> The instruments can assist staff preparing reports for the Court, by providing a clear evidence base for the judgements and recommendations made regarding a child, and inform the child care plan. (Department of Health, Cox and Bentovim, 2000b, p.1,1)

Scales and questionnaires were used by social workers undertaking a core assessment in only five cases. The rate of developmental needs identified by the core assessments suggests that the use of scales and questionnaires would have supplied additional information to inform the assessment in many more cases. It may be that without training in the use of these tools social workers lacked the confidence to use them or were not fully aware of their value. This was an issue raised by many social workers in their comments about training (see Chapter 4).

> The trainer seemed unfamiliar with all the additional tools to complete an assessment, e.g. parenting hassle scores or rather, they were not available at the time of training, which was not helpful to either the trainer or trainee. So training felt incomplete and somewhat out of control.
>
> (Social worker, hospital team)

The Alcohol Scale was most frequently used. In three cases social workers had used this scale. In two cases the Recent Life Events Questionnaire was used. The following were each used only once: Strengths and Difficulties Questionnaire, The Parenting Daily Hassle Scale, Home Conditions Scale, and the

Adult Wellbeing Scale. For the 68 core assessments audited no social worker recorded having used the Adolescent Wellbeing Scale or the Family Activity Scale.

Specialist assessments

In seven cases social workers had recorded that a specialist assessment had been commissioned.

The children

AGE OF THE CHILD

(Information available in 67 cases)

The proportion of core assessments steadily declined as the age groups rose. The largest proportion (41.8%, n=28) of core assessments involved children under the age of 5 years. Children aged 5 to 9 years accounted for 26.9 per cent (n=18), young people aged 10 to 14 years for 20.9 per cent (n=14), and young people aged 15 years and over for 10.4 per cent (n=7) of all core assessments.

GENDER OF THE CHILD

(Information available in 63 cases)

More boys (n=36, 57.1%) than girls (n=28, 44.4%) were involved in core assessments.

ETHNICITY OF THE CHILD

(Information available in 54 cases)

The majority (79.6%, n=43) of core assessments involved white children. In 9.3 per cent (n=5) of core assessments Asian children (this includes children from Pakistan, Bangladesh, India and any other Asian background) were involved. In 5.6 per cent (n=3) of cases the core assessment involved children categorised by the social workers 'any other ethnic group'; 3.7 per cent (n=2) were of mixed race; and one child was black.

The level of needs identified by the core assessment

The Core Assessment record is age-related and enables social workers to record information on the three domains of the Assessment Framework: the child's developmental needs, parenting capacity, and family and environmental factors. The record allows detailed information to be recorded, concerning the child's development and the parents' capacity, for each of the seven developmental dimensions. There is an additional section to record issues, such as domestic violence, or mental illness, that may affect parenting. Finally, a separate section allows social workers to record information on each dimension of the third domain – family and environmental factors.

CHILDREN'S DEVELOPMENTAL NEEDS AND PARENTING CAPACITY

(Information available in 41 cases)

When social workers recorded information on the Core Assessment record they noted high levels of unmet developmental need for the children and young people involved. In approximately two-thirds of cases unmet developmental needs were recorded in relation to the child's health, education, behavioural and emotional development, identity, and family and social relationships. In over three-quarters of cases social workers recorded unmet developmental needs in relation to the child's self-presentation and self-case skills (see Table 8.12, Appendix II).

In 80.5 per cent of cases (n=33) children were shown to have unmet developmental needs in at least one dimension. In 61 per cent of cases (n=25) children were shown to have unmet developmental needs in four or more dimensions.

ISSUES AFFECTING PARENTS'/CARERS' CAPACITIES TO RESPOND APPROPRIATELY TO THE CHILD'S NEEDS

(Information available in 31 cases)

Research has shown many different issues can seriously impair parents' capacity to respond appropriately to the needs of their children, including mental illness, drug and alcohol misuse, domestic violence, and history of violence etc. (see for example Cleaver *et al.*, 1999).

In 23 of the 31 cases (74.2%) where information was available, the social workers had identified that the family was experiencing one or more of these issues. In five cases the social worker had identified a single issue, in nine cases two issues, and in a further nine cases (a third of all cases where there was information) three or more of these issues had been identified.

The most prevalent issue to be recorded was a known history of violence; noted in 37.9 per cent (n=11) of cases where information was available. In some 30 per cent of cases social workers had recorded that a parent or carer was experiencing mental illness (n=9), alcohol or drug misuse (n=9), and a similar proportion were shown to have experienced childhood abuse (n=8).

In seven cases (24.1%) the social worker had noted that the parent had a learning disability (see Table 8.13, Appendix II).

FAMILY AND ENVIRONMENTAL FACTORS WHICH MAY IMPACT ON THE CHILD AND PARENTING CAPACITY

(Information available in 30 cases)

In 25 of the 30 cases (83.3%) social workers had identified aspects of the child's family and environment that impacted on the child and their parents' capacity to respond appropriately to their child's needs. The overwhelming importance of this domain on children's wellbeing and parenting capacity, already highlighted in Chapters 6 and 7, is once again highlighted by the findings.

The severity of the cases undergoing a core assessment

Assessing the severity of cases from the information contained in the Core Assessment record proved difficult. Although there were many examples of excellent recording practice, the quality of recording for core assessments was very variable unlike the consistent and systematic recording found for initial assessments mentioned earlier in this chapter. As a result, a composite of all the data available has been used to assess the severity of cases where a core assessment was carried out. This pragmatic approach provided information on 41 cases. Information was not available in the remaining 27 cases.

In these 41 cases social workers had identified severe needs (that is difficulties in three or more dimensions in all three domains) in 25 (61%) cases. In a further nine cases social workers had identified needs in three or more dimensions in two domains (22%). This suggests that social workers were generally carrying out core assessments on complex cases where there was evidence of considerable unmet need.

Summary points

- The information suggests that in approximately a third of cases the core assessment was completed within the required time.
- Social workers used a number of sources, other than the family, to gather information for the core assessment.
- In the majority of cases social workers consulted professionals working in agencies other than social services when carrying out a core assessment. Most frequently consulted were the police and health visitors.

- Social workers used scales and questionnaires to gather additional information in only five cases.
- A specialist assessment had been commissioned in seven cases.
- Child protection was the reason for over three-quarters (78.6%) of core assessments.
- Three-quarters of multiple-problem cases progressed to a core assessment.
- Core assessments tend to be used for cases involving younger rather than older children.
- Where information is available, the Core Assessment records suggest high levels of need. In 61 per cent of cases severe needs were identified in all three domains.
- In most (70.6%) cases social workers recorded that parents/carers were experiencing difficulties such as mental illness, domestic violence, drugs and alcohol problems.

Chapter summary

Sixty-eight Core Assessment records were included in the audit, accounting for just 3 per cent of all referrals. The low rate reflected:

- the continued use of existing assessment and recording systems for disabled children and child protection cases
- social workers recording detailed assessments on Initial Assessment records.

There was considerable inconsistency between the action recorded on the Initial Assessment record and the documentation found on the case-file. The inconsistencies were the result of a number of issues and in some cases reflected good practice – for example, when cases were reassigned because of decisions taken at strategy discussions or when new information on an open case came to the attention of social services. The source of the referral was also relevant. Professionals who continued to have contact with families were associated with greater consistency. In contrast, some inconsistencies resulted from poor recording, and a failure to follow Government guidance. The case-files revealed 68 initial assessments progressed to a core assessment. However, in only 31 cases had this been the recommended outcome of the initial assessment.

Referrals most likely to progress to a core assessment involved child protection concerns or parental alcohol or drug use, and referrals from other social services departments. Referrals least likely to progress to a core assessment involved parental mental illness, financial or housing problems, and referrals made by the non-professionals. Of the 61 cases categorised at the initial assessment stage as multiple-problem cases 46 progressed to a core assessment.

Social work recording of the core assessment was very variable. Basic information, such as the reason for the assessment and the identity of the professionals involved in the process, was recorded in over 80 per cent of cases. This level of recording was not sustained. In approximately half the cases social workers recorded information about the child's developmental needs, parenting capacity, and family and environmental factors. However, in only a third of cases was a plan found on the record, and in only five cases a review date noted. Recording data on the key indicators for national data collection was patchy and not routinely done. Parallel recording systems for child protection cases (the reason for most core assessments) explained much of this arbitrary recording practice.

Approximately a third of core assessments were completed on time. However, the paucity of information renders this finding unreliable.

During both the initial and core assessments social workers routinely involved other agencies. For example, in most cases at least one other agency was involved in the core assessment, and in 70.6 per cent of cases social workers involved two or more agencies. Professionals from the police and health visitors were most frequently consulted.

The scales and questionnaires were rarely used by social workers carrying out core assessments. Comments from social workers and managers (explored in Chapter 4) suggest this was because practitioners were unsure of both their value and their own ability to apply them and interpret the findings. A specialist assessment was commissioned in seven (10.3%) cases.

The audit of the Core Assessment records suggests parental involvement was poor (contradicting the experience of the families who were involved in the interview study, discussed in Chapter 3). The audit showed that social workers had recorded the views of family members about their situation in only a fifth of cases. In less than 10 per cent of cases was there evidence on the record of the parents' views of the assessment process, or a signature of a family member. These findings suggest parental involvement in the core assessment process is not yet routine practice.

In the majority of cases (78.6%) social workers carried out core assessments because there were child protection concerns. Where information was available, the social workers recorded high levels of need. In 61 per cent of cases children were found to have unmet needs in four or more developmental dimensions. In 80.6 per cent of cases parents were experiencing personal problems such as domestic violence, mental illness, or drug or alcohol use, or had a known history of violence. In practically every case (83%) social workers recorded factors within the family and environment that were likely to impact negatively on the child.

In practically two-thirds of cases (61%) severe needs had been identified in each of the three domains of children's developmental needs, parenting capacity, and family and environmental factors.

Chapter 9

The Cost of Undertaking Core Assessments

Pamela Meadows

Introduction

One of the key tasks of this research was the estimation of the cost of undertaking core assessments. At this stage we are not in a position to estimate the outcomes achieved as a result of this investment of time and resources, since any service needs identified by the assessments would only just have been put into place, and would generally not be expected to have had time to make an impact on the lives of the children and young people whose needs were being assessed. The information about costs is therefore a necessary, but insufficient, step in the process of examining the cost-effectiveness of the process.

Methodology

We asked all participating authorities for detailed information about the time taken by social workers in undertaking the various elements of the assessment, and also about the time they spent in consultation with colleagues and other professionals about the child or young person concerned. The time-sheet identified the age group of the child (0–2, 3–4, 5–9, 10–14 and 15 plus) and had columns for the other professions or organisations most likely to be consulted by social workers. The identified categories were: GPs, health visitors, other health professionals, police, housing and the child or young person's school. There was also a residual category for other consultations which might include the local education authority, a nursery or childminder or a neighbour.

In the event, four councils (one London borough, a large city in northern England, a county council in northern England and another in the south) were able to provide us with completed time-sheets. Although the number of authorities is small, they do cover a range of circumstances and conditions. We are particularly grateful to the social workers who took the time and trouble to complete our forms with the relevant information, and to the team leaders who persuaded them to do so. A copy of our time-sheet is attached at Appendix III.

We were disappointed not to have received information from any other of our participating authorities. In some cases our audit revealed that this was because few core assessments were actually completed during the period of our study. In others, core assessments were completed, but at a time of heavy workloads and the need to learn how to operate a new system, managers were reluctant to ask social workers to undertake an additional, and non-essential task. We were, however, anxious to have further information about how representative the responses we received were. In particular, we were concerned whether the cases for which we had time information might have been those that were more straightforward or atypical in other ways.

We therefore contacted all participating councils from whom we had not received any time-sheets and told them about the average level of time taken to complete the assessments by the social workers who had responded up to the time we wrote. We specifically asked whether this finding was within the typical range of experience in other councils, given that we had heard anecdotes about how time-consuming the whole process was. Thus, although we only have quantified information from four councils, this was supplemented by qualitative information from a larger number. The additional councils had also taken part in other elements of the research, and therefore had a similar experience of implementing the Assessment Framework to that in the four councils for which we had time-sheets. This verification of our estimates via a consultation process allows us to have more confidence in our findings than we might otherwise have done with such a relatively small sample base. On the basis of the quantified and the qualitative information, we have been able to build up a picture of the assessment process, and of the factors which appear to influence the amount of time each assessment requires, and we have been able to identify useful indicators for the future.

Table 9.1 Average time taken by social workers in completing a core assessment (time in hours)

Activity	Average time	Minimum time	Maximum time
Consulting school	1:26	0:00 (2)	7:00
Consulting GP	0:20	0:00 (6)	2:00
Consulting health visitor	0:59	0:00 (9)	5:30
Consulting other health professional	1:13	0:00 (5)	4:15
Consulting police	0:39	0:00 (8)	4:15
Consulting housing	0:19	0:00 (13)	3:00
Other consultation	0:54	0:00 (11)	5:20
Discussion with supervisor	1:20	0:00 (2)	5:30
Discussion with colleague	0:52	0:00 (8)	4:30
Discussion with child or young person	2:05	0:00 (2)	6:00
Discussion with parent	5:58	2:30	12:45
Consulting files	1:49	0:20	6:00
Undertaking assessment	3:50	1:30	10:00
Completing assessment forms	4:26	1:15	8:00

Note: Where the minimum time is zero the number of cases with zero values is in brackets.

Social workers' own time

We received time-sheets from 24 social workers from our four councils. Of these, 17 also identified the time involved in consulting colleagues and other professionals. The remaining seven only provided information about the social worker's own time. We also received a number of additional time-sheets that related to uncompleted assessments. While these provided some useful information, they are not included in our analysis, since we do not know how much time the uncompleted elements would involve.

The average time taken to complete a core assessment by all the social workers who responded was 21¾ hours. The median amount of time (that is the amount of time taken in the core assessment where half took more time and half took less) is very similar at 21¼. This suggests that the average is not being distorted by exceptionally high or low readings.

The time taken to carry out a core assessment forms the initial stages of social services' work with children in need. The findings from a wider study on costs undertaken by the Department of Health (Department of Health National Statistics, 2002) suggest the average time taken to carry out a core assessment is consistent with the average time social services staff or centre workers spend with children in need living with their families or independently. An average of 2.9 hours per week (rounding up to 20.3 hours over 35 working days – the time allocated to undertake a core assessment) of social service staff or centre time is spent working with children in need living with their families or independently (Department of Health National Statistics, 2002).

The longest time taken by a social worker to complete an assessment was 45 hours. The social worker concerned attached a note to the effect that this assessment involved a child protection case and that they took considerably longer than the norm. The shortest time taken by a social worker to complete an individual assessment was six hours. However, this estimate illustrates the issue of economies of scale, since the social worker concerned produced assessments for four children in the same family in a total of 24 hours. The average time per child was therefore six hours, but the whole process took much the same amount of time as a typical single case. If several children in the same family are being assessed at the same time, it is likely that interviews with parents and discussions with key professionals such as GPs may take a little longer than they would with only a single child involved. However, in the case of four children they would not take four times as long.

If we take only the 17 estimates produced by the social workers who provided the fuller details of the distribution of the time involved in the assessment process, the average time taken to complete an assessment is 26¼ hours, with a median of 25 hours, and a minimum of just over 15 hours. If we bear in mind that there is down-time involved in travelling, missed appointments, team meetings and other activities, our data suggests that each assessment involves almost a full working week for a social worker. We need, however, to recall that this takes place over a longer period of elapsed time: typically several weeks. The Assessment Framework requires social workers to complete core assessments in a maximum of 35 working days.

The range of time involved that we have found in our study is quite large: from either six or 15 to 45 hours. However, in reality most cases are clustered around the average. Out of the 17 cases for which we have full information, only four took under 20 hours and only four more than 30. The seven cases for which we had only partial information all took under 18 hours, but, as mentioned earlier, they do include a group of four siblings. Of the 17 cases for which we have the ages of the children, more than half were aged between 5 and 9. One note of caution here is that if we look at the average time taken by age group we find that this was the group whose assessments were completed by social workers in the shortest times (just over 24 hours). The longest assessments were those involving babies under the age of two. These took 33 hours on average. However, we need to exercise caution about drawing conclusions about variation by age, as most age groups had only two cases.

Table 9.2 Average time taken by social workers for core assessments involving children in different age groups

Age group	Number of cases	Time taken by social worker (in hours)
0–2	2	33:40
2–4	2	30:42
5–9	11	24:08
10–14	2	26:20

When we consulted the councils which had not provided time-sheet information about whether or not our findings were in line with their experience, several responded that the estimates looked in line with their own experience. Three responded that they or their social workers felt our estimates were a little low, but not far out of line with their experience. As some of the later returns involved more time, on average, than the earlier ones, their inclusion increased the average time taken, and therefore brought our overall estimate more closely in line with the qualitative information we received during this part of the exercise.

We did not receive any responses that suggested that our estimates were a considerable understatement of the time taken. (We did receive two interesting suggestions that we should try and correlate the time taken and the quality of the assessment derived from our audit of cases, but we were unable to do this because the time-sheet data were anonymised.) Our participating councils represent a wide range of conditions, both geographically and in terms of type of council. We, therefore, believe that the absence of any feedback suggesting that our estimates are markedly different from experience elsewhere strongly supports our conclusion that our estimates are in the right general area.

In view of our small sample, and in order to take account of the feedback that our estimates may be a little low, our presentation of costs below provides estimates on four different bases:

- 26¼ hours: the time taken by our cases for which we have full information
- 21¾ hours: the average time taken by all our cases, which reflects a high level of sibling groups
- 31½ hours: this is 20 per cent higher than the base case and allows for the possibility that our estimates are still somewhat below the true amount of time taken
- 36 hours: this reflects the probable amount of time for an individual complex case. This is the average for our five most complex cases.

Key elements of the social workers' own time

There was very little variation in the amount of time that social workers took to complete the Core Assessment records setting out their assessments. The average was 4½ hours, and most took between four and five hours. Only three took more than five hours and only two took less than four hours.

The actual assessment process (the reviewing and absorbing of the information collected, the thinking about it and coming to the decisions arising from it) took around 3¾ hours on average. There was more variation here: several cases took two hours or less, while one complex case took ten hours.

Around six hours was spent with parents. In only one case did this amount to less than 3½ hours and in only one case was the total more than twelve hours. This element of the process seems, therefore, to be fairly consistent across the social workers in our four councils.

A typical assessment involves spending two hours with the child or young person. Two of our 15 cases did not spend any time with the child or young person. Most social workers spent between 1½and three hours with the child or young person, although in one case (a preschool child) this involved six hours and in another (where the child was aged between five and nine) the social worker spent five hours with the child.

The average amount of time social workers spent consulting files was 1¾ hours, but there was considerable variation here. Some of this variation will be accounted for by differences in previous contact between the child or family and the council. If the child has not previously been in contact with the council, there will not be a file to consult. In half the cases looking at files involved an hour or less, whereas for most of the remainder around four hours would be typical, with a maximum of six hours.

Time spent in discussion and consultation with colleagues and other professionals

Where a social worker spends time consulting or discussing a case with another professional, there is a double cost involved in the assessment: the cost of the social worker's own time, and the cost of the time of the other party to the conversation, whether in person or on the telephone. Our costs include estimates for the cost of the time of these other professionals, but these estimates will be minima, since they are based only on the time spent interacting with the lead social worker, and do not include any time they might take in consulting records, writing reports, talking to each other or engaging directly with the family or young person. Thus, as with the social worker's own time, the time of other professionals entering into the assessment process will tend to be understated by the approach we have used.

In all cases where the children were of school age the social worker consulted the child's or young person's school. The two cases where there was no school consultation involved infants under the age of two. In all but three cases there was consultation either with the child or young person's GP or with a health visitor. Occasionally there was consultation with both. GP consultations were typically short (5–10 minutes) although two lasted an hour and one two hours. Health visitor consultations were generally longer. An hour was common, and three cases involved more than three hours in total. In 12 of our 17 cases there was a consultation with another health professional. We did not ask for details of who this consultation was with, but we would expect those involved to include speech and language therapists, paediatricians and child and adolescent mental health professionals. The consultation lasted over an hour on average.

In around half the cases for which we had information, there was consultation with the police. This could, of course, be because the social worker was concerned about potential danger to a child from an adult with whom he or she had contact (as would be likely in the case of infants) or it could have related to offending behaviour of the individual child. Many of these police consultations were quite short (20 minutes would be typical) but a small number took several hours.

Social workers had other consultations in around a third of the cases for which we had information. Where these took place they were generally lengthy: 2½ to 5½ hours is the main range, although a few were shorter than this.

Estimation of costs

Although social workers have always been undertaking assessments of children's needs (if only implicitly when they decide to provide them with a particular service), the Assessment Framework introduced a common process to be applied in all cases. We do not have any details of the costs of undertaking assessments under previous arrangements. It would have been helpful to have had this as a means of identifying any *additional* costs involved in using the Assessment Framework. However, since it is not possible to do this retrospectively, our estimates essentially form a baseline.

Our estimation of costs are drawn from national data on the unit costs of the time of different professional groups. Table 9.3 sets out the hourly costs which have been used, and the notes to the table set out the sources from which those costs have been derived. The information for social services and health professionals is drawn from *Unit Costs of Health and Social Care 2001* by Ann Netten and colleagues at the Personal Social Services Research Unit at the University of Kent (Netten, Rees and Harrison, 2001). This is an annual volume, supported by the Department of Health, which draws together information compiled from both administrative and research sources in a consistent way. The information for teachers is drawn from the

PriceWaterhouseCoopers study of teacher workloads undertaken for the Department for Education and Skills. That for police officers is drawn from a study of the application of economic evaluation to policing activity undertaken by the Home Office Research and Planning Unit. For the two remaining categories the costs are based on our own estimates. These are essentially relative to the professional groups for which we do have independent information.

Table 9.3 Unit hourly costs for different professional groups

Professional	Cost per hour (£)	Source of estimate
Social worker	25	Based on an hour of client-related work from Netten, Rees and Harrison (2001)
Supervisor	31	Based on an hour of client-related work for a team leader from Netten, Rees and Harrison (2001)
GP	70	Based on an hour of GMS time excluding support staff costs from Netten, Rees and Harrison (2001)
Health visitor	25	Based on hourly cost from Netten, Rees and Harrison (2001)
Other health professional	24	Hourly cost of a member of a child psychology team from Netten, Rees and Harrison (2001)
Police constable	19.25	Derived from Stockdale, Whitehead and Gresham (1999), based on a 7½ hour day and uprated by the increase in police pay between 1998 and 2000
Teacher	15	Cost of a supply teacher from PriceWaterhouseCoopers (2001)
Housing officer	15	own estimate
Other	18	own estimate

Drawing on these estimates of costs, we have calculated the cost of undertaking core assessments, both for social services departments and for all agencies taken together for the seventeen cases for which we have detailed information

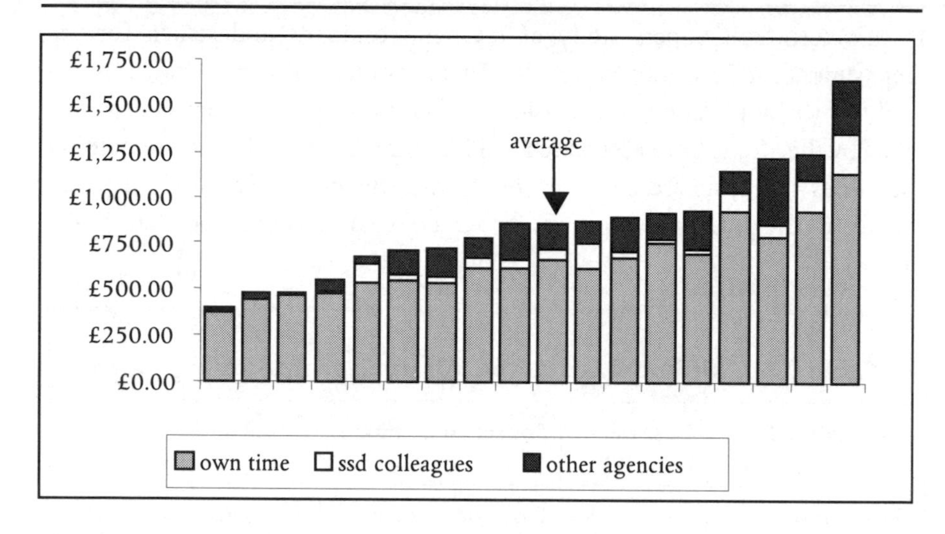

Figure 9.1 Cost of completing core assessments
Note: The figure is based on the 17 cases for which detailed information was available

about the way time was spent. The cheapest assessment cost a total of £407, of which £377 was the cost of the social worker's own time. The most expensive assessment cost £1642 in total, of which £1137 represented the cost of the social worker's own time. The average for the 17 cases was a total of £853: £657 for the social worker's own time, £63 for other colleagues in the social services department and £133 for colleagues in other agencies. The costs allocated to professionals other than the lead social worker represents only the time spent talking or working with the lead worker.

The costs above are estimated on the basis of the average time taken in the 17 cases for which we have detailed information (that is a total of 26¼ hours for the individual social worker). If, however, our seven cases for which we have no details are also included, we have a total of 21¾ hours. If the time taken to consult and liaise with other professionals represents a similar proportion of the total in these assessments as it is in the remaining 17, this would produce an average cost of a core assessment of £707 of which £544 is the social worker's own time. In reality, if 21¾ hours does represent a better estimate of the average time taken to complete a core assessment, this is probably an overestimate of the costs. This is because in the cases for which we have details, those which took the social work practitioner the shortest times tended to have much shorter amounts of time spent in consultation with other professionals (presumably because the cases were more straightforward generally), whereas our estimate assumes that these times are scaled down from the average.

If we increase our estimate of the average time taken to complete a core assessment from 26¼ hours to 28 hours, to take account of the fact that the social services departments which we consulted suggested that our results were close to their experience, but perhaps a little low, the average cost of an assessment increases to £910, of which £700 is the cost of the social worker's own time. If 28 hours is a truer average than our own estimate, our estimate based on scaling up the costs to other agencies in proportion will tend to understate their costs. As Figure 9.1 indicates, the cases that involved the highest costs in terms of social worker time also had markedly higher costs in terms of other agencies' time. In other words, more complex cases involve a disproportionately rather than a proportionately larger involvement by other agencies. However, we have used a simple scaling-up process because our sample size is really too small to be able to produce a more reliable alternative estimate of the time input of other agencies for cases that take longer.

As a second sensitivity test we assume that our estimate is 20 per cent too low. This produces an overall average assessment cost of £1025, of which £788 is the social worker's own time. Our final estimate for a core assessment in a complex case is based on the average costs derived from the five longest assessments reported in our time-sheets. Unlike the other estimates in the table, these figures are not based on scaling up the averages from the whole sample, but reflect only these five cases. The five cases are drawn from three of our four councils. It is apparent that the amount of time involved for colleagues and other agencies is significantly greater for these cases than it is for the average case. The cost of the social worker's own time is around a third higher than the base case at £900, but the cost of the time of supervisors and colleagues in the social services department is nearly doubled at £117. The cost of the time of other agencies is increased by two-thirds to £221. The effect of varying the assumptions is summarised in Table 9.4.

Overall, the social worker's own time typically accounts for more than three-quarters of the cost of completing an assessment, while the cost to other agencies is around 15 per cent of the total. However, we need to remember that this represents the minimum cost to other agencies, as it only includes the time spent with the lead social worker. Any time spent by the other agencies pursuing their own enquiries to feed into the social worker's assessment is not included.

Table 9.4 Total cost of completing core assessments under different assumptions

	Cost of social worker's own time (£)	Cost of ssd colleagues' time (£)	Cost of other agencies' time (£)	Total cost (£)
Based on cases with full details (26¼ hours)	657	63	133	853
Based on cases with partial information (21¾ hours)	544	53	101	698
Based on cases with full details plus 20% (31½ hours)	788	76	161	1025
Based on 5 most complex cases (36 hours)	900	117	221	1238

Conclusion

Our research suggests that an average core assessment costs around £900, of which around £140 is the cost to other agencies and around £760 is the cost to the social services department. This sum is consistent with the findings from the Department of Health's Child in Need survey. This shows the average weekly cost to social services departments for children supported in their families or living independently is £85 (this rounds up to £595 for 35 working days – the time in which social workers undertake a core assessment). Moreover, the cost of a core assessment is small compared with the cost of looking after a child or young person in residential accommodation (£2205 per week), or placing them with foster parents (£644 per week) (Netten, Rees and Harrison, 2001). If the care plan and subsequent service delivery produced as a result of the core assessment is more appropriate than would otherwise have been the case, there may be both improved outcomes for children, and savings from the provision of inappropriate or ineffective services. Although the estimation of the benefits, and therefore a full cost-effectiveness analysis, was outside the timescale of this project, these cost estimates provide information against which the benefits of intervention can be assessed.

Chapter 10

Conclusions and Implications for Policy and Practice

Background

The current focus of central government policy towards children and families is to offer assistance and resources at an early stage in order to prevent the development of more serious long-term problems. However, the challenge to service providers, and particularly to social workers, is to identify accurately and sensitively those families who may benefit from social work services as one aspect of that particular help. Social services assessments of children in need living with their families have tended to focus primarily on issues of abuse and neglect and the developmental needs of children have not always been recognised. Research and inspection reports (Sinclair *et al.*, 1995; Social Services Inspectorate, 1997b) highlighted the variability of social work assessments of children in need:

- practice differed within teams in social service departments and between departments
- some assessments were unfocused
- assessments were not always used to determine the content of the plan for the child.

The Assessment Framework (Department of Health *et al.*, 2000a) was developed in response to these findings to ensure that assessments of children in need focused on children's developmental needs and parental capacities within the wider family and environment. Assessments were to be undertaken in collaboration with the relevant agencies and involve children (wherever possible) and parents/carers, so that the overall assessment included the contribution of them all. This research examines the impact of the Assessment Framework on assessments of children in need and their families.

Context/climate within which the Assessment Framework was implemented

The Assessment Framework was published at a time of great change for Councils with Social Services Responsibilities. They were already experiencing a number of challenges. For example, the Human Rights Act 1998 and the Data Protection Act 1998 had been introduced, and although the Assessment Framework took account of the implications of this new legislation, managers and practitioners needed to familiarise themselves with it. In addition, councils were still coming to terms with the implementations of *Modernising Social Services* (Department of Health, 1998c). This set out a new approach to the way in which councils' social services functions would be assessed, with a focus on performance against nationally set targets. In addition, practitioners continued to experience considerable change as councils re-organised or merged social services departments with other council departments such as Education, and/or restructured children and families services. Furthermore, the Assessment Framework came at a time when all councils, but particularly those in London and the South-east, were experiencing considerable difficulties with the recruitment and retention of social work staff. As a result many councils were implementing the Assessment Framework while experiencing high levels of staff vacancies and having to employ large numbers of locum staff.

The Assessment Framework requires practitioners to record detailed information about individual children and their family in a systematic way. The ease with which this could be achieved depended on the degree to which Councils with Social Services Responsibilities had computerised their recording systems and whether existing systems had the capacity to be adapted to meet the requirements of the Assessment Framework. This factor proved to be extremely variable. While a few councils provided a computer for every practitioner, used software that allowed information to be collected and aggregated, and employed staff trained in IT skills, most were struggling with few computers, inadequate software, and staff who were not conversant with entering their information on to a computer.

Despite all these organisational barriers, the conceptual framework set out in the *Framework for the Assessment of Children in Need and their Families*

(Department of Health *et al.*, 2000a) was welcomed by social services and their partner agencies, and staff and their managers made a commitment to its successful implementation.

The scale of change required

Implementation required every one of the 24 councils involved in the study to change some aspect of their working practices. Some councils had to bring about more fundamental change than others. A key message from the findings was that there were two critical sets of factors that determined the extent and ease with which councils would implement the Assessment Framework. First, the nature of their existing structures, skills, and resources, and second, the methods used to introduce it. An exploration of these two aspects suggests that some factors were more relevant than others in enabling councils to introduce the new system. In terms of their existing structures the factors found to have particular impact on a council's ability to implement the Assessment Framework effectively were:

- effective collaborative arrangements between social services and other agencies at both strategic and practice levels
- existing good levels of theoretical and technical knowledge of staff and managers, underpinned by written guidance on assessment, information for families, and an approach to assessment that was consistent with the Assessment Framework.

The key factors that were found to be important in relation to the process of implementation were:

- the involvement of other agencies at a strategic level in the introductory process. For example, joint working relationships with other agencies that resulted in the development of joint initiatives
- training that provided staff with the space and time to internalise the required changes
- a good match between the format of the assessment record (electronic or paper) introduced by the social services department, and the availability of computers, suitable software, and the IT skills of practitioners.

Research findings

The involvement of children and families

Traditionally, social work assessments and those by other professionals have been imposed on children and families rather than carried out in a collaborative manner with families. The Assessment Framework is based on the principle of working together with children and families in order to identify both the strengths within the child, family and their community which can be built upon, as well as the difficulties and problems for which outside assistance is required.

Findings from the audit

If the findings from the audit were only considered, it would seem that little has yet changed. For example, in only a third of cases did the social worker give the family a copy of the Initial Assessment record. Furthermore, parents' and young people's views about their needs and concerns were noted in only a fifth of Core Assessment records, and their signature found on 10 per cent of those records.

Findings from the questionnaires and interviews with social work managers and practitioners

However, the findings from the questionnaires and interviews with social workers and managers reflect a rather different picture. They suggest that the implementation of the Assessment Framework and the use of the assessment records have increased the involvement of children and families in the assessment process. Professionals accounted for the increased involvement by citing the following changes in their practice:

- a more transparent and accountable relationship with the child and family
- a more focused approach to assessment
- increased consultation with the child and family
- recording the views of the child and family members
- discussing issues where parents and professionals disagree.

Social workers thought that the increased involvement of families in the assessment process had improved the quality of their assessments.

Approximately a third of social work practitioners, however, reported that the Core Assessment records were an obstacle to the involvement of families in the assessment process. The reasons cited showed considerable misunderstanding over the purpose of the assessment records. These social workers viewed the assessment records as the assessment itself, seeing the format as a questionnaire to record parents' answers to specific questions. This was contrary to the guidance accompanying the assessment records (Department of Health, 2000a) and the information given during the familiarisation sessions held by the research team. Practitioners' confusion about the purpose of the records may reflect the level of training provided by councils at the point of implementation. For example, in a third of councils training was still in the planning stages at the point of implementation. In a further third the provision of training was mainly through seminars. Although this approach is effective in providing practitioners with information, it does not help practitioners to understand the purpose of the records and how to use them in individual cases.

Findings from the interviews with parents and carers

The professionals' perception of increased family involvement was substantiated by parents' accounts of the assessment process. The sample of families included 30 referred because of suspected child abuse. A comparison of their views of the assessment process with those of families involved in suspected child abuse enquiries undertaken prior to the refocusing of children's services (Cleaver and Freeman, 1995), shows profound changes. Instead of feeling disempowered, alienated and betrayed, parents reported high levels of consultation, involvement and inclusion in all stages of the referral, assessment and planning process. For example, in approximately three-quarters of cases in the interview sample, parents reported that social workers had explained why the assessment was being carried out, how it would be done, what it would entail. An equal proportion of parents reported satisfaction over their involvement in the decision-making and planning processes.

However, parents were less certain about the efficacy of the plan. Parental satisfaction with the plan was related to:

- their having a shared perspective with social workers on the difficulties the family was experiencing
- involvement in the choice and development of the plan
- agreement with and commitment to the plan
- the plan being carried out.

Findings from the interviews with young people

The interviews with young people suggest that social work practice continues to exclude children from fully participating in decisions that are likely to affect them (Department of Health, 1994; Grimshaw and Sinclair, 1997; Sinclair *et al.*, 1995). There was little evidence of informing or consulting children and young people during the assessment and planning processes. When asked how things could be improved, young people reiterated the issues reported in much previous research (see, for example, Cleaver, 2000; Department of Health, 2001; Thoburn *et al.*, 1995). They wanted professionals to:

- take time to explain to them what is happening and why
- listen to and respect their views and experiences
- believe what they said
- talk to the people they think are important
- provide them with something to remind them of what was decided.

Ascertaining the wishes and feelings of children and young people is not always an easy task for social workers, partly because a past history of abuse and neglect may have left many children with a deep distrust of adults. In addition, the increased emphasis on case management rather than on direct work with children and families has left some social workers with little experience and even less confidence in their ability to communicate effectively and carry out direct work with children and young people (Jones, in press; Marsh and Peel, 1999).

Training and continuing professional development

The implementation of the Assessment Framework with its emphasis on direct work with children and families in order to understand the inter-relationship of the three domains of child development, parenting capacity, and family and environmental factors, highlighted deficits in the content of current social work education. Carrying out quality assessments depends, among other things, on a sound knowledge of child development and an understanding of the impact of parenting attributes and environmental factors on the children's wellbeing. The findings from the study showed that many qualifying and post qualifying social work courses had not covered these key areas of knowledge and skill adequately.

The training provided by most councils on the Assessment Framework was done through short-course, one-off training courses or through the use of seminars. The research found that these approaches to training were not able to address the gaps identified in practitioners' knowledge. A significant proportion of social workers who responded to the questionnaires expressed considerable anxiety about their ability to carry out assessments; particularly how to analyse information gathered during the assessment, how to work collaboratively with professionals from other agencies, and how to obtain parental consent to assess their child and family. Social workers also expressed concerns about their knowledge of recent legislation, such as the Human Rights Act, 1998 and the Data Prevention Act, 1998 which was being implemented at the same time as the Assessment Framework.

These findings have much wider implications for social services than the implementation of the Assessment Framework. They lie at the core of professional practice with children and families. Urgent measures are required to address these issues through qualifying training, continuing professional development, supervision and management.

Setting aside the issue of the quality of social work training, the delivery of one-off courses to introduce practitioners to a new assessment system was not the most effective way to achieve and maintain a trained and confident staff group. Difficulties arose because such an approach was not sufficiently flexible to address the following aspects:

- Understanding a new approach to assessment takes time and new issues come to light as the process becomes more established, requiring iterative training processes.
- Staffing difficulties, experienced by three-quarters of the councils, meant that when teams were not fully staffed it was not always possible for managers to release practitioners for two days.
- Staffing difficulties resulted in practitioners feeling under pressure because they were managing unallocated cases in addition to their own workload. When this happened they were less able to give the training they attended their full attention.
- Staffing difficulties also meant that some councils depended heavily on locum practitioners who did not remain in the council's employ for long.

The research showed that social services staff who were not part of community-based fieldwork teams working with children and families, such as key staff in hospitals, were often excluded from the introductory training on the Assessment Framework. The consequence of this was that they were unable to contribute effectively to the process of assessment, and felt disadvantaged and alienated from this new development.

A few councils took a more flexible approach to training – for example, through the use of mentors, action learning sets and practice workshops. This type of training was able to be accommodated more easily to the needs of the agency and those of practitioners because it involved practitioners in an iterative, developmental process that reinforced what had been learnt and allowed new issues to be addressed as they arose.

The impact on social work practice

The implementation of the Assessment Framework and the introduction of the assessment records were reported as increasing the workloads of both social work managers and practitioners. The findings suggest that the additional work for managers was related to implementing a new system rather than anything inherent in the Assessment Framework itself. Part of the increase in practitioners' workloads was related to bringing social work practice into line with the Assessment Framework. For example, with the introduction of the Assessment Framework, practitioners were required to see the child when undertaking an initial assessment, requiring more time than had previously been allocated as this had not been their usual practice. Furthermore, more time was also now required to (a) seek parental agreement before contacting professionals in other agencies, and (b) work collaboratively with children/young people and their parents. These requirements under the Human Rights Act, 1998, and the Data Protection Act, 1998 were being introduced at the same time as the Assessment Framework and had been incorporated into the Assessment Framework Guidance (Department of Health *et al.*, 2000a).

The implementation of the Assessment Framework and the introduction of the assessment records improved the quality of assessments; two-thirds of managers and over half the practitioners reported an improvement. Social workers who were unqualified or qualified for less than three years were more likely to report that the implementation of the Assessment Framework and the introduction of the assessment records had improved the quality of their assessments. This was true also for those staff who found the training relevant to their practice. Managers found that the use of the assessment records had improved the quality of social workers' record-keeping. These improvements in recording resulted in managers having greater understanding of individual cases, and increased confidence in their decision-making and planning for children in need.

Inter-agency collaboration

A key principle of the Assessment Framework is that inter-agency collaboration provides a better understanding of children's needs and circumstances, and ensures an effective service response. The findings indicate that during the early stages of implementing the Assessment Framework the degree of inter-agency collaboration increased to some extent. Approximately a third of professional staff from agencies other than social services and a similar proportion of social work practitioners reported that collaboration over assessments had increased since the implementation of the Assessment Framework.

When collaboration was thought to have increased this was attributed to a number of factors including:

- the structured way information was recorded
- a more holistic understanding of the child's needs and circumstances
- greater clarity over the roles and responsibility of agencies
- a greater willingness to share information.

Factors that hampered collaborative work included:

- a lack of agreement over the definition of children in need
- poor social work practice and particularly the failure of social workers to communicate with other professionals
- unavailability of resources identified as necessary by the assessment
- increased paperwork through having to record the assessment in a structured and systematic way (without the benefit of an adequate electronic recording system)
- general difficulties related to introducing a new system.

Once again the importance of relevant training was highlighted. When joint training between professionals from social services and staff from other relevant agencies had taken place, this was valued as was training that addressed issues which traditionally impeded collaborative work.

The findings from the questionnaires returned by professional staff from agencies other than social services suggested that there was considerable room for improvement in collaborative work. However, their views did not match the findings from the audit which showed that social workers routinely consulted professionals from one or two other agencies when undertaking a core assessment.

Discrepancies between the findings gained from interviews and questionnaires and those gathered from the audit applied to two issues: parental involvement in the assessment process, and inter-agency collaboration. The direction of the discrepancy differed, however. In relation to parental involvement, parents reported more positive views than the findings from the audit. In contrast, in relation to inter-agency collaboration, professionals held more negative views than the audit findings. These discrepancies would benefit from further exploration.

Scales and questionnaires

An innovative feature of the Assessment Framework was the publication of a set of scales and questionnaires to enrich social workers' repertoire of skills in assessing children and their families, and produce an evidence base for their judgements and decision-making (Department of Health, Cox and Bentovim, 2000b). These were piloted in a number of child care situations and modified to suit children and families and social work practitioners, and a training pack issued to support their use was developed (Cox and Walker, 2000).

At the time the audit was carried out few practitioners had received training on the purpose and use of scales and questionnaires, and the findings showed that at this early stage of implementation, they rarely used them. The comments from practitioners (explored in Chapter 4) suggest they were unsure of their value and of their own ability to apply them and interpret the findings.

Recording practice

Twenty-four councils participated in the audit. The study included an audit of 2248 referrals, identified sequentially from a given date. Over a third (n=866, 38.5%) progressed to an initial assessment, and 3 per cent (n=68) to a core assessment. Discussions with managers in the councils suggest two factors may have contributed to the low proportion of Core Assessment records found on the case-files. First, practitioners continued to use existing assessment procedures and recording formats for disabled children and child protection cases. Second, the Assessment Framework and the assessment records had not fully bedded in, and rather than undertake a core assessment practitioners were gathering very detailed information about children's development and circumstances but recording this on Initial Assessment records.

The quality of recording on both the referral form and the Initial Assessment record, in relation to administrative and case related information, was generally of a high standard. Social workers did not, however, routinely record information about two important aspects of children's lives: the child's religion (noted in only 29% of cases), and the identity of relatives not living in the child's household (noted in only 25% of cases). This suggests that social workers do not always regard this information as relevant when assessing children in need. Religion is, however, often an essential element of children and young people's sense of identity. Dutt and Phillips (2000) have written about this in relation to children in black and minority ethnic communities. Exploring and recording the identity of relatives not living in the child's household can be an essential way of identifying who is significant in a child's life. It can be also key to ensuring the safety of children, which may be of particular importance in cases of sexual abuse (Cleaver and Freeman, 1996).

The quality of social work recording on the 68 Core Assessments records was not of the same high standard found at the referral and initial assessment stage. Basic information, such as the reason for the assessment and the identity of the professionals involved in the process, was routinely recorded. In approximately half the cases, however, information about the child's developmental needs, parenting capacity and family and environmental factors was missing. Two-thirds of Core Assessment records contained no plan. A review date was found on only 7 per cent of the Core Assessment records. Finally, these poor standards of recording would have hampered the aggregation of data held by social services when completing their government statistical returns.

Parallel recording systems for child protection cases (the reason for most core assessments) explained much of the idiosyncratic recording practice found on the Core Assessment record. For example, when councils continued to operate a separate system, with different recording forms, for child protection cases, information was spread between the two sets of records. Information about the reason for the core assessment and the child's needs and circumstances may have been recorded on the Core Assessment record but the plan and review date were recorded on separate documentation. This meant that the relevant information about the case was not found during the audit and was not available in one place on a single record.

The research found that a further barrier to carrying out core assessments was the lack of computers, relevant software or skilled staff, to enable information gathered during an assessment to be recorded electronically. In addition, practitioners were reluctant to initiate core assessments in councils where Core Assessment records were paper-based, because it resulted in rewriting information recorded elsewhere, such as on the Initial Assessment record or separate child protection documentation. To introduce a comprehensive recording system successfully depends on agencies having sufficient up-to-date computers, with relevant software to allow information to transfer from one document to another, and a workforce with the confidence and skills to use it.

Inconsistency between decisions to carry out a particular assessment and the corresponding documentation found on the case-file

In only three-quarters of cases, where the referral showed that an initial assessment was to be undertaken, was an Initial Assessment record found on the case-file. Similarly, in less than half the cases where a decision to undertake a core assessment had been recorded on an Initial Assessment record, was a Core Assessment record actually found on the case-file. Conversely, 18.4 per cent of Initial Assessment records and 54.4 per cent of Core Assessment records were found on cases where this had not been the decision recorded on the referral or the Initial Assessment record respectively.

The inconsistencies found related to a number of issues:

- In some cases inconsistency reflected good practice. For example, when a decision was made to undertake a core assessment at a child protection strategy meeting, or because new information came to light on an open case.
- The level of inconsistency was related to the source of the referral. When referrals were from agencies likely to follow up decisions made after referral or initial assessment, such as health and education, consistency was greater than when referrals came from the police or non-professionals.
- Poor recording played a key role. In 41 per cent of referral forms social workers had simply failed to record anything in the further action section and there was no information about whether it was planned for the case to proceed to an initial assessment.
- Inconsistencies also resulted from social workers failing to follow government guidance laid out in *Working Together to Safeguard*

Children (Department of Health *et al.*, 1999). Child protection referrals were not recorded as undergoing an initial assessment, however brief, following a referral but progressed directly to a core assessment.

- In councils that had provided training to staff, the rate of inconsistency was less than half that of councils where training was still in the planning stages (20% compared with 50%).
- Councils with high levels of theoretical and technical knowledge had a rate of inconsistency less than a third of that found for councils with low levels of theoretical knowledge (14% compared to 60%).

The findings about poor practice reinforce the necessity of ongoing case supervision, monitoring and training when introducing any new system which will require significant changes in practice.

Keeping to the required timescales

Approximately two-thirds of referrals and initial assessments were completed on time. Although poor recording resulted in unreliable data on the timing of core assessments, the available data suggest that approximately a third were completed on time. The findings from the costings exercise indicate that carrying out a core assessment on the most complex type of case takes some 36 hours. This suggests that it is not the assessment itself that is impossible to complete within 35 working days, but organisational, staffing, and resource issues which hinder or prevent practitioners from meeting the timescales set out in the Guidance.

The ability to respond to referrals and complete initial assessments on time was associated with the type of council. Shire Counties and Metropolitan Boroughs were most likely to complete referral and initial assessments on time. London Boroughs, which had the highest rates of staff vacancies (between 37% and 49.5%), and Unitary Authorities, which were smaller, were least likely to respond to referrals and complete initial assessments within the timescales required under s7 guidance (Department of Health *et al.*, 2000a).

The research indicates that a number of organisational factors supported practitioners to complete referrals and initial assessments on time. These included:

- good levels of theoretical and technical knowledge (that is written guidance on assessment, information for families and an approach to assessment that is consistent with the Assessment Framework prior to implementation)

- effective inter-agency working at strategic and practice levels prior to implementation
- the development of inter-agency initiatives, such as joint protocols or inter-agency referral and assessment forms.

The profile of cases referred to children's social services

The children

The sample of 2248 referrals included equal proportions of boys and girls. The balance of genders continued for those children for whom initial assessments and core assessments were undertaken.

As might be expected, children under 5 years accounted for the largest proportion of referrals (approximately a third). However, young people aged 15 years and over constituted 14 per cent of the sample. The pattern was similar for those children who went through to initial and core assessments. For example, in the sample of core assessments 41.7 per cent related to children less than 5 years, and 10.4 per cent involved young people 15 years and over.

The source of the referral

Almost a third (29.5%) of all referrals came from non-professionals, that is, young people, parents, relatives, friends and neighbours. Health and the police were the most frequent source of professional referrals, followed by other social services departments and education.

Non-professionals referred more than twice the proportion of children than any individual professional group, in every age group except children less than 5 years. Referrals for this age group were more likely to come from health (29.2%) than from non-professionals (23.3%).

Non-professionals were also the main source of referrals for children from both the black and white communities, but not children from Asian communities. Health referred the largest proportion of Asian children and children of mixed race. This anomaly may reflect the poor health experienced by Pakistani and Bangladeshi communities (Nazroo, 1997) and/or a lack of awareness in Asian communities of what social services are available (Qureshi *et al.*, 2000).

The reason for the referral

Child protection concerns accounted for practically a third (30.3%) of all referrals. The profile of referrals varied considerably between the participating councils. Councils where the proportion of child protection referrals was low, had much higher rates of referrals for domestic violence and other parenting issues. This may reflect the fact that two-thirds of the councils in the study reported that they were restricting services to children with high levels of needs (those in need of protection or accommodation/care). This suggests that the thresholds for accepting referrals operated by different councils may still be influencing how professionals describe their concerns when referring children and families to social services (Department of Health, 1995a).

The reason for the referral was associated with the age and gender of the child. The relationship with the child's age followed an expected pattern. For example, the proportion of child protection referrals decreased as the age group of the children increased, disabled children fell equally between most age bands, and issues around parental control generally featured older children.

The association between the reason for referral and the gender of the child was also understandable, because it mirrored differences within the child population. For example, higher proportions of disabled children who are boys were reflected in the profile of referrals.

Re-referrals

In order that central government can know whether children and families referred to social services get an appropriate service response, councils are required to supply information on the percentage of referrals that are repeat referrals to the same social services department within 12 months (Quality Protects 7.1). Re-referrals accounted for 16.4 per cent of all referrals.

The re-referral group showed both similarities and differences to the total sample of referrals. For example, the reasons for referral in the two groups were similar. The ethnicity of the child did, however, differentiate the two groups. Black and mixed-race children were over-represented in the re-referral group. It is of note that, proportionately, cases involving black and mixed-race children were less likely to progress to a core assessment than children from other ethnic groups. This suggests greater attention should be paid to assessing children from these communities to ensure equality of access to services.

Referrals and requests for services from the non-professionals were less likely to progress either to an initial or a core assessment than cases emanating from professional sources. This suggests that referrals from non-professionals should be accorded more importance and given equal weighting to referrals from professionals. Research indicates that when they are not, children can be placed at risk of significant harm (Cleaver *et al.*, 1998; Gibbons *et al.* 1995).

The overview of child protection studies (Department of Health, 1995a) stressed the importance of taking seriously referrals from non-professionals. It is, therefore, very worrying that seven years on, concerns reported by family members, neighbours and friends are still considered less significant than those from professional agencies.

The outcome of referrals

Decisions about further action to take (if any) were recorded on the referral form. In practically half (46.2%) the cases, the recorded further action was an initial assessment. In 30 per cent of cases, social workers either provided the family with information, or referred them to another agency, or carried out some other action such as accommodating the child. In the latter cases information about the child was held in different recording systems and no Initial Assessment record was completed. Finally, in almost a quarter of cases (23.9%), social workers had recorded that no further action was to be taken.

Cases that progressed to an initial assessment (n=866)

Although the recorded action in practically half the cases was an initial assessment, in only 38.5 per cent of cases were the records of these assessments found on the files. The largest proportion of initial assessments was carried out following child protection referrals. Nonetheless, less than half (46.5%) of all referrals where there were child protection concerns progressed to an initial assessment.

Two factors were associated with cases progressing from referral to initial assessment: the age of the child, and the reason for the referral. Referrals involving children under the age of 15 years and referrals with concerns about parental alcohol/drug use, and parental mental illness were more likely than others to progress to an initial assessment. This raises questions about what is happening when child protection referrals are made to social services, how decisions are being made about the agency's response to such concerns, what level of priority they are being given, and how the decisions of duty staff are being monitored.

Referrals least likely to progress to an initial assessment involved young people aged 15 years or older, police referrals relating to domestic violence, and referrals related to financial or housing problems. The low rates of initial assessments on cases referred for financial and housing problems (environmental factors) suggest the impact of these issues on children's health and wellbeing and on parenting capacity remains underestimated and not yet fully understood (see, for example, Aldgate and Tunstill, 1995; Ghate and Hazel, 2002; Quilgars, 2001).

The Initial Assessment record has sections for social workers to record the findings from their assessment in relation to the three domains of the Assessment Framework: children's developmental needs, parenting capacity, and family and environmental factors. Each domain is subdivided so that information related to individual dimensions can be noted, such as the child's health, education, emotional and behavioural development, and so on.

The audit shows that in cases where an initial assessment was undertaken the information recorded about the child's developmental needs and circumstances showed that this was an entirely appropriate decision. For example, difficulties in relation to family and environmental factors were noted in two-thirds of initial assessments, with issues around family functioning and family history being the most prevalent. In half the cases social workers identified the child as having developmental needs, most frequently in relation to the child's family and social relationships. In a third (33.8%) of cases social workers identified difficulties in parenting capacity with issues in the dimension of 'ensuring the child safety' most commonly recorded. Finally, in approximately three-quarters of cases social workers identified factors within the family known to affect parenting capacity. These included parental mental illness, learning disability, problem drug and alcohol use, a history of violence or child abuse, having been in care during childhood, and domestic violence.

The research team took the view that where the Initial Assessment record showed families were experiencing severe difficulties in all three domains, this would warrant a decision following the initial assessment to undertake a core assessment. Severity was defined as:

- a child identified as experiencing developmental needs in three or more dimensions (such as health, education, and family and social relationships)
- parenting capacity identified as inadequate in three or more areas (such as basic care, emotional warmth, and guidance and boundaries)

- difficulties identified in relation to two or more of the family and environmental factors (such as family history and functioning, and income).

Sixty-one cases fulfilled these criteria and were categorised as having multiple problems. These children could be regarded as some of the most vulnerable in our society and accounted for 2.7 per cent of all referrals and 7 per cent (n=61) of all initial assessments.

Outcome of initial assessments

Social workers recorded that no further action was necessary in practically half (45%) of all the initial assessments in the sample. Of the other cases the action most frequently recorded was to provide some form of social services provision to the child and family (29% of all cases). However, a social worker was assigned to only 14.5 per cent of all cases. In a quarter of cases, the recorded action was a referral to another agency.

In 9.1 per cent of all the initial assessments, the recorded action was to proceed to a core assessment. It is of great concern that in 10 of the 61 cases that were identified by the research team as being multiple-problem cases, and, therefore, requiring more in-depth assessment and a plan of intervention, no further action was recorded by the social workers.

Cases that progressed to a core assessment (n= 68)

The cases most likely to progress to a core assessment were child protection referrals and those for parental alcohol or drug misuse. The source of the referral was also relevant: referrals from other social services departments were found to be more likely to progress to a core assessment. Referrals least likely to progress to a core assessment involved parental mental illness, financial or housing problems, and referrals made by the non-professionals.

Of the 51 cases categorised by the research team as multiple-problem cases and where social workers had recorded that the case would progress to a core assessment, only 36 were found to have done so. Thus, in 15 cases out of 61 (i.e. a quarter of such cases) which had been identified by the research team from information recorded at initial assessment as having multiple problems likely to impair a child's development, no further assessment was undertaken. This suggests that either the information gathered during the initial assessment was not used to inform decision-making and future plans, or the information gathered was not given due weight. This has major management and training implications, including issues of who makes decisions about further assessment and action, how these are approved and monitored by the agency, and what training and supervision is given to practitioners.

In the majority of cases (78.6%), core assessments were carried out because the child was considered to be at risk of suffering significant harm. Where information was recorded on the Core Assessment record, the social workers identified high levels of need. For example, in 61 per cent of cases children were found to have unmet needs in four or more developmental dimensions. In 80.6 per cent of cases parents were experiencing personal problems such as domestic violence, mental illness, or problem drug or alcohol use, or had a known history of violence. In most cases (83%) social workers recorded factors within the family and environment that were likely to have a negative impact on the child, and the parents' capacity to meet their needs.

In practically two-thirds of the core assessments (n=25), severe needs (that is in three or more dimensions) had been identified in all three domains: children's developmental needs, parenting capacity, and family and environmental factors. This suggests that core assessments were carried out in cases that warranted an in-depth assessment. However, there was a proportion of cases where the information recorded on the Initial Assessment record would suggest that the child might have benefited from a core assessment, but did not receive one.

The cost of undertaking a core assessment

This is the first time any attempt has been made to cost a key area of social work activity with children and families. From 24 responses supplied by four councils, the findings suggest that the time and cost of undertaking core assessments varied considerably depending on the complexity of the case and whether there were one or more children in the family being assessed. The cost to social services ranged from £377 to £1137. On average the cost to social services in undertaking a core assessment was £760. An additional £140 was the cost of the time professionals from other agencies spent in communicating with the social worker. This did not include the time other professionals spent in pursuing their own enquiries, and, therefore, in collecting the information given to the social worker. The total cost for all agencies involved is, therefore, considerably higher than the average of £900 recorded in this study.

The cost of assessment since the implementation of the Assessment Framework has to be seen in the context of a wider study undertaken by the Department of Health on costs through its annual Children in Need survey. The findings from the current study would suggest that the cost of a core assessment is not significantly more than the cost of the time spent working with children in need supported in their families or living independently, which is on average £85 per week (Department of Health National Statistics, 2002). With the Assessment Framework the requirement is for the process of assessment to be more structured and undertaken within a clear time-frame.

Since these were some of the first core assessments undertaken following the introduction of the Assessment Framework, caution must be applied to the costs and time spent on different aspects of the core assessment activity. They provide a helpful and useful baseline, however, for further exploration as the system becomes more fully integrated into social services.

Implications for policy and practice: turning policy into practice

Resources

To turn new government policy into practice depends on a transparent implementation programme, the process of which has been agreed by both central and local government. Moreover, adequate resources are needed for the success of any implementation programme. In the case of the implementation of the Assessment Framework there was a transparent implementation programme drawn up and communicated to councils through the regional development workers appointed under the Quality Protects programme. In addition, assessment was a priority in the Quality Protects programme and funding was available to councils as part of the overall drive to improve the quality of services to children in need and their families. Finally, there was a range of materials specifically commissioned to support local implementation. These included a training pack (NSPCC and the University of Sheffield, 2000), scales and questionnaires (Department of Health, Cox and Bentovim, 2000b) and assessment records (Department of Health and Cleaver, 2000) to support the collection of information during the assessment process, as well as the funding of a consultation process. A feature of these materials was that they were designed to assist direct work with children and families.

Nonetheless, the research shows this was not enough and many of the councils did not develop a corresponding plan of implementation that addressed all aspects of the implementation, involved staff from all relevant agencies fully, and was adequately resourced and sustained over time.

Training

Research shows that implementing new government policy is an iterative process requiring continual training and reinforcement so that people understand the theory and knowledge base that underpins it, their own role, and the changes that will result from it. The particular needs of staff within the organisation and other agencies have to be properly identified and understood so that the training can be tailored to their needs. The research suggests that training should have been initially targeted at first-line managers in order for them to have the knowledge and confidence to support practitioners in this new approach in assessing children's needs and circumstances.

Leadership

The Assessment Framework applies to a wider group of agencies than social services. Strong leadership is essential and chief officer commitment must be in place from the outset in order to:

- provide the strategies, direction and vision within social services
- negotiate the necessary commitment at a senior enough level from other agencies.

The commitment of senior managers and practitioners working in agencies other than social services is essential and using a multi-agency group to drive the implementation of the policy was one well-used strategy. In some councils existing groups that had been established for a different purpose, such as the Area Child Protection Committee, were utilised. Although this has the advantage of building on existing partnerships and ways of working, it could lead to a confusion of purpose.

A further significant component of successful implementation was the appointment of a dedicated project officer with responsibility for overseeing the implementation of the Assessment Framework. The project officer has to operate at both a strategic and operational level, be able to influence the way resources are allocated, command respect both within social services and with other relevant agencies, and be able to win the hearts and minds of those involved in implementation. Consequently careful consideration needs to be given to the level at which the post is established and the extent to which it is integrated within the line management of the agency.

Managing the implementation

The research shows that the task of implementing the Assessment Framework was very difficult because it was a whole new way of thinking about children and families and working with them which had implications throughout the whole organisation including in adult services.

During the consultation and dissemination of the Assessment Framework, a number of practitioners and managers reported that they were already undertaking assessments in line with the conceptual framework underpinning the Assessment Framework. However, during the process of implementation it became clear that there was a wider gap between what social work professionals thought they were doing in relation to the assessment of children and families and what was required under the Assessment Framework. The findings revealed that many managers and practitioners were overwhelmed by the task. This was compounded by the context in which they were working: the new performance agenda, increased accountability and scrutiny, organisational turbulence, and a crisis in recruitment and retention of social work and other public-sector staff. The research also showed insufficient acknowledgement of the significance of the task ahead and the difficulties social services were facing.

The findings suggest that senior managers adopted different strategies to implement the Assessment Framework. For example, some developed a plan or sanctioned a plan that went part way to implementation but did not encompass all that was required. Others treated it as if it was a very straightforward piece of policy implementation. This meant that they did not recognise the scope of the changes required and as a result in many councils there were one-off training events on particular issues but no overall training and development plan sustained over time.

Creative innovative solutions such as the use of mentors working alongside front-line practitioners were found to have had a number of advantages. They were shown to have supported front-line workers through the changes, raised morale, offered advice on particular cases, and raised the quality of record-keeping.

The findings would suggest that social workers were not always carrying out core assessments of cases that the initial assessment had indicated were necessary. Although this is of considerable concern, it should be borne in mind that the research took place within one year of the council implementing the Assessment Framework and the findings, therefore, reflect a system yet to be bedded into the day-to-day practice of front-line workers. Indeed, the findings suggest that once social workers completed their first core assessment they became more optimistic about their ability to undertake further core assessments, albeit in a more appropriate manner.

Direct work with children and families

The research shows that the implementation of the Assessment Framework has had a profoundly positive impact on the experiences of parents involved in assessments, particularly when there were child protection concerns. It is interesting that this was not fully recognised by practitioners. This suggests that even quite small changes in practice can have apparently disproportionate effects on the experiences of families of the public services. The importance of greater collaboration, a more honest approach about the reason and purpose of the assessment, what would be recorded, and the likely outcome, have been underestimated by social services. Social workers should be encouraged and supported in working openly with parents because other research has shown that this can have long-term beneficial effects even in the most adverse circumstances (Cleaver and Freeman, 1995; Farmer and Owen, 1995; Jones and Ramchandani, 1999). To ensure that families, regardless of their circumstances, can have equal opportunity of understanding the system, councils must ensure they provide information covering all aspects of the new policy and procedures in a variety of different formats and languages.

Whereas these positive benefits were identified in work with parents, the same effect was not apparent in work with children and young people and there is no doubt that this remains an area of major difficulty for many practitioners. This suggests that the focus during the last two decades on managing cases has been to the detriment of encouraging practitioners to undertake not only direct observation of children but also to engage with children and young people to explore their understanding of what is happening to them and to find out what they want to happen next. Councils should develop clear policies to ensure that young people are routinely informed and involved in decisions about them at all stages of assessment, planning, intervention and reviewing. Consulting and involving young people should not be a luxury but constitute an essential part of any work that involves them.

Messages for successful implementation

At the time of the study most councils were characterised by major problems in recruitment and retention of staff, innumerable organisational changes, and low levels of IT provision, and were having to respond to the demands of the

Government's performance agenda. Moreover, there were some significant new pieces of legislation affecting the rights of citizens, such as the Human Rights Act 1998 and the Data Protection Act 1998, which required modifications to current policies and practice for Councils with Social Services Responsibilities. In spite of this backdrop some councils were able to make considerable progress in implementing the Assessment Framework. The research findings suggest that the essential features for successful implementation include:

- Senior management commitment at an agency and inter-agency level. Strong leadership is essential and chief officer commitment must be in place from the outset.
- Senior management recognition of how the implementation of the Assessment Framework fits within their children services strategy – for example, the inter-relationship with training and continuing professional development, the council's strategy for IT, policies on staff supervision and the use of mentors, and the implementation of the Human Rights Act 1998 and the Data Protection Act 1998.
- The establishment of an inter-agency implementation group that involves staff from other agencies and voluntary bodies at a sufficient level of seniority and influence to commit their organisation to collaborative strategies for implementation.
- The appointment of a dedicated project manager at a sufficiently senior level within social services to plan, co-ordinate, steer, and promote the implementation process.
- An acknowledgement of the critical strategic relationship between the IT infrastructure of children's services and the capacity within the organisation to implement the Assessment Framework. The council's technical capacity and the version of the assessment records need to match. For example, using an electronic format to record information requires practitioners to have regular access to computers, and the skills to use the particular IT package. Any mismatch has the potential to lead to dissatisfaction and frustration amongst social services staff.
- A recognition that staff need an underpinning knowledge of child development, factors that affect parental capacity, and the impact on children and their parents of environmental factors. Such a knowledge base enables managers and practitioners to understand

the conceptual framework underpinning the Assessment Framework and implement it.

- The provision of opportunities to address any identified gaps in practitioners' knowledge and skills base. Many of the cases practitioners are working with are extremely complex and require a highly skilled workforce.
- Training that is responsive to the needs of staff and directly relates to the issues raised by managers and practitioners during the implementation process. Training that has an iterative relationship between the identified needs of staff and the programmes offered.
- Recognition that managers and practitioners have different levels of competence in relation to the knowledge and skills required to undertake direct work with children and families and manage the staff.
- Training programmes, supervision and the use of mentors to support staff during the implementation phase. Such an approach ensures that practitioners understand what is required of them, are supported in making any necessary changes in their practice, and that problems and issues are dealt with promptly. To accomplish this, managers and mentors need to be trained before practitioners in order for them to have the knowledge and confidence to support practitioners in this new approach to assessing children's developmental needs and circumstances.
- Training on the Assessment Framework that is offered not only on a single agency but also on a multi-agency basis. Training needs to address traditional barriers to collaborative work. Staff from all agencies value such an approach that was also seen to enhance their practice.
- A coherent system for recording information about assessments for all children in need, including disabled children and those in the child protection system. The information for the plan and review must be kept in the same place as the core assessment because this enables information from the assessment to inform the plan, and children with high levels of need to progress to a core assessment.
- The establishment of mechanisms to monitor the implementation of the Assessment Framework. When these are in place any difficulties can be identified at an early stage and the necessary

steps to address them taken. Monitoring also ensures decisions are appropriate at each stage in the assessment process.

- Comprehensive guidance for practitioners on the process of assessment including: inter-agency procedures and practice, information sharing between agencies, recording policies and procedures, and guidance on involving children and families.
- Equal weight given to referrals irrespective of whether they come from a professional or non-professional source.
- The offer of a range of services under s17 *Provision of services for children in need, their families and others*, of the Children Act 1989. When this occurs referrals are more likely to be made in relation to the specific difficulties experienced by the parents, e.g. domestic violence and parental substance misuse, than in terms of the child's safety. This reflects a situation where councils have responded to the refocusing debate in the mid-1990s and are providing need-led services.

Appendix I

Aims and Methods

The research had three main aims:

1. To explore the assessment process as set out in the *Framework for the Assessment of Children in Need and their Families* (Department of Health *et al.*, 2000a).
2. To consider whether the assessment records facilitate assessments which consider the child's developmental needs, parenting capacity, and family and environmental factors.
3. To estimate the costs incurred in conducting assessment using the assessment records.

In the process of meeting these aims, the study sought to answer the following questions:

- Which type of families receives initial or core assessments?
- During a core assessment, which members of the family are involved, which agencies are consulted, and what information is gathered and recorded?
- How effective are the assessment records in identifying objectives and developing a plan?
- What are the views of service users and social workers, of assessments conducted under the Assessment Framework (operationised using the assessment records)?
- Are the assessment records effective in capturing the key data on children as specified in Quality Protects?
- What are the costs of carrying out assessments and recording the information on the assessment records?

It should be recognised that this study was undertaken at a time when the participating councils were in the process of implementing the Assessment Framework, and by a research team who have been involved in the development of the system. The findings therefore, although showing which strategies are associated with more successful implementation, only offer indications of how the Assessment Framework impacts on professional practice and the experiences of children and families. The study does not provide an objective evaluation of the Assessment Framework or evidence of the long-term effects of the assessment on the outcomes for children and families.

The authors believe that, once the Assessment Framework has been fully embedded within social services, and professionals in other relevant agencies are conversant with it, an objective evaluation should be carried out. Such an evaluation must be undertaken by a research team who, unlike the present one, have not been involved in the research that underpins the Assessment Framework, the development of the assessment records, or the training or implementation of the Assessment Framework.

Selecting the councils

The original study was solely funded by the Department of Health under their research initiative The Costs and Effectiveness of Services to Children in Need. The available resources restricted the study to three London Boroughs. The aim was to ensure the boroughs differed along the following dimensions:

- use of the formal child protection system
- proportions of children looked after
- implementation of Section 17 of the Children Act 1989
- ethnically diverse community.

Government statistics, Key Indicators Graphical System (KIGS, Department of Health, 1998), and Aldgate and Tunstill's work on the s17 (Aldgate and Tunstill, 1995) were used to select the councils.

During the dissemination of the Assessment Framework a number of additional Councils with Social Services Responsibilities expressed a keen interest to be involved in the research study. In December 1999, with the agreement of the Department of Health, a letter was sent to every council inviting them to join the research project. This letter described the aims and methods of the study and offered councils the opportunity to participate, for a specified fee. Twenty-two councils joined the study (one withdrew halfway through the research). As a result, the findings from this study are based on research carried out in 24 English councils.

The 24 participating councils were very varied. An exploration of the ONS classification of Local and Health Authorities of Great Britain (1999) showed that the participating councils differed on a range of variables; only two were classified as extremely or very similar. The councils differed on the following dimensions:

- the type of council
- the proportion of resources allocated to work with children in need
- their performance ratings
- the communities they served.

The sample consisted of five Outer London Boroughs, three Inner London Boroughs, seven Metropolitan Districts, three Unitary Authorities and six Shire Counties. The councils showed wide differences (ranging from 8% to 74%) in the proportion of their gross expenditure assigned to work with children in need. Government statistics categorise councils by the proportion of gross expenditure allocated to children in need, into three groups: high, average and low. Ten of the research councils were categorised as low, nine as average, and five as high in relation to the proportion of gross expenditure allocated to children in need.

The Social Services Inspectorate published social services performance ratings for councils for the year April 2001 to March 2002 (Social Services Inspectorate, 2002). There are four star ratings that are the product of an assessment process. 'Assessment includes evidence from inspections and reviews, monitoring and performance indicators, to form an overall picture of performance over time on both qualitative and quantitative aspects of performance' (Social Services Inspectorate, 2002). The research councils represented all four ratings. One council was classified as three-star, eight as two-star, 14 as one-star, and one gained zero stars.

Furthermore, the councils differed in the type of communities they served. For example, the proportion of the population that ascribed themselves to the white ethnic group showed much variation. At one extreme in a number of County and Unitary Authorities 99 per cent of the population described themselves as white. In contrast in two London Boroughs approximately a third of the population (32.3% and 30.3%) did not classify themselves as white. In one Borough after white, the largest ethnic group people assigned themselves to was Indian and in the other, black Caribbean (1991 Census – Ethnic group of residents).

Working in partnership with the councils

A research study that depends on the implementation of new government policy and social work practice will generate considerable anxiety and resistance from practitioners. The research team met with both senior and line managers in every participating social services department, and in some cases senior practitioners were also involved. These meetings were used to explain the aims and methods of the study, to outline the timetable, to address any concerns raised, and to gain the commitment, agreement and co-operation of the staff. Participating councils agreed to use the Department of Health referral and assessment records. When councils needed to adapt the records to meet their own departmental needs for data collection, changes had to be in the form of additions. It was made clear to managers that no part or item of the Department of Health assessment records should be changed or deleted.

In addition, time was spent exploring current structures and systems within children's social services. The aim was to identify issues that posed potential difficulties to implementing the Assessment Framework. For example, in some social services departments staffing levels within particular teams, or the role of teams, would have made complying with the requirements of the Assessment Framework extremely difficult.

The sessions with managers and senior practitioners were also used to establish an acceptable and workable access procedure for contacting parents and children for the interview part of the research.

Finally, the identification of a member of staff in the social services department responsible for liaising with an identified member of the research was established.

Organising the study

The research took place prior to the Assessment Framework being mandatory. As a result, the participating councils were at different stages of implementing the Assessment Framework at the time they joined the study. The research therefore focused both on the process of implementation – the *developmental stage* – and the subsequent impact of the Assessment Framework on social work assessments – the *research stage.*

The developmental stage

This part of the study concentrated on supporting councils in their implementation of the Assessment Framework and introduction of the assessment records, and involved a number of processes.

FAMILIARISATION SESSIONS

The experience of the introduction of the Looking After Children materials highlighted the importance of training when introducing new assessment tools. Prior to introducing the Assessment Framework every social worker and line manager needed to (a) familiarise him or herself with the assessment records, and the questionnaires and scales that accompanied them, and (b) learn how best to use them. Because previous research has shown how crucial is the commitment of middle management to the success of research which explores practice, specific training for this group was provided (Cleaver *et al.*, 1998). Training on the Assessment Framework and how to carry out an assessment was not the responsibility of the research group, indeed the NSPCC had developed *The Child's World* to enable trainers to accomplish this task.

The research group was responsible for conducting a series of four half-day familiarisation sessions in each participating council. The familiarisation sessions assumed that training on the Assessment Framework had already been undertaken and their main focus was the assessment materials and how they could best be used.

In order to ensure that these sessions were consistent across all the councils, a training pack was developed. This pack was given to each participating council to allow the training officer within the council to make use of the materials in future training sessions. A copy was also made available on the research website.

Although the aim was to cover the same ground in every participating council, it was also important to ensure the familiarisation sessions met the needs of particular groups. Meetings and discussions were held with management and the training sections in every social services department to plan the content and timing of the sessions.

What quickly became apparent was that staff in the councils differed considerably in their knowledge of the Assessment Framework. For example, in some councils at the time the familiarisation sessions were held, no training on assessment had been carried out and copies of the Assessment Framework had yet to be distributed. As a consequence, social workers had little understanding of the Assessment Framework and the concepts and principles which underpin it. In contrast, other councils had run a number of courses on the Assessment Framework targeted at a wide range of staff, and social workers were using the assessment records on a regular basis.

Attendance at the familiarisation sessions highlighted the variation both in the number of attendees, their status and profession. In some councils the sessions were over-subscribed, in others attendance was disappointing. Both practitioners and line managers attended in some councils, in others line managers were absent. A broad range of practitioners were represented in some councils, including workers from family centres, long-term teams, disability teams, CAMS, and adult services. In others attendance was much narrower, dominated by specific groups such as those responsible for referrals and initial assessments or long-term work. The content of the sessions was modified to meet the needs of particular groups. A typical programme for a half-day session is included at http://www.jkp.com.

A MULTI-AGENCY SESSION

To assist participating councils in implementing the Assessment Framework, the research team gave a presentation about the Assessment Framework and the research at a multi-agency conference. This was arranged by the council to meet their specific requirements. As a result these sessions varied considerably. Some were run as a conference to *introduce* the Assessment Framework to both social services staff and staff from other agencies. Other councils put on a conference to *launch* the Assessment Framework and the assessment-recording forms. Some councils held large conferences with a range of speakers covering topics such as: Children's Needs – Parenting Capacity; the impact of new legislation; child protection and the Assessment Framework; Family Group Conferences; and assessing attachment. In other councils the format was very different: although there were short formal presentations, the emphasis was on small, focused group work.

THE DEVELOPMENT OF AN ELECTRONIC VERSION OF THE ASSESSMENT-RECORDING FORMS

A key issue raised during many of the meetings, familiarisation sessions and multi-agency conferences was the possibility of the assessment records being produced in an electronic format. In response to this an electronic version of the assessment records using Adobe software was developed. The electronic version of the assessment records offers councils and practitioners the following advantages:

- It allows practitioners to complete the forms directly on the computer using active check boxes and text fields.
- It avoids repetition, by enabling basic factual information to be transferred from Referral and Initial Information records through to Core Assessment records, e.g. name, address, and date of birth.
- It assists managers in monitoring compliance and completion of the assessment records.
- It encourages practitioners to use the assessment records and thus helps to ensure that the records have been sufficiently trialed prior to the development of the Integrated Children's System.

Although the electronic version of the assessment records offered considerable advantages for social workers, the system had limitations. It was a 'stand alone' system, not linked to individual councils' IT systems, nor to any electronic version of the Looking

After Children materials. In addition, to use the electronic version of the assessment recording forms required councils to purchase Adobe software. The copyright of the prototype electronic version of the assessment-recording forms resides with the Department of Health.

Electronic data collection and analysis is an integral part of the Integrated Children's System. The prototype electronic version of the assessment records provided valuable information for the development of the Integrated Children's System. Work on identifying the key data set was headed up by representatives within the Department of Health. The research team assisted with the specification for the data required for electronic data collection on the Integrated Children's System, with regard to the assessment of children in need.

Following the introduction, familiarisation sessions and the multi-agency day each council implemented the Assessment Framework and undertook to trial the Department of Health's assessment records. The original expectation had been that every participating council would implement the Assessment Framework and start using the assessment records by August 2000 – ahead of the Government requirement of April 2001. However, things rarely proceed as planned. In several of the participating councils the implementation of the Assessment Framework was linked to a departmental, or divisional, re-organisation which delayed their start. Indeed, only a quarter (n=6) of the councils had implemented the Assessment Framework by August 2000, and four did not achieve implementation until April 2001.

THE FIRST AUDITS

The idea of implementing the Assessment Framework and using the assessment records from August 2000 was to allow an initial audit to be undertaken six months after implementation. The aim of this audit was to support councils in the process of implementation by identifying areas in the assessment process where they were encountering difficulties. The first audit was intended to include approximately 30 core assessments from each council. The core assessments and all the paperwork that preceded them (in some cases this would be a referral and initial assessment and in others, where core assessments had been carried out on open cases, no earlier paperwork would be available) would be audited.

However, the audit revealed two issues that impacted on the ability to keep to this objective:

1. The delay in implementing the Assessment Framework meant that some councils had, at the time of the audit, undertaken few core assessments. In fact the delay in implementation in one council meant they could not be included in the initial audit. Although councils had committed to using all the Department of Health referral and assessment records (with or without minor alterations) many were using a combination of their own existing forms and the Department of Health's assessment records. For example, some councils continued to use their original referral form and introduced the Department of Health's assessment records, others adopted only the core assessment record.

2. As a result it was not always possible to identify 30 core assessments or to audit all the related non-Department of Health referrals and assessment forms in every participating council. This meant that in some councils the audit concentrated primarily on initial assessments and in others the focus was on core assessments. In the end the initial audit included 241 referral forms, 251 Initial Assessment records and 394 Core Assessment records.

Once the first audit had been completed a meeting was held with relevant managers in each council to disseminate the findings; each council was given a copy of the report.

REGIONAL CONFERENCES

To support councils in the process of implementing the Assessment Framework the research group held a series of one-day regional conferences. The first series of conferences took place during December 2000 and the second series in September 2001. Each participating council was invited to send ten delegates. The recommendation was that six places would be used by social services to enable both practitioners and managers to attend and two places would be offered to colleagues in education and two places to colleagues in the health service. A total of 247 people attended the first series of conferences: 173 representatives from social services, 46 health professionals and 28 from education. The second series was less well attended with 139 people: 103 from social services, 24 from health and 12 from education.

The aims of the conferences were twofold. First, to feed back early findings from the research and, second, to enable the councils to share experiences, both challenges and methods of overcoming them, in implementing the Assessment Framework. Each conference included:

- a brief presentation from a representative from the Department of Health to explain recent relevant policy developments
- a brief feedback session led by the project director and a member of the research team
- a short presentation by the councils on topics chosen by them (included in the second series of conferences)
- workshops with a predetermined focus.

The focus of the workshops had been established in consultation with the councils. Councils were expected to send at least one delegate to each workshop.

A summary of the key issues raised during the conferences was fed back to the participating councils.

TELEPHONE INTERVIEWS WITH MANAGERS

In order to understand the context in which councils were working and how they implemented the Assessment Framework, a telephone interview was conducted with a manager from each of the councils. These interviews sought information on the following issues:

- the structure of the council

- the social services processes and practices in relation to work with children, prior to implementing the Assessment Framework
- the changes to departmental structures and the processes used to implement the Assessment Framework.

These interviews took approximately one hour.

The research stage

To address the three main aims of the research and the consequent questions (outlined at the start of the chapter) the study used a combination of methods. These included *postal questionnaires* aimed at professionals from both social services and other relevant agencies, *interviews* with families and professionals, and an *audit* of social work case-files.

POSTAL QUESTIONNAIRES

Questionnaires were designed to elicit the experiences and views of professionals to the implementation of the Assessment Framework and the introduction of the assessment records (a copy of these are included at http://www.jkp.com). The questionnaires were produced in paper and electronic form. All questionnaires were sent to the link professionals in the social services department who took responsibility for distributing them both within their own department and to other relevant agencies such as health and education. The findings are based on the returned questionnaires from 215 social work practitioners, 93 social work managers, and 153 professionals from other agencies.

The questionnaires for social workers sought information on the following issues:

- background information about the professional's work career
- training attended on the Assessment Framework
- experiences of using the Referral and Initial Information record, the Initial Assessment record and the Core Assessment record
- the link between the assessment records and the Looking After Children materials.

The manager's questionnaire focused on rather different areas and sought information on the following issues:

1. Implementing the Assessment Framework.
2. The impact of the Assessment Framework and the use of the assessment records on:
    - gathering management information
    - supervising staff and monitoring individual cases
    - the quality of social workers' assessments and recording
    - working with other agencies
    - involving families in assessments
    - the link between the assessment records and the Looking After Children materials.

The questionnaire for professionals from agencies other than social services mainly focused on issues relating to inter-agency work and sought information on:

1. Professionals' familiarity with the Assessment Framework and the assessment records.
2. The impact of the Assessment Framework on:
    - the way they record information
    - the degree and quality of inter-agency co-operation on the assessment of children in need
    - the degree and quality of inter-agency co-operation on the delivery of services for children in need.

THE INTERVIEW STUDY

The original plan had been to carry out an interview study of 50 cases drawn from the three participating London Boroughs. With the extension of the study to include 24 English councils a decision was taken, after consultation with the Research Advisory Group, to include three cases from each participating council – giving an expected sample of 72 cases. Unfortunately it was not possible to reach this target. The final interview sample included 52 cases from 22 councils.

Interviews, whenever possible, were carried out with children over the age of 10 years, a parent or carer, the social worker who carried out the assessment and, when relevant, the professional who had made the referral. A total of 50 parents or carers took part in the case study (the study sample included two unaccompanied asylum seekers), eight young people, 52 social workers and 13 other professionals.

To qualify for inclusion in the sample, families must have been involved in a core assessment. The sample was composed of an index child from each family. Purposive sampling was used to ensure that sample included cases involving children from each of the five age groups (0–2; 3–4; 5–9; 10–14; and 15 years and over) and children with disabilities.

Gaining access to families

An accessing procedure was worked out with each council during early meetings with management. This involved the following stages:

1. The council placed general information about their involvement in the research where clients could easily find it. For example, in some councils a notice was posted in the waiting room, in others the council produced a flyer which was given to families, in others still information was included in general information and publicity for service users such as in a Family Centre newsletter.
2. The research team produced a letter addressed to parents. This letter informed them about the study and the possibility that at a future date they might be asked to participate in the research. The letter also informed families who did not wish to participate how to ensure that their name was

not passed on to the research team. Once a decision had been taken by the social worker to carry out a core assessment, the social worker gave a copy of this letter to the family.

3. The data from the first audit was used to identify cases recently referred to the council where a core assessment has been carried out. Six cases were selected sequentially from a given date, chosen to include a distribution of different-aged children and, whenever possible, a disabled child. The social worker then took responsibility for contacting the families (if they had not already withheld their name) to ask if they wished to be involved in the study. When families agreed, the social worker passed on to the research team the name, address and, when available, the telephone number of the family.

4. A member of the research team then contacted the family. The first contact was used to explain the purpose of the study, potential contribution of the family, and how long it would take. It was made clear to parents that, although the researcher would be unable to intervene with social services on their behalf, their contribution to the study would be of future benefit to parents like themselves. The researcher also took time to explain issues of confidentiality and anonymity. When the case involved a child over the age of 10, parents were asked if they would give permission for their child also to contribute to the research. Before giving their consent, the issues that would be covered in the child's interview were discussed and they were assured that their child would be free to stop the interview at any time. Permission was also sought for the researcher to read the family case-file and interview the current social worker and any other professional who had been involved in the assessment.

Interviews

To interview parents and young people successfully about sensitive issues depends on the ability to establish a feeling of trust quickly (Cleaver and Freeman, 1995). Careful selection and training of the interviewers was essential. The research interviewers were either qualified social workers or child psychologists. Police checks were carried out prior to any interviews taking place. All members of the research team carried an identity card issued by the University of London. A team of four interviewers were trained by the author to ensure their interviews were research-focused sessions rather than therapeutic interventions.

Interviews were carried out with the parent(s), whenever possible children over the age of 10 years, social workers and other professionals involved in the assessment process. By interviewing family members and professionals it was hoped that individual accounts, which may be shaped by their experiences, could be balanced by the views of others. The interviews were informal events that mirrored as far as possible normal social interactions (Burgess, 1984; Hammersley and Atkinson, 1983).

Interviews with parents Interviews with parents were carried out in their own home. Considerable efforts were made to engage with fathers as well as mothers. This resulted in five cases where the father or stepfather was the sole parent interviewed, and in a further two cases where both parents were interviewed. The following areas were covered in the interview:

- previous experience of social work services
- the current reason for contact with social services
- the quality of preparation prior to the assessment
- parents' understanding of the cause and purpose of the assessment
- parental involvement and participation in the assessment process
- the adequacy of the assessment – did it cover all the issues they believed were relevant
- parents' understanding of the core assessment objectives and plans, and their perceived relevance.

Interviews with social workers Interviews with relevant social workers were conducted at their convenience and in their own offices. The interviews lasted for about one hour and covered the following issues:

- the circumstances surrounding the referral
- what was done to prepare the family for the assessment
- how the initial assessment was carried out. This included an exploration of issues such as: working with other agencies, involving the family, and working within the required time-frame
- how the core assessment was carried out. This covered the same issues included in the exploration of the initial assessment process but went on to explore the analysis and planning stages.

Interviews with other professionals involved in the assessment Interviews with other professionals were also carried out in their own office and at their convenience. This interview took approximately an hour and covered the following issues:

- their degree of familiarity with the Assessment Framework and the assessment records
- previous experience of referring the study family to social services
- their involvement in the current referral of the family
- the degree of involvement in the assessment of the family
- the degree of involvement in establishing the objectives and plans for the family
- their evaluation of the assessment process in this case.

Interviews with young people (children over 10 years)

> The trouble was they never explained anything to us. They just treated us like babies and we weren't. We needed to know what was going on, what was happening, how things would work out… (O'Quigley, 2000, p.10)

> Children in our society are not accustomed to having their views taken into account in their everyday lives at home and at school. We do not live in a culture which supports participation by children. (Schofield and Thoburn, 1996, p.62)

Previous research has all too often revealed that professional decisions about young people's lives fail to take account of the views of the young people themselves. It was therefore felt that a study on the impact of a new framework for the assessment of children in need must include the experiences of young people. But involving young people can be difficult because they are not used to being listened to. Research has also shown that interviewing young people must be done with great sensitivity to ensure they are empowered to give the answers they want to give, rather than the answers they think they should give (Hill *et al.*, 1996). It was important, therefore, to ensure that the young people understood that the questions were not a test, there were no right or wrong answers, and that what we wanted to know was their thoughts or feelings about things.

The process of selecting and involving young people in the study When the identified case involved a child over the age of 10 years the researcher discussed the possibility of interviewing the young person with the social worker. In cases where the social worker felt it would be inappropriate the researcher then made a judgement as to whether or not to include the case in the sample or seek to replace it. For example, in two cases the social worker felt it would be inappropriate to attempt to interview two young people with severe, mute autism; these cases were, nonetheless, included in the study although the young person was not interviewed.

When the parent was first approached, permission to interview children over the age of 10 years was sought. In some cases parents did not wish their child to be involved. In general, this was because parents felt their already traumatised child would not benefit from further questioning. In all cases parents' wishes were respected, and the case included in the study, but the young person was not interviewed. When parents consented to the involvement of their child, the researcher approached the young person to seek their agreement to be interviewed.

Special attention was given when seeking the agreement of young people to develop an explanation that would be meaningful to them and which took account of their cognitive development and linguistic ability. For example, we talked about the research in terms of writing a book that would help social workers understand the experiences of young people who have contact with social services, and to do this we needed their help. In seeking their agreement the interviewer explained the limits of confidentiality and the responsibility of all adults to ensure that children are safe (Morrow and Richards, 1998). With this exception young people were assured that everything they said would be treated in confidence and they would not be identified in any report.

Interviews were always carried out at the young person's home. The interviews took approximately an hour and explored similar issues to those covered in the interview with parents.

THE SECOND AUDIT

The plan was to audit 100 sequential referrals to social services from an identified date approximately three months prior to the audit, and all subsequent assessment records. Each council with social services responsibility was asked to identify 100 referrals and all subsequent documentation. However, this did not always result in the expected number of cases because in some councils administrative staff experienced difficulties in locating the identified case- files.

The councils involved in the study included both large rural counties and small London Boroughs. To ensure that the sample reflected the range and type of cases coming into children's social services, when the 100 referrals accounted for less than one week's work a further consecutive 100 referrals was requested. There were only two councils where this applied. Furthermore, one council was extremely small and had received only five referrals within one calendar month; all these were included in the audit. Finally, the referrals from one council could not be included because operational reasons had prevented the identification of 100 consecutive referrals. The final audit included 2248 referrals, 866 Initial Assessment records, and 68 Core Assessment records.

The Initial Assessment record has a space for the social worker to record the start and end date of the assessment. The researchers used this data to calculate whether initial assessments were completed within the required seven working days. In working on this data it had been assumed that social workers' recording would have been in line with the recommendations of the Assessment Framework: "An initial assessment is deemed to have commenced at the point of referral to the social services department."(Department of Health *et al.*, 2000a, p.31, 3.9)

However, in some cases researchers identified a considerable time lapse between the point of referral and the commencement of the initial assessment. To see if this affected the findings significantly, in half the councils the timing of the initial assessment was calculated from the point of referral. A comparison between the two types of calculation showed no significant differences.

The second audit explored the following issues:

- the proportion of children referred to social services for whom (a) an initial assessment was undertaken and (b) a core assessment had been completed
- how comprehensively the assessment records were completed
- the frequency and identity of other tools used in completing the assessment
- the frequency and identity of other agencies involved in the assessment
- the characteristics of the families
- the match between the information collected during the assessment and the recorded objective and plans.

DOCUMENTARY EVIDENCE

Councils' policy and administrative procedures will inevitably affect the assessment, decision-making process and service provision as well as the costs incurred. To take account of their impact, these were scrutinised.

Costing the assessments

This study is concerned with evaluating the costs incurred in using a particular method of assessment rather than another. However, in all assessments the key element is social-worker time. Thus, although any method will have indirect and direct overhead costs associated with it, the ratio between direct and indirect costs will not change. It was sufficient to collect information on the amount of time each social worker devoted to carrying out a core assessment.

Specifically designed time-sheets enabled social workers to record the time taken in completing all aspects of the core assessment. These were produced both in paper and electronic format. The electronic version of the time-sheet collated the time taken to undertake the various tasks needed to complete the core assessment. Both paper versions and an electronic version were distributed to all participating councils.

An integral part of the original Department of Health-commissioned research, based in three councils, was costing. These councils understood that, by agreeing to participate, social workers would need to record the time taken to carry out core assessments. In addition, in many of the councils which chose to join the study senior and line managers saw the advantage of gaining information on costs and agreed to supply some limited information.

The intention was to collect data on costs no sooner than six months after councils had implemented the Assessment Framework. The aim of this strategy was to try and gain a picture of costs that avoided any distortion resulting from social workers' uncertainty of using a new system. Unfortunately, the delay in implementation, already discussed, affected the councils' ability to co-operate with this part of the study. Difficulties arose because many of the social workers that would be undertaking the work had also been involved in organisational changes and felt overwhelmed. As a result the costing data is based on 24 completed time-sheets from four councils.

The production of a prototype electronic version of the assessment records

This work was commissioned from a design team who worked in close collaboration with the Department of Health and the research team. The brief given to the design team stated that the electronic records had to have the following characteristics:

1. They must be able to be filled in on screen on councils' existing computer systems and completed or partially completed records must be saveable to the users' local discs.
2. They must be printable, both once filled in and when blank, from councils' existing computer systems. Blank printed assessment records must be a direct alternative to the Department of Health's printed assessment records. The records must also be as technically self-explanatory and easy to use as possible.
3. They must be able to transfer common information from one record to another.

The chosen software format for the assessment records was Adobe Portable Document Format (PDF) because of its stability, wide range of controls over the appearance and operation of the electronic forms, extensive support for Internet protocols and its robust set of security features.

This format was trialled in four councils and alterations and additions made in the light of feedback. For example, the revised electronic version had the ability to aggregate information gathered during the assessment process that would be required for the Department of Health annual returns. The new version was also subjected to a trial in two councils and further revisions made.

The specification was written which will enable a third party to take the existing set of electronic forms and modify them so that they can submit all their data, via a user's existing Internet connection, to a remote database. The remote database will allow access to the database information by social services' practitioners, managers, Department of Health employees and research groups. Levels of access and control of the database will depend on the user's security level.

An Internet-ready set of electronic forms has been mocked-up for demonstration purposes. The data access website has also been mocked-up and trialled with council social service managers. They submitted feedback that has been taken into account when finalising the site. This work was finished in July 2001 and submitted to the Department of Health.

MANAGING THE DATA

The study was exploratory rather than evaluative in that it's aim was to scrutinise a new framework for the assessment of children. The study used three main methods of information gathering:

1. An audit of social work case-files.
2. A questionnaires survey involving social work managers, practitioners and other professionals in relevant agencies.
3. A case study based on interviews with young people, parents, and relevant professionals.

The data from one source could be used as evidence to show, for example, the proportion of referrals that progressed to an initial or core assessment. On the other hand, data from a number of sources could be used to create a more comprehensive understanding of an issue. For example, in relation to the impact of the Assessment Framework on direct work with families, the audit provided information on the number of cases where parents' views had been recorded on the assessment record – showing what was recorded. The social work managers' and practitioners' questionnaires explored the difficulties and advantages of involving parents and young people in the assessment process – giving insights into why it was happening. Finally, the interviews explored parental and young people's reports of their involvement in the assessment process – revealing the experiences of parents and young people.

The data gathered from the three methods of investigation were subjected to both quantitative and qualitative methods of analysis. The audit was analysed using SPSS (Statistical Package for the Social Sciences). The size of the sample allowed tests of significance to be applied.

The questionnaires for social work managers, practitioners and other professionals included both closed and open questions. The replies to the closed answers were also analysed using SPSS. However, because the questionnaire samples were relatively small, subdivisions resulted in many of the cell sizes being too small for tests of significance. The data were, therefore, analysed principally by frequency counts of the variables and simple cross-tabulations.

The numbers in the interview sample were small (n=52) and it would be misleading to assume that they are representative of the entire population of children in need. Hence, no attempt was made to attach sophisticated statistics to these findings. Qualitative methods were used to extract meaningful themes from the data in a way which represented the experiences of children, parents and social workers (see, for example, Lofland and Lofland, 1971). The data were used in a descriptive manner to aid the understanding and interpretation of the findings from both the questionnaires and the audit.

Cost estimation is a relatively underdeveloped area of research, but we have built upon the work of Beecham (1999), Beecham and Knapp (1995), Knapp and Robertson (1989) and Netten *et al.*, (2001). The Children in Need Activity and Expenditure Collection planned for the year 2000 gave a valuable baseline of the average costs of assessment nationally. This was used as a baseline for comparing the costs incurred when social workers use the Core Assessment records in carrying out assessments. If the data was not available in time the PSSRU Unit Cost figures (Netten, Dennet and Knight, 1998) was used to develop an approximation to a baseline.

A series of meetings were held which enabled the emerging findings from both the implementation stage of the study and the research to inform the development of the Integrated Children's System.

Summary

The study had three main aims:

- to explore the assessment process as set out in the Assessment Framework
- to consider whether the assessment records facilitate assessments which consider children's developmental needs, parenting capacity, and family and environmental factors
- to estimate the costs incurred in conducting assessment using the assessment records.

The study was funded under the Department of Health's research initiative The Costs and Effectiveness of Services to Children in Need. The available funds restricted the focus to three London Boroughs. Keen interest to participate in the study was expressed by other councils. With the agreement of the Department of Health an open invitation was extended to councils to join the study for a specified fee. As a result the sample increased from three to 24 councils. The councils differed on a range of variables and represented eight regions.

The study encompassed two stages. Stage one was *developmental* and focused on the process of implementation. Stage two was the *research* and examined the impact of the Assessment Framework on social work assessments.

In each council the developmental stage encompassed the following:

- four sessions with line managers and practitioners to familiarise them with the purpose and use of the assessment records
- the development of a training pack, used during the familiarisation sessions and made available to each council
- an introductory research presentation at a multi-agency conference
- the development of an electronic version of the assessment records that was made available to each council
- an initial audit of approximately 30 Core Assessment records and all previous paperwork
- a series of one-day regional conferences during December 2000 and September 2001 to allow professionals from all the relevant agencies in the participating councils to be briefed about the progress of the research and to share experiences
- interviews with managers to establish the context in which councils were introducing the Assessment Framework and the process of implementation.

The research stage used a combination of methods. Postal questionnaires were designed to collect data on the experiences of social work managers, practitioners, and professionals from other agencies, of the Assessment Framework and the use of the assessment records. An identified link person in each council was responsible for distributing the questionnaires both within the social services department and to the other agencies. Returns were received from 93 social work managers, 215 social work practitioners, and 153 professionals from agencies other than social services.

The intention had been to include three cases from each of the 24 councils in the interview sample. However, cases were not always forthcoming and the final sample was made up of 52 families. The sample included 50 parents or carers, 8 children over the age of 10 years, 52 social workers and 13 other professionals involved in the case. The focus of the interviews was to explore how the family experienced assessments and the degree of their participation. The audit included 2248 referrals to social services (in the majority of cases this represented 100 referrals from each participating council) and 866 subsequent Initial Assessment and 68 Core Assessment records.

Specifically designed time-sheets, in both paper and electronic formats, were given to social workers for them to record the time spent on individual activities during the assessment process. Although managers saw the value of gathering information that would allow the costs of assessments to be estimated, getting practitioners to complete the time-sheets proved problematic. Twenty-four completed time-sheets from four councils were returned to the research team.

A prototype electronic version of the assessment records was commissioned from a design team. These enabled information to be entered on screen and common data to be transfered from one record to another. The format was subjected to two short trials in six councils and revised in the light of feedback. A specification was written to enable data to be submitted to a remote database via an Internet connection. Levels of access and control of the data base would depend on the user's security level. An Internet-ready set of electronic forms was developed for demonstration purposes and the result of this work has been submitted to the Department of Health.

The data was subjected to both quantitative and qualitative methods of analysis. The size of the audit enabled tests of significance to be applied, whereas the data from the questionnaires were principally analysed by frequency counts and simple cross-tabulations. Interviews were subjected to qualitative methods of analysis that enabled themes to be identified. Cost estimation built upon the work of economists such as Beechman (1999).

A series of meetings enabled the emerging findings from this study to inform the development of the Integrated Children's System.

Appendix II

Tables

Tables for Chapter 3: Involving families in the assessment process

Table 3.1 The relationship between the quality of assessments and family involvement in core assessments

	The quality of assessments				
Family involvement in the assessment process	**Improved**	**No effect**	**Deteriorates**	**Total** n=	%
Increased	66%	12.8%	21.3%	47	100
Had not increased	31%	34.5%	34.5%	58	100
Total	49	26	30	105	100

Note: 111 cases missing.

Table 3.2 The age of the children/young people involved in the interview sample

Age of children/young people	Percentage of case study
0 to 2 years	17.3
3 to 4 years	23.1
5 to 9 years	21.2
10 to 14 years	23.1
15 years and over	15.4

Table 3.3 The reasons for contact/referral to social services (n=52)

Reason for referral*	Present case study n=52	
	Number	Percentage
Child protection concerns	30	57.6
Parental mental illness	14	26.9
Parental drug/alcohol misuse	8	15.3
Domestic violence	7	13.4
Child/young person beyond control	16	30.7
Unaccompanied asylum seeker	2	3.8
Disabled child	12	23
Housing/financial problems	9	17.3
Other	6	11.5

Note: Categories are not mutually exclusive.

Table 3.4 A comparison between the suspected child abuse cases in the present case study and the Cleaver and Freeman 1995 study in relation to the reason for referral

Main reason for referral	Present case study		Suspected child abuse sample (Cleaver and Freeman, 1995)	
	n=30	Percentage	n=61	Percentage
Physical abuse	13	43.3	27	44.2
Sexual abuse	6	20.0	21	34.4
Emotional abuse	1	3.3	6	9.8
Neglect	10	33.3	7	11.4

Table 3.5 A comparison between the suspected child abuse cases in the present case study and the Cleaver and Freeman 1995 study in relation to the age group of the child

Age group of the children	Present case study n=30	Suspected child abuse sample n=61 (Cleaver and Freeman, 1995)
	Percentage	Percentage
Less than 5 years	53.3	39.3
5 to 9 years	23.3	37.7
10 years and over	23.3	22.9

Table 3.6 Parents views on the efficacy of child in need plans		
The plans are helping/will help the family	**Number**	**Percentage**
Definitely will help	19	45.2
Will help so some extent	7	16.6
Not sure/don't know	6	14.2
Will not help at all	10	23.8
Total	42	100

Note: In 8 cases parents were not aware of any plans. Two cases involved unaccompanied asylum seekers.

Tables for Chapter 4: The experiences of social service managers and practitioners

Table 4.1 The proportion of social work questionnaires coming from different social work teams

Type of social work team	Social work practitioners		Social work managers	
	Frequency	Percentage	Frequency	Percentage
Not completed	2	0.9	1	1.1
Not applicable	0	0	1	1.1
Referral and assessment	44	20.5	21	22.6
Area, district or locality	87	40.5	31	33.3
Long term team	40	18.6	18	19.4
Disabled children	22	10.2	9	9.7
Family centre	10	4.7	2	2.2
Other	10	4.7	10	10.7
Total	215	100	93	100

Note: The 20 cases classified as 'Other' (both social workers and managers) included CAMHS (7 cases), hospital teams (7 cases), child protection teams (2 cases), family resource teams (3 cases) and unaccompanied asylum seekers (1 case).

Table 4.2 The number of years social workers have been qualified

Years qualified	Frequency	Percentage
Not qualified	22	10.3
<5 years	69	32.2
<10 years	53	24.8
<15 years	34	15.9
<20 years	22	10.3
20 years and over	14	6.5
Total	214	100

Note: Missing data in 1 case.

Table 4.3 Social workers' practice experience in the field of child and family work

Years of practice experience	Frequency	Percentage
<5 years	74	34.9
<10 years	47	22.1
<15 years	45	21.2
< 20 years	19	8.9
20 years and over	27	12.7
Total	212	100

Note: Missing data in 3 cases.

Table 4.4 The relationship between the type of team and their experience of training events

Type of team	Experience of training events			
	Good	Could be better	Poor	Total
Referral and assessment % within each team	10 34.5	17 58.6	2 6.9	29 100
Area, district or locality % within each team	13 19.1	41 60.3	14 20.6	68 100
Long term % within each team	9 32.1	15 53.6	4 14.3	28 100
Other % within each team	14 51.9	12 44.4	1 3.7	27 100
Total count % within each team	46 30.3	85 55.9	21 13.8	152 100

Table 4.5 Managers' reports on the consistency in using the recording forms within their teams (n=89)

Type of team	Consistently used		Not consistently used		Total
	Number	Percentage	Number	Percentage	Number
Referral and assessment	20	95	1	5	21
Area, district or locality	27	87.1	4	12.9	31
Long term	9	50.0	9	50.0	18
Disabled	7	87.5	1	12.5	8
Other	11	100	0	0	11

Note: 4 cases missing. $\chi^2(4)=18.987$. $p<.001$.

Table 4.6 The proportion of managers from different teams who consider the records useful in monitoring social work practice

Type of team	Proportion of managers finding the records useful in monitoring practice %
Referral and assessment	78.9
Area, district or locality	53.6
Long term team	40.0
Disabled children	33.3
Other	72.7

Note: 'Other' on the whole refers to specialist teams and includes managers working in CAMHS, hospital teams, child protection teams, family resource teams and unaccompanied asylum seekers.

Table 4.7 The relationship between time since qualification and perceived impact of the recording forms on the quality of assessments

	Social workers' perception of the quality of their assessments			
Time since qualified	Improved	No effect	Impaired	Total
Not qualified or < 3 years	44 72.1%	14 23%	3 4.9%	61 100%
Qualified >3 years	67 47.9%	51 36.4%	22 15.7%	140 100%
Total	111 55.2%	65 32.3%	25 12.4%	201 100%

Pearson Chi-square 10.902 (2) $p<.004$.

Table 4.8 The relationship between perceived usefulness of the training and perceived impact on the quality of assessments

	Perceived impact on the quality of assessments			
Perceived usefulness of training	**Improved**	**No effect**	**Impaired**	**Total**
Of little or no use	41 54.7%	21 28%	13 17.3%	75 100%
Fairly or very useful	31 75.6%	9 22%	1 2.4%	41 100%
Total	72 61.3%	30 26.9%	14 12.1%	116 100%

Pearson Chi-square 7.121 (2) p<.028.

Table 4.9 Practitioners' experience in using the Referral and Initial Information record for more than one child within the same family

Completing a Referral and Initial Information record on more than one child in the same family				
Statement	**Disagree**	**Neither agree nor disagree**	**Agree**	**Total**
Completing separate referral forms on individual children did not take any longer	64 77.1%	2 2.4%	17 20.5%	83 100%
Completing separate referral forms led to unnecessary duplication of information	19 22.9%	9 10.8%	55 66.3%	83 100%
Completing separate referral forms provided a clear focus on the needs of individual children.	30 36.1%	33 39.8%	20 24.1%	83 100%

Note: Completing separate referral forms provided a clear focus on the needs of individual children.

Table 4.10 Practitioners' experience in using the Initial and Core assessment records for more than one child within the same family						
	Disagree		**Neither agree nor disagree**		**Agree**	
	%	%	%	%	%	%
	Initial	**Core**	**Initial**	**Core**	**Initial**	**Core**
Led to unnecessary duplication of information	12.3	19.2	15.4	18.2	72.2	62.6
Impairs the quality of the assessment	30.3	30.8	38.2	35.1	31.4	34
Provided a clear focus on the needs of individual children	20.4	21.0	35.2	33.6	44.3	45.2

Table 4.11 Social workers' experience of the Initial Assessment record on decision making				
Decision-making at the initial assessment stage				
Statement	**Disagree**	**Neither agree nor disagree**	**Agree**	**Total**
The initial assessment record helped me decide if the child was 'in need'	32 22%	39 27%	74 51%	145 100%
The initial assessment record helped me identify the immediate action needed	38 25%	48 32%	65 43%	151 100%
The initial assessment record is useful to know if a core assessment is appropriate	41 27.5%	50 33.5%	58 39%	149 100%

Tables for Chapter 6: Referrals: findings from the audit

Table 6.1 The rate of recorded information on the referral form

Information to be recorded	Number of cases where information was recorded	Proportion of cases where information was recorded %
Parent aware of referral	1405	62.5
Reason for referral	2190	97.4
Child's name	2236	99.5
Child's address	2219	98.7
Child's age or date of birth	2162	96.2
Child's gender	2023	90.0
Child's religion	654	29.1
Child's ethnicity	1677	74.6
Principal carer	1634	72.7
Other household members	1563	69.5
Interpreter required	791	35.2
Source of referral	2162	96.2
Referrer's address	1514	67.4
Significant relatives not part of the household	582	25.9
Further action	2040	90.7
Start and end date	1799	80.0
Name of worker	2137	95.1
Name of team manager	1818	80.9

Table 6.2 Relationship between the reason for referral and parent's awareness of the referral being made			
Main reason for referral	**Parental awareness of the referral**		
	Number	**Percentage**	**Total**
Parental alcohol/drugs	15	41.7	36
Child protection	211	49.6	425
Domestic violence	63	58.9	107
Other parenting issues	140	61.7	227
Other issues	110	65.5	168
Parental mental illness	40	67.8	59
Housing problems	46	76.7	60
Financial problems	69	82.1	84
Child beyond control	134	85.4	157
Disabled child	63	95.5	66
Total	891	64.1	1389

χ^2 (9) = 123.865 p<.000.

Table 6.3 Referrals made by professionals: Relationship between the reason for referral and parent's awareness of the referral being made			
Main reason for referral	**Parental awareness of the referral**		**Total**
	Number	**Percentage**	
Parental alcohol/drugs	8	42.1	19
Domestic violence	30	48.4	62
Child protection	121	58.4	207
Parental mental illness	20	58.8	34
Other issues	43	64.2	67
Other parenting issues	65	66.3	98
Child beyond control	37	78.7	47
Housing problems	9	81.8	11
Disabled child	25	96.2	26
Financial problems	9	100	9
Total	367	63.3	580

Table 6.4 Relationship between source of referral and parent's awareness of the referral being made

Source of referral	Parental awareness of the referral		Total
	Number	Percentage	
Health	205	77.4	265
Education	64	50.8	126
Police	103	52.6	196
Non-professionals	324	73.8	439
Other	71	40.3	176
Other social services departments	112	64.4	174
Total	879	63.9	1376

$\chi^2(5) = 102.141.\ p<.000.$

Table 6.5 The age group of children referred to social services

Age group of child	Number referred	Proportion of all referrals %
less than 5 years	753	34.8
5–9 years	526	24.3
10–14 years	582	26.9
15 years and over	301	14

Table 6.6 The ethnicity of children referred to social services

Race of child	Number	Percentage
Black	111	7.2
Asian	98	6.4
White	1227	80
Mixed race	69	4.5
Other	25	1.6
Total	1530	100

Table 6.7 The source of cases referred to social services		
Source of referral	**Number**	**Percentage**
Health	385	17.8
Education/nursery/childminder	227	10.5
Police/probation	372	17.2
Parent/carer	438	20.3
Child/young person	63	2.9
Other non-professionals	136	6.3
Other	256	11.8
Other social services department	285	13.2
Total	2162	100

Note: 'Other' sources include anonymous referrals and those from neighbours and voluntary bodies.

Table 6.8 The association between the source of the referral and the age group of the child

	Age of child				
Source of referral	**<years**	**5 to 9 years**	**10 to 14 years**	**15 years & over**	**Total**
Health	29.2% (212)	13.8% (71)	9.1% (51)	13.5% (39)	17.9% (373)
School/nursery	5.8% (42)	14.2% (73)	14.6% (82)	8% (23)	10.5% (220)
Police/ probation	14.3% (111)	15.0% (77)	21% (118)	17.4% (50)	17% (356)
Non-professionals	23.3% (169)	28.5% (146)	34.4% (193)	37.8% (109)	29.5% (617)
Other	12.9% (94)	13.3% (68)	8.9% (50)	11.5% (33)	11.7% (245)
Other social services	13.5% (98)	15.2% (78)	11.9% (67)	11.8% (34)	13.3% (227)
Total	100% (726)	100% (513)	100% (561)	100% (288)	100% (2088)

Note: Percentages given are the percentage within particular age group that are from that source.
$\chi^2(15)=154.203.p<.000.$

Table 6.9 The source of referrals involving children from different ethnic groups

Ethnicity of child	Source of referral						
	Health	**Education**	**Police**	**Non-professionals**	**Other**	**Social services**	**Total**
Black	18.7%	14.0%	7.5%	29.9%	16.8%	13.1%	100% 107
Asian	26.6%	10.6%	13.8%	20.2%	12.8%	16.0%	100% 94
White	16.2%	11.2%	16.7%	32.8%	11.4%	11.6%	100% 1189
Mixed	29.4%	11.8%	10.3%	25.0%	8.8%	14.7%	100% 68
Total	17.7% 258	11.4% 166	15.6% 227	31.4% 458	11.8% 172	12.1% 177	100% 1458

$\chi^2(15) = 28.979.\ p<.016.$

Table 6.10 The main reason for referral

Reason for the referral	Number	Percentage
Child protection concerns	663	30.3
Domestic violence	214	9.8
Parental alcohol/drug misuse	61	2.8
Parental mental illness	91	4.2
Other parenting issues	337	15.4
Disabled child	92	4.2
Child/young person beyond parental control	238	10.9
Financial problems	119	5.4
Housing problems	105	4.8
Unaccompanied asylum seeker	25	1.1
Other	245	11.2
Total	2190	100

Table 6.11 Relationship between the reason for referral and the age group of children					
Main reason for referral	**Age group of child**				
	5 years	**5 – 9 years**	**10 – 14 years**	**15 years & over**	**Total**
Child protection	34.1%	27.7%	28.0%	10.2%	639
Domestic violence	45.6%	25.7%	23.8%	4.9%	206
Parental alcohol/drugs	50.9%	33.3%	8.8%	7.0%	57
Parental mental illness	53.4%	25.0%	20.5%	1.1%	88
Other parenting issues	47.7%	25.1%	20.7%	6.5%	323
Disabled child	32.2%	28.9%	27.8%	11.1%	90
Child beyond control	9.0%	13.7%	47.9%	29.5%	234
Financial problems	37.8%	24.3%	15.3%	22.5%	111
Housing problems	36.9%	18.4%	9.7%	35.0%	103
Other issues	24.4%	21.7%	34.9%	19.0%	258
Total	34.9% 735	24.3% 512	27.1% 572	13.8% 290	2109 100%

χ^2 (27) = 312.101. p.$<$000.

Table 6.12 Relationship between the reason for referral and the gender of the child			
Main reason for referral	**Gender of the child**		
	Female	**Male**	**Total**
Child protection	50.3%	49.7%	160
Domestic violence	49.7%	50.3%	177
Parental alcohol/drugs	59.3%	40.7%	54
Parental mental illness	58.3%	41.7%	84
Other parenting issues	45.5%	54.5%	297
Disabled child	33.7%	66.3%	83
Child beyond control	38.6%	61.4%	223
Financial problems	59.4%	40.6%	106
Housing problems	40.9%	59.1%	93
Other issues	50.9%	49.1%	220
Total	48.2% 938	51.8% 1009	1497 100%

χ^2 (9) = 31.525. p$<$.000.

Table 6.13 Relationship between the reason for referral and the source of referral

Main reason for referral	Source of referral						
	Health	Ed.	Police	Non-professionals	Other	Social services	Total
Child protection	14.5%	15.5%	21.1%	21.1%	14.7%	18.4%	640
Domestic violence	10.9%	1.5%	57.2%	21.1%	7.0%	7.5%	201
Parental alcohol/ drugs	39.0%	5.1%	18.6%	20.3 %	3.4%	13.6%	59
Parental mental illness	47.2%	4.5%	5.6%	25.8%	5.6%	11.2%	89
Other parenting issues	25.0%	12.3%	8.4%	30.4%	10.5%	13.3%	332
Disabled child	32.2%	10.0%	0	43.3%	7.8%	6.7%	90
Child beyond control	9.4%	7.7%	14.5%	55.1%	2.6%	10.7%	234
Financial problems	9.3%	1.9%	0	71.3%	13.0%	4.6%	108
Housing problems	11.8	0	2.9%	52.0%	23.5%	9.8%	102
Other issues	15.6%	16%	11.4%	24.0%	19.8%	13.3%	263
Total	17.8% 377	10.4% 221	17% 361	29.7% 630	11.9% 253	13% 276	2118 100%

Table 6.14 Further action arising from the referral

Further action	Percentage	Total number
Initial assessment	46.2	939
Referral to another agency	6.8	139
Provision of information	16.8	342
Other action	15.5	315
No further action	23.8	484

Note: 'Other action' could include the child becoming accommodated, or the child protection enquiries being undertaken. The figures do not add up to 100 per cent because in some cases social workers had recorded more than one further action. For example, in some cases an initial assessment was recommended and a referral was made to another agency. All cases categorised as no further action are cases where no other action was recorded – i.e. no action had been taken.

Table 6.15 Relationship between the age group of the child and the recorded further action being an initial assessment			
Age group	**An initial assessment**		
	Number	**Percentage**	**Total**
5 years	311	47.5	680
5 – 9 years	230	47.6	483
10 – 14 years	273	51.7	528
15 years and over	92	36.6	266
Total	906	16.9	1957

χ^2 (3) = 21.308 $p<.000$.

Table 6.16 Relationship between the age group of the child and the recorded further action being the provision of information			
Age group	**The provision of information**		
	Number	**Percentage**	**Total**
<5 years	124	18.2	681
5 – 9 years	65	13.5	483
10 – 14 years	72	13.6	528
15 years and over	70	26.3	266
Total	331	16.9	1958

χ^2 (3) = 25.696. $p<.000$.

Table 6.17 Relationship between the ethnicity of the child and the recorded action being an initial assessment			
Age group	**An initial assessment**		**Total**
	Number	**Percentage**	
Black	28	35.0	80
Asian	30	36.6	82
White	573	49.7	1153
Mixed	29	49.2	59
Total	660	48.0	1374

χ^2 (3) = 11.057 $p<.011$.

Table 6.18 Relationship between the reason for referral and the recorded action being an initial assessment

Main reason for referral	An initial assessment		
	Number	Percentage	Total
Child protection	339	55.8	607
Domestic violence	74	36.6	202
Parental alcohol/drugs	42	73.7	57
Parental mental illness	45	54.9	82
Other parenting issues	150	48.4	310
Disabled child	50	56.8	88
Child beyond control	104	48.1	216
Financial problems	19	18.3	104
Housing problems	30	33.3	90
Other issues	74	30.8	240
Total	927	46.4	1996

χ^2 *(9) = 116.203 p<.000.*

Table 6.19 Relationship between the reason for referral and the recorded further action being referral to another agency (omitting those where an Initial Assessment had also been recorded)

Main reason for referral	Referral to another agency		
	Number	Percentage	Total
Child protection	13	2.2	604
Domestic violence	8	4.0	201
Parental alcohol/drugs	0	0	57
Parental mental illness	8	9.8	82
Other parenting issues	16	5.2	310
Disabled child	12	13.6	88
Child beyond control	27	12.5	216
Financial problems	8	7.7	104
Housing problems	9	10.0	90
Other issues	12	5.0	240
Total	113	5.7	1992

Note: In two cases the reason for referral had not been given, and in 24 cases an initial assessment had also been the recorded action.

χ^2 *(9) = 54.591 p<.000.*

Table 6.20 Relationship between the reason for referral and the sole recorded further action being provision of information			
Main reason for referral	**The provision of information**		
	Number	**Percentage**	**Total**
Child protection	42	6.9	608
Domestic violence	46	22.8	202
Parental alcohol/drugs	6	10.5	57
Parental mental illness	6	7.3	82
Other parenting issues	47	15.2	310
Disabled child	6	6.8	88
Child beyond control	25	11.6	216
Financial problems	29	27.9	104
Housing problems	29	32.2	90
Other issues	46	19.2	240
Total	282	14.1	1997

χ^2 *(9) = 93.192 p<.000.*

Table 6.21 Reason for referral and the recorded action being written description under 'Other'			
Main reason for referral	**An initial assessment**		
	Number	**Percentage**	**Total**
Child protection	105	17.2	607
Domestic violence	17	8.4	202
Parental alcohol/drugs	3	5.3	57
Parental mental illness	11	13.4	82
Other parenting issues	26	8.4	310
Disabled child	8	9.1	88
Child beyond control	23	10.6	216
Financial problems	28	26.9	104
Housing problems	7	7.8	90
Other issues	51	21.3	240
Total	279	14.0	1996

Table 6.22 Relationship between the reason for referral and the recorded further action being no further action

Main reason for referral	No further action		
	Number	Percentage	Total
Child protection	127	21.0	605
Domestic violence	62	30.8	201
Parental alcohol/drugs	6	10.5	57
Parental mental illness	13	15.9	82
Other parenting issues	80	25.8	310
Disabled child	9	10.2	88
Child beyond control	49	22.7	216
Financial problems	38	36.5	104
Housing problems	19	21.1	90
Other issues	68	28.3	240
Total	471	23.6	1993

χ^2 *(9) = 38.842. p<.000.*

Tables for Chapter 7: Initial Assessments: findings from the audit

Table 7.1 The relationship between the reason for referral and consistency between the recorded action on the referral form being an initial assessment and an initial assessment found on the case file

Reason for referral	Consistency between recorded action and on the referral form and an initial assessment on file		
	Recorded action was an initial assessment	Initial Assessment record found on the case file	Percentage
Child protection concerns	339	253	74.6
Domestic violence	74	55	74.3
Parental alcohol/drug misuse	42	30	71.4
Parental mental illness	45	39	86.7
Other parenting issues	150	113	75.3
Disabled child	50	35	70.0
Child/yp beyond control	104	86	82.7
Financial problems	19	16	84.2
Housing	30	21	70.0
Other	74	52	70.2
Total	927	700	75.5

Table 7.2 The relationship between the source of referral and consistency between the recorded action on the referral form being an initial assessment and an initial assessment found on the case file

Source of referral	Consistency between recorded action and an initial assessment on file		
	Recorded action was an initial assessment	Initial Assessment record found on the case file	Percentage
Health	186	148	79.6
Education	104	81	77.9
Police	148	97	65.5
Non-professionals	257	194	75.5
Other	95	71	74.7
Other social services departments	125	97	77.6
Total	915	688	75.2

Table 7.3 Association between reason for referral and case progressing to initial assessment

Reason for referral	Referral led to an initial assessment		Referral did not lead to an initial assessment		Total
Child protection concerns	308	46.5%	355	53.9%	663
Domestic violence	66	30.8%	148	69.2%	214
Parental alcohol/drug misuse	35	57.4%	26	42.6%	61
Parental mental illness	47	51.6%	44	48.4%	91
Other parenting issues	135	40.1%	202	59.9%	337
Disabled child	40	43.5%	52	56.5%	92
Young person beyond parental control	101	42.4%	137	57.6%	238
Financial problems	17	14.3%	102	85.7%	119
Housing problems	31	29.5%	74	70.5%	105
Other	66	24.4%	204	75.6%	270
Total	846	38.6%	1344	61.4%	2190

χ^2 *(9) = 97.147. p<.000.*

Table 7.4 Association between source of referral and case progressing to initial assessment

Source of referrer	Referral led to an initial assessment		Referral did not lead to an initial assessment		Total
Health	185	48.1%	200	51.9%	385
School/nursery	98	43.2%	129	58.8%	227
Police/Probation	116	31.2%	256	68.8%	372
Non-professionals	228	35.8%	409	64.2%	637
Other	93	36.3%	163	58.9%	285
Other social services department	117	41.1%	168	58.9%	285
Total	837	38.7%	1325	61.3%	2162

χ^2 (5) = 28.506. p<.000.

Table 7.5 The rate of recorded information on the Initial Assessment record

Information to be recorded	Number of cases where information recorded	Proportion of cases where information recorded %
Reason for initial assessment	834	96.3
Child's health needs	759	87.6
Child's educational needs	738	85.2
Child's emotional and behavioural needs	714	82.4
Child's identity and social presentation	691	79.8
Child's family and social relationships	748	86.4
Parents' basic care	726	83.8
Parents' ensuring safety	698	80.6
Parents' emotional warmth	678	78.3
Parents' stimulation	651	75.2
Parents' guidance and boundaries	660	76.2
Parents' stability	666	76.9
Issues affecting parenting capacity	646	75
Family history and functioning	706	81.5
Social resources	702	81.1
Housing	722	83.4
Employment and income	692	80.4
Summary of initial assessment	780	91
Further action	752	86.8
Family given a copy of assessment	521	60.2
Time taken to complete the assessment	710	82.0
Name of worker	789	91.1

Table 7.6 Relationship between reason for initial assessment and assessment done within seven working days

Reason for initial assessment	Percentage completed on time	Total number
Child protection concerns	67.3	272
Domestic violence	50.9	53
Parental alcohol/drug misuse	76.9	26
Parental mental illness	69.4	36
Other parenting issues	66.0	103
Disabled child	61.3	31
Child/young person beyond parental control	64.6	82
Financial problems	78.6	14
Housing	80.8	26
Unaccompanied asylum seeker	87.5	8
Other	61.5	39
Total	66.4	690

Note: Information missing on 176 initial assessments.

Table 7.7 The main reason for referral compared with the reason for the initial assessment

Reasons for referral or initial assessment	Proportion of referrals %	Proportion of initial assessment %
Child protection concerns	30.3	38.8
Domestic violence	9.8	7.1
Parental alcohol/drug misuse	2.8	4.0
Parental mental illness	4.2	5.6
Other parenting issues	15.4	14.9
Disabled child	4.2	4.6
Child/young person beyond parental control	10.9	12.1
Financial problems	5.4	2.0
Housing problems	4.8	3.7
Unaccompanied asylum seeker	1.1	1.7
Other	11.2	5.5
Total	100	100

Note: Information missing from 242 cases.

Table 7.8 Age group of children involved in an Initial Assessment

Age of child	Number	Percentage
less than 5 years	299	35.8
5–9	210	25.1
10–14	242	28.9
15 and over	85	10.2
Total	836	100

Note: Information missing from 30 cases.

$\chi^2(3) = 16.579.\ p<.001.$

Table 7.9 Ethnicity of children involved in an Initial Assessment

Ethnicity	Number	Percentage
White	508	81.4
Black	37	5.9
Asian	40	6.4
Mixed	31	5.0
Other	8	1.2
Total	624	100

Note: Information missing from 242 cases.

Table 7.10 Proportion of cases where the child's developmental needs were identified

Developmental need	Number	Percentage	Total
Health	187	24.6	759
Education	254	34.4	738
Emotional and behavioural development; Self care skills	296	41.4	714
Identity and social presentation	179	25.9	691
Family and social relations	372	49.7	748

Note: Totals vary because social workers did not systematically record information in every section.

Table 7.11 Proportion of cases where difficulties in relation to parenting capacity were identified

Parenting capacity	Number	Percentage	Total
Basic care	84	11.5	726
Ensuring safety	236	33.8	698
Emotional warmth	137	20.2	678
Stimulation	109	16.7	651
Guidance and boundaries	199	23	660
Stability	252	30.2	666

Note: Totals vary because social workers did not systematically record information in every section.

Table 7.12 Issues affecting parenting capacity

Issue	Number	Percentage
Physical illness	48	7.4
Mental illness	109	16.9
Physical disability	9	1.4
Learning disability	17	2.6
In care during childhood	5	0.8
Childhood abuse	10	1.5
History of child abuse	28	4.3
History of violence/domestic violence	107	16.6
Alcohol/drug problems	75	11.6
Other	63	9.8
No problems identified	175	27.1

Note: Information missing from 220 cases.

Table 7.13 Proportion of cases where difficulties in relation to family and environmental factors were identified

Family and environmental factors	Number	Percentage	Total
Family history and functioning	460	65.2	706
Social resources	283	40.3	702
Housing	213	30.0	722
Employment and income	191	27. 6	692

Note: Totals vary because social workers did not systematically record information in every section.

Table 7.14 Issues affecting parenting capacity in multiple-problem cases (n=61)	
Issues affecting parenting capacity	**Number**
Physical illness	4
Mental illness	11
Learning disability	6
Childhood abuse	3
History of child abuse	3
History of violence/domestic violence	9
Alcohol/drug use	6
Other issues	3
No issues identified	5

Note: Information on 50 cases.

Table 7.15 Association between multiple-problem cases and the reason for initial assessment			
Reason for initial assessment	**Number**	**Percentage**	**Total**
Child protection concerns	15	4.6	324
Domestic violence	4	6.8	59
Parental alcohol/drug use	1	3.0	33
Parental mental illness	5	10.6	47
Other parenting issues	12	9.7	124
Disabled child	2	5.3	38
Child/young person beyond control	17	16.8	101
Financial problems	0	0	17
Housing problems	3	9.7	31
Other	1	1.7	60
Total	60	7.2	834

Note: Information missing from 32 cases.

Table 7.16 Recommended further action following the Initial Assessment		
Recommended further action	**Number**	**Percentage**
No further action	342	45
Services to be provided	220	29.0
Referral to another agency	197	25.0
Strategy discussion to be held	34	4.5
Immediate legal action	5	0.7
Core assessment	69	9.1
Specialist assessment to be commissioned	6	0.8
Allocation to a social worker	110	14.5

Note: Information missing from 107 cases. The categories are not mutually exclusive. For example, children and families may be given both a service and be referred to another agency.

Table 7.17 Recorded further action in multiple-problem cases (information available for 759 cases)			
	Summary of recorded further action		
Profile of case	**Some action taken**	**No further action**	**Total**
Multiple-problem cases	47 (82.5%)	10 (17.5%)	57 (100%)
Single-problem cases	370 (52.7%)	332 (47.3%)	702 (100%)
Total	417 (54.9%)	342 (45.1%)	759 (100%)

Note: Information missing from 107 cases.
χ^2 *(1)=18.847. p<.000.*

Tables for Chapter 8: Core Assessments: findings from the audit

Table 8.1 The relationship between the reason for referral and consistency between the recorded further action on the Initial Assessment record and a core assessment found on the case file

Reason for referral	Consistency between recorded further action on the Initial Assessment record and an core assessment on file		
	Recorded further action was a core assessment	Core Assessment record found on the case file	Percentage
Child protection concerns	27	13	48
Domestic violence	12	8	66.6
Parental alcohol/drug misuse	8	3	37.5
Parental mental illness	3	0	0
Other parenting issues	8	2	25.0
Disabled child	1	1	100
Child/yp beyond control	4	3	75.0
Housing	1	0	0
Other	3	0	0
Learning disability	1	0	0
Not completed	1	1	100
Total	69	31	44.9

Table 8.2 Association between reason for the referral and case progressing to a core assessment

Reason for referral	Referral led to a core assessment		Referral did not lead to a core assessment		Total
Child protection	44	6.4%	635	93.5%	679
Domestic violence	10	4.4%	213	95.5%	223
Parental alcohol/drug misuse	4	6.3%	59	93.6%	63
Other parenting issues	3	0.9%	348	99.1%	351
Disabled child	2	2%	94	97.9%	96
Child/yp beyond parental control	3	1.3%	241	98.7%	244
Total	66	4.0%	1590	96.0%	1656

Table 8.3 Association between source of referral and case progressing to a core assessment

Source of referral	Referral led to a core assessment		Referral did not lead to a core assessment		Total
Health	13	3.2%	393	96.7%	406
School	7	2.9%	230	97.0%	237
Police	11	2.8%	377	96.1%	388
Non-professionals	8	1.2%	648	98.8%	656
Other	4	1.5%	261	98.5%	265
Other social services dept	22	7.2%	284	92.8%	306
Total	65	2.9%	2193	97.1%	2258

Table 8.4 The rate of recording child's developmental needs (n=68)

Child's developmental needs	Decisions recorded through the use of tick boxes		Information recorded through the use of free text	
	Number	Percentage	Number	Percentage
Health	33	48.5	31	45.6
Education	30	44.1	23	33.8
Behavioural and emotional development	32	47.1	29	42.6
Identity	30	44.1	24	35.3
Family and social relationships	30	44.1	27	39.7
Social presentation n=40 (does not apply to children <5yrs).	17	42.5	14	35.0
Self-care n=40 (does not apply to children <5 yrs).	15	37.5	11	27.5

Table 8.5 The rate of recording parental capacity to meet the child's developmental needs (n=68)

Child's developmental needs	Decisions about parental capacity recorded through the use of tick boxes		Information about parental capacity recorded through the use of free text	
	Number	Percentage	Number	Percentage
Health	30	44.1	28	41.2
Education	27	39.7	26	30.2
Behavioural and emotional development	31	45.6	26	30.2
Identity	31	45.6	24	35.3
Family and social relationships	30	44.1	26	38.2
Social presentation = 40 (does not apply to children <5yrs).	17	42.5	17	42.5
Self care = 40 (does not apply to children <5yrs).	16	40.0	12.0	30

Table 8.6 Rate of recording information in the short summary sections (n=68)

Child's developmental needs	Summaries of the child's needs and parents' responses	
	Number	Percentage
Health	41	60.3
Education	40	58.8
Behavioural and emotional development	41	60.3
Identity	35	51.5
Family and social relationships	37	54.4
Social presentation = 40 (does not apply to children <5yrs).	22	55
Self-care = 40 (does not apply to children <5yrs).	18	45

Table 8.7 The rate of recording family and environmental factors (n=68)

Family and environmental factors	Some information recorded	
	Number	Percentage
Family history	35	51.4
Family functioning	29	42.6
Wider family	36	52.9
Housing	38	55.9
Employment	35	51.4
Income	29	42.6
Family's social integration	32	47.1
Community resources	26	38.2

Table 8.8 The rate and quality of recording in the three main summary sections (n=68)

Main summary sections	Not completed		Some information recorded		Strengths and needs identified	
	Number	Percentag e	Number	Percentage	Number	Percentage
Child's needs	39	57.4	8	11.8	21	30.9
Parenting capacity	41	60.3	9	13.2	18	26.5
Family and environmental factors	40	58.8	9	13.2	19	27.9

Table 8.9 The completion rate and quality of recording for the analysis section (n=68)

The quality of the analysis	Number	Percentage
Not completed	26	38.2
Only descriptive information recorded	18	26.5
Child's needs identified and service provision recorded	24	35.3

Table 8.10 The completion rate and quality of recording for the objectives and plans (n=68)

	Child's objectives & plans		Parent's objectives & plans		Wider family and environmental factors objectives & plans	
	Number	Percentage	Number	Percentage	Number	Percentage
Not completed	45	66.2	53	77.9	51	75.0
Does not relate to identified needs	3	4.4	23	4.4	1	1.5
Relates to some identified needs	16	23.5	10	14.7	12	17.6

Table 8.11 Agencies consulted during the core assessment

Identity of agency	Cases where agency consulted	Cases where agency not consulted
Health visitor	29 (42.6%)	39 (57.4%)
GP	22 (32.4%)	46 (67.6%)
School/nursery	24 (35.3%)	44 (64.7%)
Education Welfare Officer	2 (3%)	66 (97%)
Police or probation	40 (58.8%)	28 (41.2%)
Other consultants	35 (51.5%)	33 (48.5%)

Table 8.12 Children's developmental needs identified by the core assessment

Developmental dimension	Unmet need	No unmet need	Total
Health	26 (63.4%)	15 (36.6%)	41
Education	26 (65.0%)	14 (35.0%)	40
Behavioural and emotional needs	28 (68.3%)	13 (31.7%)	41
Identity	22 (62.8%)	13 (37.2%)	35
Family and social relationships	25 (67.6%)	12 (32.4%)	37
Social presentation (relates only to children over the age of 5 years).	17 (77.3%)	5 (22.7%)	22
Self-care skills (relates only to children over the age of 5 years).	16 (88.9%)	2 (11.1%)	18

Note: Information available in 41 cases.

Table 8.13 Issues affecting parenting capacity identified at the core assessment

Parenting issue	Identified problem	No identified problem	Total
Physical illness	5 (16.6%)	25	30
Mental illness	9 (29.0%)	22	31
Physical disability/sensory impairment	3 (11.1%)	24	27
Learning disability	7 (24.1%)	22	29
Period in care during childhood	4 (13.8%)	25	29
Childhood abuse	8 (29.6%)	19	27
Known history of child abuse	3 (12.0%)	22	25
Known history of violence	11 (37.9%)	18	29
Problem drinking/drug use	9 (30.0%)	21	30

Note: Information available in 31 cases.

ELEMENT OF ASSESSMENT	LIASION WITH OTHER AGENCIES														LIASION WITHIN SOCIAL SERVICES				LIASION WITH YOUNG PERSON AND FAMILY						OTHER ACTIVITIES						TOTALS	
	School		**GP**		**Health visitor**		**Other health professional**		**Police**		**Housing**		**Other**		**Supervisor**		**Colleagues**		**Young person**		**Parent**		**Meeting**		**Consulting files**		**Assessing evidence**		**Completing forms**			
	hr	min	hr	min	hr	min	hr	min	hr	min	hr	min	hr	min	hr	min	hr	min	hr	min	hr	min	hr	min	hr	min	hr	min	hr	min	hr	min
INFORMATION GATHERING																																
Details		r		r		r		r		r		r		r		r		r		r		r		r		r		r		r		
Background		r		r		r		r		r		r		r		r		r		r		r		r		r		r		r		
Health																r		r		r		r		r		r		r		r		
Education																		r		r		r		r		r		r		r		
Emotional and Behavioural																																
Identity																																
Family/ Social relationship																																
Social presentation																																
Self-care																																
Family and environment																																
CHILD IN NEED PLAN																																
Summary																																
Young person's/ Parents contribution																																
Analyse assessment																																
Draw up objectives																																
Agree with other agencies																																
Agree with supervisor																																
Agree with service user																																
AGENCY TOTALS (DETAILS, BACKGROUND, ASSESSMENT)																																

References

Adcock, M. (1998) 'Significant harm: implications for local authorities.' In M. Adcock and R. White (eds) *Significant Harm: its management and outcome.* Croyden, Surrey: Significant Publications.

Aldgate, J. and Bradley, M. (1999) *Supporting Families Through Short Term Fostering.* London: The Stationery Office.

Aldgate, J. and Tunstill, J. (1995) *Making Sense of Section 17: Implementing Services for Children in Need within the 1989 Children Act.* London: HMSO.

Bee, H. (2000) *The Developing Child,* 9th Edn. London: Allyn and Bacon.

Beecham, J. (1999) *The Exploration of Unit Costs in Child Care Services: Estimating Unit Costs* (Draft Report to the Department of Health).

Beecham, J. and Knapp, M.R.J. (1995) 'The cost of child care assessment.' In R. Sinclair, L. Garnett and D. Berridge (eds) *Social Work Assessment with Adolescents.* London: National Children's Bureau.

Birchall, E. and Hallett, C. (1995) *Working Together in Child Protection.* London: HMSO.

Brandon, M.M. and Lewis, A. (1996) 'Significant harm and children's experiences of domestic violence.' *Child and Family Social Work, 1,* 1, 33–42.

Bullock, R. (1995) 'Change in Organisations: Likely Problems in Implementing Looking After Children.' In H. Ward (ed.) *Looking After Children: Research into Practice.* London: HMSO.

Burgess, R.G. (1984) *The Research Process in Educational Settings.* Lewes: Falmer.

CCETSW (1992) *Paper 31: The Requirements for Post Qualifying Education and Training in the Personal Social Services.* London: CCETSW.

Children Act 1989. London: HMSO.

Children and Young People's Unit (2001) *Building a Strategy for Children and Young People, Consultation Document.* London: Children and Young People's Unit.

Cleaver, H. (2000) *Fostering Family Contact.* London: The Stationery Office.

Cleaver, H. and Freeman, P. (1995) *Parental Perspectives in Cases of Suspected Child Abuse.* London: HMSO.

Cleaver, H. and Freeman, P. (1996) 'Child abuse which involves wider kin and family friends.' In P. Bibby (ed.) *Organised Abuse: The Current Debate.* London: Arena, 231–244.

Cleaver, H., Unell, I. and Aldgate, A. (1999) *Children's Needs – Parenting Capacity: The impact of parental mental illness, problem alcohol and drug use, and domestic violence on children's behaviour.* London: The Stationery Office.

Cleaver, H. and Walker, W. (2000) *Using the Assessment Records with Children and Families.* www.frameworkresearch.org.uk.

Cleaver, H., Wattham, C. and Cawson, P. (1998) *Assessing Risk in Child Protection.* London: NSPCC.

Colton, M., Drury, C. and Williams, M. (1995) *Children in Need.* Aldershot: Avebury.

Corrick, J., Jones, D. and Ward, H. (1995) *Looking After Children, Management and Implementation Guide.* London: HMSO.

Cox, A. and Walker, S. (2000) *The Home Inventory: A training approach for the UK.* Brighton: Pavilion.

Department of Education and Science (1988) Circ.4/88 *Working Together for the Protection of Children from Abuse: Procedures within the Education Service.*

Department of Health (1988) *Protecting Children. A guide to social workers undertaking a comprehensive assessment.* London: HMSO.

Department of Health (1991a) *The Care of Children: Principles and Practice in Guidance and Regulations.* London: HMSO.

Department of Health (1991b) *Child Abuse: A study of inquiry reports 1980–1989.* London: Department of Health.

Department of Health (1994) *The Children Act Report 1993.* London: HMSO.

Department of Health (1995a) *Child Protection: Messages from Research.* London: HMSO.

Department of Health (1995b) *The Challenge of Partnership on Child Protection: Practice Guide.* London: HMSO.

Department of Health (1996) *Focus on Teenagers: Research into Practice.* London: HMSO.

Department of Health (1998a) *Quality Protects: Objectives for Social Services for Children.* London: Department of Health.

Department of Health (1998b) *Quality Protects: Framework for Action.* London: Department of Health.

Department of Health (1998c) *Modernising Social Services: Promoting independence, improving protection, raising standards.* London: The Stationery Office.

Department of Health (1999a) *The Government's Objectives for Children's Social Services.* London: Department of Health.

Department of Health (1999b) *Modernising Health and Social Services: National Priorities Guidance.* London: Department of Health.

Department of Health (2000a) *Framework for the Assessment of Children in Need and their Families, Guidance Notes and Glossary for: Referral and Initial Information Record, Initial Assessment Record and Core Assessment Record.* London: The Stationery Office.

Department of Health (2000b) *Assessing Children in Need and their Families: Practice Guidance.* London: The Stationery Office.

Department of Health (2001) *The Children Act Now: Messages from Research.* London: The Stationery Office.

Department of Health and Cleaver, H. (2000) *Assessment Recording Forms.* London: The Stationery Office.

Department of Health, Cox, A. and Bentovim, A. (2000b) *Framework for the Assessment of Children in Need and their Families, The Family Pack of Questionnaires and Scales.* London: The Stationery Office.

Department of Health, Department for Education and Employment, Home Office (2000a) *Framework for the Assessment of Children in Need and their Families.* London: The Stationery Office.

Department of Health, Home Office, Department for Education and Employment (1999) *Working Together to Safeguard Children: A guide to inter-agency working to safeguard and promote the welfare of children.* London: HMSO.

Department of Health, Home Office, Department for Education and Employment (2001) *Safeguarding Children in whom Illness is Induced or Fabricated by Carers with Parenting Responsibilities, Supplementary Guidance to Working Together to Safeguard Children.* London: Department of Health.

Department of Health National Statistics (2002) *Children in Need in England: Final results of a survey of activity and expenditure as reported by Local Authority Social Services' Children and Family Teams for a survey week in February 2000.* www.doh.gov.uk/public/cinresults .htm.

DiClementi, C. (1991) 'Motivational Interviewing and the Stages of Change.' In W. Miller and S. Rollnick (eds) *Motivational Interviewing.* London: Guildford Press.

Dutt, R. and Phillips, M. (2000) 'Assessing black children in need and their families.' In Department of Health, *Assessing Children in Need and their Families, Practice Guidance.* London: The Stationery Office, 37–70.

Education Act 2002. London: HMSO.

Farmer, E. and Owen, M. (1995) *Child Protection practice: Private risks and public remedies.* London: HMSO.

Farrington, D.P. (1987) 'Epidemiology.' In H.C. Quay (ed.) *Handbook of Juvenile Delinquency.* New York: Wiley, 33–61.

Freeman, P. and Hunt, J. (1998) *Parental Perspectives on Care Proceedings.* London: The Stationery Office.

Ghate, D. and Hazel, N. (2002) *Parenting in Poor Environments.* London: Jessica Kingsley Publishers.

Gibbons, J., Conroy, S. and Bell, C. (1995) *Operating the Child Protection System.* London: HMSO.

Goodyer, I.M., Cooper, P.J., Vize, C.M. and Ashby, L. (1993) 'Depression in 11–16-year-old girls: The role of past parental psychopathology and exposure to recent life events.' *Journal of Child Psychology and Psychiatry, 34,* 1103–1115.

Government statistics (1998) *Key Indicators Graphical System (KIGS).* London: Department of Health.

Graybeat, C. (2001) 'Strengths-Based Social Work Assessment: Transforming the Dominant Paradigm.' *Families in Society: The Journal of Contemporary Human Services, 82,* 3, 233–242.

Gregg, P., Harkness, S. and Machin, S. (1999) *Child Development and Family Income.* York: York Publishing Services Ltd.

Grimshaw, R. and Sinclair, R. (1997) *Planning to Care: Regulation, Procedure and Practice under the Children Act 1989.* London: National Children's Bureau.

Hague, G. and Malos, E. (1994) 'Children, domestic violence and housing: the impact of homelessness.' In A. Mullender and R. Morley (eds) *Children Living with Domestic Violence: Putting Men's Abuse of Women on the Child Care Agenda.* London: Whiting and Birch Ltd.

Hall, P., Lond, H., Parker, R. and Webb, A. (1975) *Change, Choice and Conflict and Social Policy.* London: Heinemann.

Hallett, C. (1995) *Interagency Coordination in Child Protection.* London: HMSO.

Hammersley, M. and Atkinson, P. (1983) *Ethnography: Principles in Practice.* London: Tavistock Publications.

Handy, C. (1978) *Gods of Management.* London: Arrow.

Hill, M., Laybourn, A. and Borland, M. (1996) 'The ethics of social research with children, an overview.' *Children and Society, 10,* 2, 129–144.

HM Treasury (2001) *Tackling child poverty: giving every child the best possible start in life.* London: The Public Enquiry Unit.

HM Treasury (2003) 'Every Child Matters'. Cm. 5860. London: The Stationery Office.

Home Office (1998) *Supporting Families: A Consultation Document.* London: The Stationery Office.

Horwath, J. (2001) (ed.) *The Child's World: Assessing Children in Need.* London: Jessica Kingsley Publishers.

Horwath, J. and Morrison, T. (2000) 'Identifying and implementing pathways for organizational change – using the Framework for the Assessment of Children in Need and their Families as a case example.' In *Child and Family Social Work, 5,* 245–254.

Howe, D. (1986) *Social Workers and their Practice in Welfare Bureaucracies.* Aldershot: Gower.

Jack, G. (2001) 'Ecological Perspectives in Assessing Children and Families.' In J. Horwath (ed.) *The Child's World: Assessing Children in Need.* London: Jessica Kingsley Publishers, 79–97.

Jaffe, P., Wolfe, D. and Wilson, S. (1990) *Children of Battered Women.* London: Sage.

James, G. (1994) *Department of Health Discussion Report for ACPC Conference: Study of Working Together 'Part 8' Reports.* London: Department of Health.

Jenkins, J.M. and Smith, M.A. (1990) 'Factors protecting children living in disharmonious homes: Maternal reports.' *J. Am. Acad., Child Adolescent Psychiatry, 29,* 1, 60–69.

Johnson, G. and Scholes, K. (1989) *Exploring Corporate Strategy Text and Cases.* London: Prentice Hall.

Jones, H., Clark, R., Kufeldt, K. and Norrman, M. (1998) 'Looking After Children: Assessing Outcomes in Child Care: The Experience of Implementation.' *Children and Society, 12,* 212–222.

Jones, P.H.D. (in press) *Communicating with Children.*

Jones, P.H.D. and Ramchandani, P. (1999) *Child Sexual Abuse: Informing practice from research.* Abingdon, Oxon: Radcliffe Medical Press.

Kennedy, M. and Wonnacott, J. (2003) 'Disabled Children and the Assessment Framework.' In M.C. Calder and S. Hackett (eds) *Assessment in child care: Using and developing frameworks for practice.* Dorset: Russell House Publishing, 172–192.

Knapp, M. and Robertson, E. (1989) 'The cost of child care services'. In B. Kahan (ed.) *Child Care Research, Policy and Practice.* Oxford: Open University Press.

Lofland, J. and Lofland, L. (1971) *Analysing Social Settings: A Guide to Qualitaive Observations and Analysis.* Belmont: Wadsworth.

Malos, E. and Hague, G. (1997) 'Women, Housing, Homelessness and Domestic Violence.' *Women's Studies Intervention Forum, 20,* 3.

Marchant, R. and Jones, M. (2000) 'Assessing the needs of disabled children and their families.' In Department of Health, *Assessing Children in Need and their Families, Practice Guidance.* London: The Stationery Office, 71–112.

Marsh, P. and Peel, M. (1999) *Leaving Care in Parnership: family involvement with care leavers.* London: The Stationery Office.

Morley, R. and Mullender, A. (1994) 'Domestic violence and children: What do we know from research.' In A. Mullender and R. Morley (eds) *Children Living with Domestic Violence: Putting Men's Abuse of Women on the Child Care Agenda.* London: Whiting and Birch Ltd.

Munro, E. (1998) 'Improving Social Workers' Knowledge Base in Child Protection Work.' *British Journal of Social Work, 28,* 89–105.

National Assembly for Wales (2001) *Children First.* Norwich: The Stationery Office.

Nazroo, J.Y. (1997) *The Health of Britain's ethnic minorities. Findings from a national survey.* London: Policy Studies Institute.

Netten, A., Dennett, J. and Knight, J. (1998) *Unit Costs of Health and Social Care.* University of Kent: Kent.

Netten, A., Rees, T. and Harrison, G. (2001) *Unit Costs of Health and Social Care 2001.* Canterbury: Personal Social Services Research Unit, University of Kent.

NSPCC and The University of Sheffield (2000) *The Child's World: Assessing Children in Need. Training and development pack.* London: NSPCC.

Office for National Statistics (ONS) (1999) *ONS Classification of Local and Health Authorities of Great Britain.* www.statistics.gov.uk/neighbourhood.

O'Quigley, A. (2000) *Listening to children's views: The findings and recommendations of recent research.* York: York Publishing Services Ltd.

Orford, J. and Velleman, R. (1990) 'Offspring of parents with drinking problems: drink and drug taking as young adults.' *British Journal of Addiction, 85,* 779–794.

Ovreveit, J. (1986) *Improving social work records and practice.* London: BASW.

Owers, M., Brandon, M. and Black, J. (1999) *Learning How to Make Children Safer: An Analysis for the Welsh Office of Serious Child Abuse Cases in Wales.* Norwich: University of East Anglia/Welsh Office.

Packman, J. and Hall, C. (1998) *From Care to Accommodation.* London: The Stationery Office.

Parker, L., Lamont, D.W., Wright, C.M., Cohen, M.A., Alberti, K.G. and Craft, A.W. (1999) 'Mothering skills and health in infancy: The thousand families study revisited.' *Lancet, 353,* 9159, 1151–1152.

Pascale, R. (1990) *Managing on the Edge: How the Smartest Companies Use Conflict to Stay Ahead.* New York: Simon and Schuster.

Peters, T. and Waterman, R. (1982) *In Search of Excellence: Lessons from America's Best New Companies.* New York: Harper and Row.

Pont, C. (2001) 'Summary of child care inspection findings (1992–1997) on assessment.' In Department of Health, *Studies informing the Framework for the Assessment of Children in Need and their Families.* London: The Stationery Office, 181–195.

PriceWaterhouseCoopers (2001) *Teacher Workload Study.* London: Department for Education and Skills (http://www.teachernet.gov.uk/bank.cfm?section=1974).

Quilgars, D. (2001) 'The Environment.' In J. Bradshaw (ed.) *Poverty: The Outcomes for Children.* London: Family Policy Studies Centre, 91–101.

Qureshi, T., Berridge, D. and Wenman, H. (2000) *Where to turn? Family support for South Asian communities.* London: National Children's Bureau.

Robbins, D. (2001) 'Assessment in child protection and family support: report of an SSI study'. In Department of Health, *Studies informing the Framework for the Assessment of Children in Need and their Families.* London: The Stationery Office, 139–180.

Rose, W. (2001) 'Assessing Children in Need and Their Families: An Overview of the Framework.' In J. Horwath (ed.) *The Child's World.* London: Jessica Kingsley Publishers, 35–50.

Rose, W. (2002) 'Achieving Better Outcomes for Children and Families by Improving Assessment of Need.' In T. Vecchiato, A.N. Maluccio and C. Canali (eds) *Evaluation in Child and Family Services: Comparative Client and Program Perspectives.* New York: Aldine de Gruyter.

Rutter, M. (1990) 'Commentary: some focus and process considerations regarding effects of parental depression on children.' *Developmental Psychology, 26,* 60–67.

Rutter, M. and Quinton, D. (1984) 'Parental psychiatric disorder: Effects on children.' *Psychological Medicine, 14,* 853–880.

Ryan, M. (2000) *Working with Fathers.* Abingdon, Oxon: Radcliffe Medical Press.

Rydelius, P.A. (1983). 'Alcohol and family life.' Quoted in T. Lindstein (1996) *Working with Children of Alcoholics.* Stockholm: Stockholm University, School of Social Work.

Schofield, G. and Thoburn, J. (1996) *Child Protection: The Voice of the Child in Decision-making.* London: Institute for Public Policy Research.

Seden, J. (1995) 'Religious persuasion and the Children Act.' *Adoption and Fostering, 19,* 2, 7–15.

Seden, J. (2001) 'Assessment of children in need and their families: a literature review.' In Department of Health, *Studies informing the Framework for the Assessment of Children in Need and their Families.* London: The Stationery Office, 1–80.

Sharland, E., Seal, H., Croucher, M., Aldgate, J. and Jones, D. (1996) *Professional intervention in child sexual abuse.* London: HMSO.

Shemmings, D. (1991) *Client Access to Records: Participation in Social Work.* Aldershot: Averbury/Gower.

Sinclair, R. (2001) 'The language of need: social workers describing the needs of children.' In Department of Health *Studies informing the Framework for the Assessment of Children in Need and their Families.* London: The Stationery Office, 81–138.

Sinclair, R. and Bullock, R. (2002) *Learning from Past Experience: A Review of Serious Case Reviews.* London: Department of Health.

Sinclair, R., Garnett, L. and Berridge, D. (1995) *Social Work and Assessment with Adolescents.* London: National Children's Bureau.

Social Services Inspectorate (1996) *Children in Need: Report of an SSI Inspection of Social Services Departments' Family Support Services 1993/95.* London: Department of Health.

Social Services Inspectorate (1997a) *Assessment, Planning and Decision-making in Family Support Services.* London: Department of Health.

Social Services Inspectorate (1997b) *Messages from Inspections: Child Protection Inspections 1992/1996.* London: Department of Health.

Social Services Inspectorate (1999) *Recording With Care: Inspection of Case Recording in Social Services Departments.* London: Department of Health.

Social Services Inspectorate (2002) *Performance Ratings for Social Services in England 2001– 2002.* London: Department of Health.

Spencer, N., Taylor, J., Baldwin, N. and Read, J. (2001) 'The impact of poverty and deprivation on caring for infants and children.' In R. Gordon and E. Harran (eds) *Fragile handle with care protecting babies from harm.* Leicester: NSPCC, 29–42.

Stevenson, O. (2000) 'The mandate for inter-agency and inter-professional work and training: legal, practical, professional and social factors.' In M. Charles and E. Hendry (eds) *Training Together to Safeguard Children: Guidance on Inter-agency Training.* London: NSPCC, 5–13.

Stockdale, M.J.E., Whitehead, C.M.E. and Gresham, P.J. (1999) *Applying economic evaluation to policing activity.* London: Home Office Police Research Series, Paper 132.

The Bridge (1995) *Paul: Death through neglect.* London: The Bridge Child Care Consultancy Service.

Thoburn, J., Lewis, A. and Shemmings, D. (1995) *Paternalism or Partnership? Family Involvement in the Child Protection Process.* London: HMSO.

Thoburn, J., Wilding, J. and Watson, J. (2000) *Family Support in Cases of Emotional Maltreatment and Neglect.* London: The Stationery Office.

Triseliotis, J., Borland, M., Hill, M. and Lambert, L. (1995) *Teenagers and the Social Work Services.* London: HMSO.

Velleman, R. (1993) *Alcohol and the Family.* Institute of Alcohol Studies Occasional Paper. London: Institute of Alcohol Studies.

Velleman, R. and Orford, J. (1999) *Risk and Resilience: Adults who were the children of problem drinkers.* Singapore: Harwood Academic Publishers.

Ward, H. (1995) 'Research Messages for Implementation.' In H. Ward (ed.) *Looking After Children: Research into Practice.* London: HMSO, 109–128.

Ward, H. (1998) 'Using a Child Development Model to Assess Outcomes of Social Work Interventions with Families.' In *Children and Society, 12,* pp.202–211.

Wigfall, V. and Moss, P. (2001) 'More than the Sum of its Parts? A study of a multi-agency child care network.' London: National Children's Bureau.

Subject Index

Entries in italics refer to illustrations, boxes or tables

Author Index